Gifted Children

A Guide for Parents and Teachers

Virginia Z. Ehrlich

Trillium Press
New York

**To my daughers, Diana, Lucy and Laurel...
And my husband, to whom I owe so much for the joys of my life**

This Edition Copyright © 1985, Trillium Press, Inc.
All Rights Reserved.

Trillium Press
Box 921
Madison Square Station
New York NY 10159
(212)–684–7399

Printed in the United States of America
ISBN: 0–89824–020–4

Contents

Preface v

1
Words, Words: What Do They Mean? *1*

2
Identifying Gifted/Talented Children *17*

3
Trials and Tribulations of Being Gifted *37*

4
Schooling: When, Where, Why? *59*

5
School Days: What to Expect *75*

6
Parents' Roles in Educating Gifted/Talented Children *103*

7
Teachers' Roles in Educating Gifted/Talented Children *115*

8
Careers for the Gifted and Talented *129*

9
Tests: Intelligence, Achievement, Aptitude *149*

10
The Law and Gifted Children *161*

11
Sources of Information *173*

Appendix: The Gifted and Talented Children's Education Act of 1978 *185*

References *191*

Index of Eminent Personalities *197*

General Index *198*

Preface

I think I have enjoyed the better aspects of two worlds. I had a good career rather early in life. Then I concentrated on homemaking and child rearing while my children were growing up, but I kept in touch with my field by reading and free-lance work I could do mostly at home and/or at my own convenience. I resumed a full-time career when my youngest child was in high school and I completed my doctoral studies.

It seems that I have learned most about the nature and nurture of the gifted from observing and living with my own daughters and from their friends. The area we lived in had excellent public schools at the time, with a fine teaching staff and a commitment to the education of the gifted. As an educator and research psychologist, I was able to view the scene from a professional perspective, which of course was constantly modified by my parental involvement.

I learned a great deal by frequent classroom observations and discussions with teachers and administrators, and especially from the many gifted youngsters who seemed to make my home their general meeting place. As a parent-professional, I was a most willing listener when they "griped" about their schools and learning experiences. They gave me frank insights into the educational process from kindergarten through graduate school.

A second source of information came from reading the biographies and autobiographies of eminent persons. This hobby was an outgrowth of work on intelligence testing which I began under some of the most famous educators of our times as an undergraduate at Teachers College, Columbia University, where I am presently an adjunct professor in education of the gifted. I read the books with a special purpose in mind: to find out what impact experiences in early childhood and youth had had on the later development of these outstanding personalities.

My work experience began with the development of tests of intelligence and achievement. I learned my profession as an apprentice learns a craft, under the guidance of master teachers. My formal education, of course, was merely an extension of the intense interest I had developed in the nature of intelligence and its manifestations.

When I had the opportunity in later years to join a project on the education of the gifted in New York City, I needed little urging to accept the assignment. This led to my becoming a Research Associate and Director of Gifted Child Studies in the New York City public schools, a position I held for eighteen years. During that time, I was able to work on and initiate research on the gifted; complete a manual entitled *Teaching Literature to the Gifted: K-6*, which I had begun during my teaching days; and create the Astor Program for Gifted Children, which was originally funded by the Vincent Astor Foundation.

Throughout all this time, I have been an active parent, member and officer of parents' associations, editor of their journals and bulletins. At one time I was involved in the work of a parent group that serviced all of Upper Manhattan in New York; this area contained three large city school districts with twenty elementary schools, six junior high schools, and four vocational and academic high schools (including the famous High School of Music and Art) within its borders. I edited their newspaper, which reached 40,000 families and which received the Freedoms Foundation Award. These parents' association activities gave me insight into parents' feelings and pupil home life which no amount of professional experience or university training in sterile lecture halls could provide. This training and experience helped me to organize my thinking and to discipline my observations.

Even now, as mother to three married daughters and proud grandmother to seven grandchildren, I remain the professional-practitioner, shifting gears according to my location and enjoying every bit of each role. My interest in the gifted has been a lifelong hobby and profession, and I am always pleased when I have a chance to share my experiences with others. I hope that you—parents, teachers, administrators, and friends of the gifted—will find some substance in my views.

Dr. Virginia Z. Ehrlich is an adjunct professor and research director of Astor Program Studies at Teachers College, Columbia University. She was a pioneer in early childhood education of the gifted, and is the creator of the Astor Program for Gifted Children at the prekindergarten/primary level, which has become an international model for such programs. A former director of gifted programs in the New York City public school system, Dr. Ehrlich has done extensive research, lecturing, and writing on the subject of gifted children.

Words, Words: What Do They Mean?

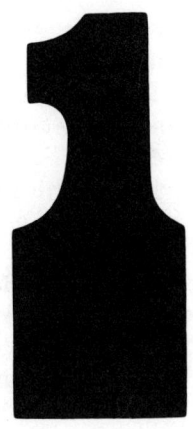

Mrs. Barnes has been waiting patiently for this day. Her son Danny is such a problem, and she must speak to the teacher about him. At last, Open School Week has arrived, and she will have ten minutes of the teacher's undivided attention. These parent interviews are being held in the regular classroom, where parents can look at the bulletin boards and browse through the students' notebooks and special projects while they wait their turn to talk to the teacher.

Danny's teacher, Myra Mason, seems to be very well organized but definitely harassed and overworked. She wants to do a good job, but too many factors seem to converge and interfere with her efforts. The district sets policies that are hard to understand; the principal makes heavy demands and runs a "tight ship"; the class is large and the children have such varied needs. In spite of her industry and devotion, Myra Mason is a little overwhelmed by the pressure she faces. She speaks knowingly, but in a hurried fashion, and resorts to the jargon of the profession to say a lot in a little time.

"Mrs. Barnes, your son Danny is an absolute genius. His mental age is over fourteen years, and his IQ is above 160 on the WISC. Of course, he didn't do as well on the performance part of the test as he did on the verbal, but his score was outstanding on both parts. Too bad he's such an underachiever. We were thinking of putting him into the enriched program rather than the accelerated, but, really, his class performance is *so* low! Even though he is very creative and a divergent thinker, he cannot be considered for the accelerated class unless we can make him stop daydreaming in class. Of course, it is hard when you have such a heterogeneous group. These gifted children do ask for so much attention.... [Pause for a quick breath!] What do you think?"

This sudden question catches Mrs. Barnes off balance and she blurts out, "About what?"

Actually, she's been trying to sort out all the words whose meanings, somehow, do not coincide with her own understanding of them. Is this a good report about her boy or isn't it? If he's a "genius," why can't he do the work? If he was so outstanding in the "performance" section of the WISC (whatever that may be), why is his "performance" in school so low? If the teacher thinks he's so "creative," why isn't he allowed to be in an "enriched" program? And again, why, if he is such a genius, can't he be accelerated, if she has all those words straight?

Mrs. Barnes, who knows how mischievous and stubborn her son can be, takes refuge in an old concern: "Is he well behaved?"

"Oh, yes," the teacher replies. "If only he wouldn't spend so much time daydreaming. Of course, he always knows the answers, whenever I call on him."

Ten minutes isn't a very long period in which to discuss your son's problems with his teacher or to resolve anything, especially with a roomful of parents waiting their turn. Besides, Danny is such a good kid that his mother has no desire to air his frailties before the community—and there really isn't much privacy in this session. So she brings her questions to a polite conclusion, trying to accentuate the positive traits she thinks the teacher will value in her son, and goes home to ponder the whole thing.

All these words! They don't mean the same thing to the teacher as they do to her. Is it good or bad to be a divergent thinker? How can you be a genius and an underachiever at the same time? These and other questions trouble Mrs. Barnes. If only she were like Mr. Johnson. He would just bellow: "Hold on there, sister! What do you mean by *this* or *that*?" He would not leave a parent–teacher conference more befuddled than when he started.

The harassed teacher reverts to jargon because it is the fastest way to get a lot said in a very little time. But we have a few extra minutes, so let us see if we can't decipher the code and make some sense out of what sounds like *non*-sense.

GENIUS

Actually, the term *genius* is seldom used in educational circles. It is a term reserved for those very rare beings whose knowledge and abilities seem limitless and incredibly outstanding. We tend to assign the term to artists, musicians, writers, and poets such as Michelangelo, Beethoven, and Shakespeare, and occasionally to scientists who make noteworthy contributions to our knowledge, such as Einstein. These are eminent persons whose accomplishments we recognize as being unique. They are *achievers*.

Educators at one time ascribed the term *genius* to any child with an IQ or score of over 140 on a special test, the Stanford-Binet Intelligence Test. This occurred simply because Lewis Terman used that designation for the thousand gifted children he studied in his famous book *Genetic Studies of Genius*, first published in 1926 (67). As a matter of fact, this definition of genius has found its place in *Webster's Third New International Dictionary* (p. 946): "4c: a person endowed with transcendent mental superiority, inventiveness, and ability.... a person with a very high intelligence quotient usu. in the range of 140 or above **Syn:**... GIFT." Before that, children with similarly high scores were called "Terman" children because of his work in adapting the Binet-Simon tests from the French.

GIFTED AND TALENTED

The more common term in use today is *gifted* coupled with *talented*; however, there is still great disagreement as to what these terms mean. They are often defined in terms of the goals of special programs. Congress, in order to pass legislation that would authorize allocations of funds for education of the gifted, arrived at a very broad definition, which was suggested by a special study (46, p. 2) on the status of education for the gifted in the United States.

The statement reads:

> Gifted and talented children are those identified by professionally qualified persons who by virtue of outstanding abilities are capable of high performance. These are children who require differentiated educational programs and/or services beyond those normally provided by the regular school program in order to realize their contribution to self and society.
>
> Children capable of high performance include those with demonstrated achievement and/or potential ability in any of the following areas, singly or in combination:
> 1. general intellectual ability
> 2. specific academic aptitude
> 3. creative or productive thinking
> 4. leadership ability
> 5. visual and performing arts
> 6. psychomotor ability
>
> It can be assumed that utilization of these criteria for identification of the gifted and talented will encompass a minimum of 3 to 5 percent of the school population.

It is in the nature of these broad definitions that they themselves require definition. In fact, there is not very much agreement among the professionals on what each of the terms means, and later legislation at the federal level uses the following language:

> For the purposes of this part, the term "gifted and talented children" means children and, whenever applicable, youth, who are identified at the preschool, elementary, or secondary level as possessing demonstrated or potential abilities that give evidence of high performance capability in areas such as intellectual, creative, specific academic, or leadership ability, or in the performing and visual arts, and who by reason thereof, require services or activities not ordinarily provided by the school. (Gifted and Talented Children's Education Act of 1978, Section 902.)

These definitions combine the terms *gifted* and *talented*.

It may be easier to define these terms in language that reflects the application of the words. Like P. W. Bridgman, Nobel Prize winner in physics, one might agree that the "true meaning of a term is to be found by observing what a man does with it, not by what he says about it" (32, p. 52). For example, one may regard talent as any specialized skill or ability in a particular field of endeavor, such as the creative and performing arts or sports, where the behavior involves some physical component of muscular coordination, visual acuity, manual dexterity, and so on. These outstanding American personalities would be considered talented: Daniel French, sculptor; Winslow Homer, painter; Maria Tallchief, dancer; Sammy Davis, performer; Isaac Stern, violinist; Jim Thorpe, athlete.

The term *giftedness* may be reserved for intellectual prowess, as is shown by scores on conventional intelligence tests, and which is characterized by an ability to see and grasp relationships, proficiency in verbal and abstract thought, persistence, intellectual curiosity, versatility and adaptability, and creative thought. As examples of this definition, one may cite these legendary "geniuses": Alexander the Great, king of Macedon, military strategist, empire builder; René Descartes, philosopher, scientist, mathematician; John Stuart Mill, philosopher, logician, economist; Albert Einstein, mathematician and theoretical physicist.

The categories are not mutually exclusive, and many gifted persons are known for both their intellectual capacities and their display of special talents. A noteworthy example is Leonardo da Vinci. On the other hand, there are many talented persons whose intellectual prowess is not outstanding.

In the following sections, the meanings of other terms used in identifying and educating the gifted will be examined.

INTELLIGENCE

There have been many theories about the nature of intelligence. Early in the century, psychologists thought that intelligence was an independent entity or "factor" in human traits. Spearman, of England, labeled it the g factor, and this is a theory that still prevails among many psychologists. In the United States, Thurstone tried to analyze intelligence into its component subfactors. This research was made possible by the introduction into the field of statistics of a technique known as *factor analysis*. With this technique it is possible to break down and identify the structure of a concept into factors or components. Using intelligence tests, Thurstone derived six factors of human intelligence, which he labeled *primary mental traits*. These were verbal ability, numerical ability, spatial ability, memory, reasoning, and word fluency.

As the statistical technique of factor analysis became more refined and with the development of computers to perform the laborious calculations involved, psychologists analyzed mental traits further. Guilford (29) hypothesized a cube with 120 cells, each describing one mental trait. He called his theory *Structure of the Intellect* or *SOI*; in it he identified a large number of these factors of intelligence. When schools speak of training in the SOI, they are saying that they are trying to teach children or provide exercises in some aspect of Guilford's structure, such as spatial orientation, general reasoning, auditory cognition (oral speech), or verbal comprehension (meaning of words). Mary Meeker (49) is a strong exponent of this theory. She has described elaborate techniques for developing and strengthening many of the factors in Guilford's cube.

There are several physiological theories of intelligence. To some, it means the number of neuron cells in the brain that can register, store, process, or retrieve information like a giant computer. Some believe that the number and "health" of these cells vary from individual to individual and that this accounts for the variability in human intelligence. Arthur Jensen (39), whose work on intelligence has stirred up a good deal of controversy, has recently proposed another theory which in a way supports the Spearman theory of an inherited g factor. Jensen proposes that intelligence is a function of the reaction time of each of the millions of nerve cells in the brain.

There are probably elements of truth in each of the ideas put forth by these careful scientists, but the reality is that the way the mind works remains one of the great mysteries of life.

Educators usually go along with theories that bear a close relation to practical results. If a theory of intelligence leads to techniques that help us understand the full range of a child's abilities, if it allows us to estimate levels of performance, we use applications of that theory in educating children. We know, for example, that tests of vocabulary are good clues to a child's academic ability and performance in school, so we use vocabulary as one of the "predicting" tools. Capacities to see analogies, to reason logically, or to recognize absurdities, for example, are linked to performance in intellectual tasks, so we use these traits as indices to a child's ability.

It is doubtful that we shall arrive in our lifetime at a precise and ultimate definition of intelligence, and it is even less likely that we shall ever have a perfect tool or instrument for measuring it. We can deal only in approximations and estimates. Realizing these limitations, we will use our information with the appropriate cautions.

THE INTELLIGENCE QUOTIENT

There is probably no term in the educational field that has led to more controversy—and to more misuse and misinterpretation—than the IQ, or intelligence quotient. Volumes have been written and endless articles generated on this one subject, and it promises to continue to be a fertile topic for discussion.

The IQ originated with the work of Alfred Binet and Théodore Simon, Frenchmen who were charged by their government in 1904 with the task of finding a way of classifying retarded children (66). Their work led to a complex system of tests that reflected multiple aspects of a child's development touching on physical, social, and intellectual growth. In fact, studies of these tests have been reported in more than one thousand articles (5). Studies have shown that the tests tap more than forty aspects of the human intellect.

Binet's work was one of the most impressive contributions to the field of educational psychology. His tests were developed on the basis of the child's growth patterns, to each of which he assigned values in terms of "months." As the child succeeded at a task (test), a number of months was added to his or her mental age. Thus, a boy who is 72 months old and who performs successfully all tests covering the first six years would receive a mental age score of 72. We divide his mental age (MA) by his chronological age (CA) and multiply this by 100 to obtain an intelligence quotient (IQ):

$$\frac{MA}{CA} \times 100 = IQ$$

Thus, our six-year-old who is performing at his appropriate age level has an IQ of 100:

$$\frac{72}{72} \times 100 = 100$$

If the six-year-old had performed at a level below his chronological age, his IQ would have been below 100. For example, if CA = 72 months and MA = 54 months, then IQ = (54 ÷ 72)100, or 75. If he had performed at a level above his chronological age, then CA = 72 months, MA = 108 months, and IQ = (108 ÷ 72)100, or 150.

There have been some changes in the method of arriving at IQs so that they can be dealt with in statistical calculations, and now one speaks of *deviation IQs*. This refers to the distance between the average IQ of the population at large and the obtained IQ along the base of the normal curve. The normal curve is bell shaped and has special mathematical properties; it has been found to describe the distribution of many human traits. Height, for example, is distributed in the shape of a normal curve. There are a few very short people and a few very tall people, with most clustering around the middle height, or average. Gamblers use applications of the normal curve when they quote odds on throwing dice. Any gambler will tell you that 7s will come up more frequently than any other combination and that 12s (boxcars) or 2s (snake eyes) are rarest. The same odds apply to IQs, which also follow the distribution of the normal curve, more or less. Most IQs cluster around the average of 100 or, more accurately, between 84–85 and 115–116. As a matter of fact, over 68 percent of the population theoretically has IQs in this range. Table 1 lists the proportions of the population in each range of IQs based on a Stanford-Binet Intelligence Test administered to 3184 subjects.

Psychologists rarely assign IQs over 166 to 170 when using the Stanford-Binet test, because they feel that it is impossible to estimate the abilities of a child who does that well on the test. The odds of finding children with IQs over 168 are about 28 in 1,000,000.

The Stanford-Binet (S-B) can be used for children from the ages of two up to about sixteen. The alternate tests to Stanford-Binet are the Wechsler scales. These tests yield two scores, verbal and performance, which we combine to yield an IQ. The S-B, WAIS, WISC-R, and WPPSI

TABLE 1. Proportion of Subjects by IQ Levels

IQ Range	Percentage of Subjects
160–169	0.03
150–159	0.2
140–149	1.1
130–139	3.1
120–129	8.2
110–119	18.1
100–109	23.5
90–99	23.0
80–89	14.5
70–79	5.6
60–69	2.0
50–59	0.4
40–49	0.2
30–39	0.03

Adapted from L. M. Terman and M. A. Merrill, *Measuring Intelligence* (Boston: Houghton-Mifflin, 1937).

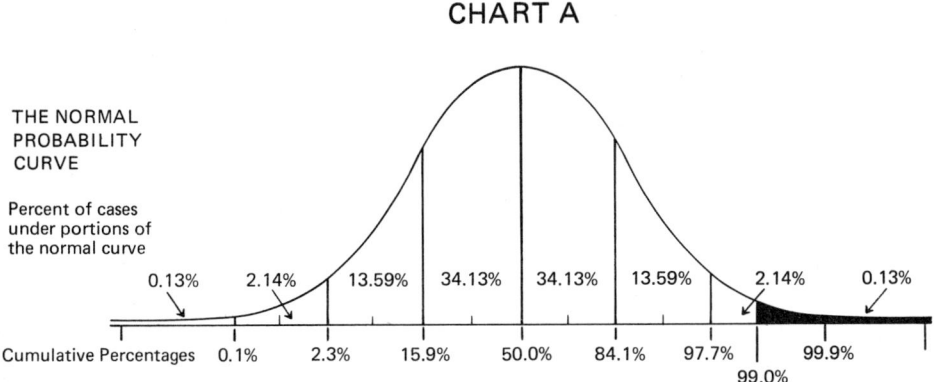

are individual tests that must be administered by a trained psychologist. There are also several group tests that yield IQ scores.

There are several other intelligence tests that require individual administration, such as the Leiter Performance Scales and the Raven's Progressive Matrices, but the Stanford-Binet and Wechsler are the two most commonly used.

The hitch in all of this is that the IQs derived from these tests are not directly comparable with each other. An IQ of 160 on the Stanford-Binet is not the same as an IQ of 160 on the WISC or on any of the other so-called group tests. This is the major reason psychologists prefer not to give parents a "number" interpretation of their child's ability and usually describe the child in terms of percentiles—the proportion of the population below the child's attained IQ. A child with an IQ above the 99th percentile exceeds 99 percent of his or her age peers in intellectual ability. On a distribution of the normal curve, the child's IQ will be found in the shaded portion, shown in Chart A of the normal probability curve. The area under the curve represents the total population; the shaded portion shows the part of the population with IQs exceeding those of 99 percent of the total population.

ACHIEVERS, UNDERACHIEVERS, AND OVERACHIEVERS

The Achiever

The achiever is a child who does well in school, meeting teacher standards of accomplishment. This child does all his or her work, gets good grades, and fits the general conception of a good student. The work performed is consistent with the school's estimate of the child's ability levels or intelligence quotient.

The Underachiever

The underachiever is a child whose schoolwork is not consistent with the teacher's estimate of his or her ability to learn. Or the reference point may be not the teacher's opinion but rather an IQ score. Thus, a child with a comparatively high IQ will be expected to read or perform in other subjects at a level that is consistent with that IQ. Part of this expectation is based on a statistical correlation between high IQ and performance in school subjects such as reading and mathematics.

As is to be expected, there are many slips between statistical data and application of the conclusions based on them. Statistics is a science that deals with averages and probabilities. Few bother to analyze statistical data in the kind of detail that will show the many deviations from the average. For example, if a statistical study shows that the odds against the occurrence of an event are 95 in 100, there are still at least 5 chances in 100 that the event *will* happen. Gambling casinos would go out of business if this were not the case. In the same way, even though high reading and mathematics abilities are correlated with high IQ, for many students this is not a reasonable or even true-to-life expectation, and the odds justifying the conclusion are far lower than 95 in 100.

It does sometimes happen that children of estimated high ability do not perform well in school. The discrepancy should be investigated to determine, for example, if there are physical, social, or emotional causes that may be inhibiting the children's learning. For example, in one of the programs for very superior children, there was a little girl who was extremely capable. The tests showed this as did all the observations and interviews. Occasionally in class, she made the kind of contribution that reflected a very high thinking level and a spark that one would be tempted to label "genius." Unfortunately, this little girl (she was only six and one-half) was beset with worries about death and self-destruction. She spoke frequently of hurting or poisoning herself, stating, "Oh, what's the use, I'll be dead tomorrow." Little Candy was much too young for such a tragic outlook on life, and the obsession affected all her work. She definitely was an underachiever. Candy was placed under therapy, but, more importantly, her mother was urged to see a therapist since it was she who suffered with the death obsession and had transmitted it to her child.

Parents, then, need to distinguish between true underachievement, which may be caused by serious problems that need attention, and the misapplication of the term to children who are merely behaving like "people," with normal variations in performance.

The Overachiever

The overachiever is a figment of someone's imagination. If a child performs at a higher level than we would normally have expected, then our estimates were wrong, not the child's performance.

There are some children who work at maximum capacity and their work reflects this effort. They may be positively motivated or, as sometimes occurs, they may be driven by parental ambition to unusual effort. But, whatever the reason, the performance cannot exceed the capacity. There is an inherent contradiction in terms when the word *overachiever* is thus applied.

CREATIVITY: CONVERGENT VS. DIVERGENT THINKING

The current fad in educational circles is teaching for "creativity." Elaborate techniques for identifying the creative child have been developed and curricula proposed purporting to foster this seemingly desirable trait.

What is creativity? Very simply, it may be considered to be the capacity to reorganize information and experiences in a way that is unique or different from anything previously known to the creator. For example, when Fleming recognized the mold on his culture plate as an agency for destroying harmful bacteria, he identified the curative properties of penicillin. Many other scientists had seen the mold Fleming first saw, but they did not reorganize their information in the creative way he did. In a similar way, Cézanne saw the geometric patterns in landscapes as dominant features in an artistic composition and introduced a new style of painting. Einstein reorganized a vast body of scientific knowledge and interpreted it in a revolutionary principle of relativity. The child who, *without training*, suddenly discovers that two and three make five and that four and one also make five is performing a creative act. Have you noticed the wonderful look of discovery in the face of a child who comes to you and says: "Daddy, you know what? When I mixed my blue and yellow paint, I got a green color. It's like magic! I mixed a lot of colors, and I got a lot of different colors. That's what happens when you mix colors, you know!"

There are some well-known advocates of creativity education, including Torrance (74, 75), Getzels and Jackson (26), Gowan (28), and Khatena (41). Among them, they have written many books and articles in the field and also have developed some tests to be used to identify creativity.

There are several issues related to creativity that still need to be resolved. One is the relationship between creativity and intellectual capacity. They are not independent traits, but it is possible for someone to be highly gifted intellectually without necessarily being highly creative. The converse is not true. It is not likely that someone will be highly creative without having at least above average or superior intellectual abilities. The capacities to identify problems, process and reorganize information, and create new or novel solutions or adaptations are intellectual activities necessary to the creative process. Most research studies lead to this conclusion.

It is important to note that creativity (creative or original thinking) applies to all fields of endeavor, including the physical sciences, the humanities, and the social sciences as well as the more commonly associated areas of music, the performing arts, and the visual arts.

Two terms have come into usage that are indirectly related to creativity: convergent and divergent thinking.

Convergent Thinking

A student who is a convergent thinker will process information along conventional, known, or preestablished patterns. "Two and two are four." "The earth revolves around the sun." "The earth is a sphere!"

Divergent Thinking

On the other hand, the divergent thinker sees things "creatively." This person processes the same information everybody else has but arrives at different conclusions. "The earth is not flat," proclaimed Columbus, "It is a sphere." "No, the sun does not revolve around the earth. It is the earth that revolves around the sun!" announced the then-heretical Galileo, and was persecuted for his divergent thinking. "My teacher is dumb!" your daughter announces, "She's got all her facts mixed up!" A heretical, unconventional, nonconforming statement from a pupil—who is probably right and who is, very likely, a clear as well as a divergent thinker.

HOMOGENEOUS AND HETEROGENEOUS GROUPING

Pupils can be grouped in full-time classes or subject areas in one of two ways. First, they may be grouped according to ability for all or part of the day or week, and may be taught all their work in these homogeneous groups. A grouping may be based on IQ, reading and/or mathematics ability, ability in other subject areas, interests, and many other factors. Occasionally, interest or talent in a visual or performing art may be the basis of grouping. Stuyvesant High School in New York City is an example of full-time homogeneous grouping according to ability levels, especially in mathematics and science. The Cleveland major works classes are grouped by intellectual ability for part of each day.

Heterogeneous grouping usually means that classes are organized with children of all ability levels except, usually, the retarded. The IQ ranges in such classes may be from 75 to 170+. Reading abilities may span a range of six to eight grades. Mathematics abilities may have a narrower range but still cover several grade levels.

ENRICHMENT AND ACCELERATION

Enrichment

Enrichment has been the golden promise held out to parents of gifted children over the years, and it usually remains just that—a promise. Enrichment has acquired a multitude of meanings and has suffered innumerable misapplications. Among its many meanings, these are but a few. Enrichment may mean the addition of an extra subject in the curriculum, extra trips to special-interest locations, additional topics covered in the individual curriculum areas, or more homework. Ideally, it means that the pupil's education will be broader in scope, exploring topics in greater depth and at higher levels of difficulty and involving many activities not covered in the regular program.

Acceleration

The term *acceleration* can have several meanings in actual application. It may mean having a child "skip" a grade, from grade four to six, for example, without covering the work of the intervening grade. This was a common practice early in this century. Acceleration can mean combining the work of three school years in two years. In New York City, for example, junior high school pupils can complete all the work of grades seven through nine in two years, in what is known as the SP (Special Progress) classes. It can mean permitting a student to advance in a single subject area at his or her own pace or by doing the work of a higher grade in the subject while remaining in unaccelerated classes for all other subjects. The Advanced Placement program of the College Entrance Examination Board (CEEB) is an example of this for high school students.

Dr. Julian Stanley of The Johns Hopkins University is an advocate of acceleration-in-subject with respect to mathematics. He also advocates general acceleration through the grades for students who can cover all the subject areas at a rapid pace (64). A youngster in the New York City school system who taught himself calculus at the age of seven was accelerated in the subject by having a local college professor tutor him in mathematics while he remained in his regular class. When he was nine, he was recommended to Dr. Stanley. Under the latter's guidance, the young man accelerated his entire schooling by finishing college at age fifteen.

We are not discussing here the merits or demerits of acceleration in any of its forms, but merely exploring its many meanings. (See p. 48 for a discussion of the advantages and disadvantages of acceleration.)

Let us return to Danny and his mother. Just what was the teacher trying to say?

This is not as simple to answer as one would like to believe. The teacher certainly did not have the time to explain all the terms and discuss their implications. In her own way, she was trying to give Mrs. Barnes both a positive and a negative report, limited by her own problems in coping with a difficult class.

It seems that Danny is really very intelligent. He likes to think and can reason and do abstract thinking better than most children his own age. With an IQ of 160, he has the capacity to do better schoolwork than most of his classmates. In fact, there are not likely to be more than one or two like him in a population of ten thousand students. He is not performing in his formal studies as well as one might expect from a boy of his ability (underachieving) and he does a lot of daydreaming. Perhaps he is bored? It is very likely, since the pace of the class must be quite slow and there is no evidence that he is being given any special attention commensurate with his abilities.

Evidently his teacher does not appreciate his classroom discussions and contributions, since they do not conform with her expectations. (He is creative and a divergent thinker.) In a class of children with such diverse abilities (heterogeneous grouping), such contributions are not often appreciated by either the teacher or the students.

It is too bad that the teacher can find no way of enriching Danny's experiences within her class, but surely she should not deny him the opportunity in another class. The alternatives, enriching or accelerating, depend on all the factors mentioned in the discussion on those topics, and no ten-minute public interview is adequate for exploring them.

Jargon, technical terminology, and specialized meanings are characteristic of every profession. They are the shorthand of communication when there is mutual agreement about the meaning of terms. Unfortunately, in the human sciences, there are some terms about which there is very little agreement and which lead us all into confusion. However, there is a common ground of meaning for most of the terms used, and we must try to use them in a manner that will be clear to the public without insulting its intelligence.

SUGGESTED READINGS

The following books are collections of essays or reports written by eminent workers in the field of the gifted dating from the early history of the subject during this century through the present time. These readings will be useful supplements to this and most of the other chapters in this book.

BARBE, WALTER B., and JOSEPH S. RENZULLI, eds. *Psychology and Education of the Gifted.* 2nd ed. New York: John Wiley, Halsted Press, 1975.

BEREDAY, GEORGE Z. F., and JOSEPH A. LAUWERYS, eds. *The Gifted Child.* The Yearbook of Education. New York: Harcourt Brace Jovanovich, Inc., 1962.

COLANGELO, NICHOLAS, and RONALD T. ZAFFRANN, eds. *New Voices in Counseling the Gifted.* Dubuque, Iowa: Kendall/Hunt, 1979.

DENNIS, WAYNE, and W. MARGARET. *The Intellectually Gifted: An Overview.* New York: Grune & Stratton, 1976.

FRENCH, JOSEPH L., ed. *Educating the Gifted: A Book of Readings.* Rev. ed. New York: Holt, Rinehart & Winston, 1964.

GOWAN, JOHN C., and E. PAUL TORRANCE, eds. *Educating the Ablest: A Book of Readings on the Education of Gifted Children.* Itasca, Ill.: F. E. Peacock, 1979.

PASSOW, A. HARRY, ed. *The Gifted and the Talented: Their Education and Development.* Seventy-Eighth Yearbook of the National Society for the Study of Education. Part I. Chicago: University of Chicago Press, 1979.

STANLEY, JULIAN C., WILLIAM C. COX, and CECILIA H. SOLANO, eds. *The Gifted and the Creative: A Fifty-Year Perspective.* Baltimore, Md.: Johns Hopkins University Press, 1977.

Identifying Gifted/Talented Children

A social worker associated with a prestigious Eastern medical facility was concerned about a child who seemed to her to be gifted but whose mother felt that the child was very likely a victim of PKU (phenylketonuria), a genetic disease with symptoms of retardation. The problem that was worrying everyone was that the child was so active she could not eat or sleep.

This is what the social worker reported. The baby is very alert, notices everything in sight, and responds to everything that happens around her by turning her head, reaching out, or making sounds. Actually, she repeats sounds and simple words, and already has a language of her own. She can stand and will walk if you hold her hands. She is extremely active and seems to understand everything one says to her. Unfortunately, her excessive alertness and responsiveness to the environment are interfering with her feeding and sleeping. She is only four and one-half months old!

Retarded? Hardly! This child is showing the signs of possible intellectual advancement, although at an incredibly early age.

On the other hand, one very confident mother was already making school plans for her eight-month-old baby. He had had a social smile at only two weeks and had sat up early; he stood alone, repeated sounds, possessed a spoken vocabulary of about eight words: *mama, dada, bread, milk, ball, water, dog,* and *apple* (papple), and had a vocabulary of understood language that was much larger. The mother wanted to know where there was a school in which she could place this very bright child. At eight months!

Other parents, more practical, want to register their children early in any school that may be available, so that at the "appropriate" time they will be accepted in these rare places.

As director of a program in the public school system, I was expected to respond to the public's need for information, even though we did not reach infants and nursery school children. These parents had a real need and, because I was eager to foster an active interest on behalf of the gifted, I tried to encourage parents who suspected giftedness in their children and who cared enough to make inquiries about them. I knew only too well the tragedy of gifted children whose abilities were not recognized or were ignored, and whose lives had been sadly damaged because of this neglect.

Let us meet some more gifted children. Little Beth comes into my office and gives me a cheerful greeting: "Hi!" She is completely at ease. She notices everything. "Is that a coleus plant?" she asks, pointing toward the windowsill. "Yes, it is, Beth. All of the plants on the windowsill are coleus plants." "Oh, I know that," she observes, "but I've never seen one with whitish leaves." "Yes, it is a little unusual," I reply. Beth is just four years old. She has an IQ of about 155 or more. She asks, "May I look at this book?" taking a copy of *Jennie's Hat* (40) off my "temptation" table. That is where I keep books, games, and other items that children may pick up, look at, or respond to in some way. Beth sits quietly reading the book (about fourth-grade level), while I chat with her mother about a special program for children like Beth. Beth giggles and shows her mother the well-laden hat that Jennie is wearing, explaining the theme of the story to her.

This poised, cheerful, sociable child is a joy to behold. She really can read and very well, too. Her language is mature and sensible, and she sounds like a miniature grown-up. I don't need a test to tell me she's bright. Her behavior, her use of language, and her reading ability have already given me clues. Actually, the psychologist confirms what I have already guessed. Beth has a very high IQ, at a level that will be found in only one out of every ten thousand children of her age.

Mickey, who is also about four, refuses to come into my office. He strikes at his mother and then races down the hall in pursuit of his own private demons. We retrieve him and bribe him back with soft-spoken words and an offer of a cookie. But he is restless, hopping from one thing to another, tugging at his mother's clothing, interrupting a rather futile attempt at conversation. Our psychologist, an expert in her own way with reaching all types of children, gives Mickey a firm command, puts a gentle arm around his shoulder, and marches him off. Her firmness and authoritative manner have caught him off guard. But it doesn't last. Mickey will not attend. He climbs on chairs and wants to sit on the windowsill in the testing room. "I can't control him," his mother complains, and scolds him along with a threat to beat him if he doesn't stop. "I can't do anything with him. He's always asking questions, breaking things. He never sits still."

The magician, otherwise known as our psychologist, has somehow managed to get some responses to her questions, and she returns with a smiling, momentarily cherubic Mickey, who is proudly clutching a drawing he made for her. The psychologist announces, "Dr. E., will you *look* at this *terrific* picture Mickey made. Will you *look* at all those *details!*" The praise is in her voice as well as in her words. She is showing me a drawing of a man in which this four-year-old has demonstrated his remarkable observational ability by the attention he has given to all parts of the body and clothing. He explains that this is a picture of his father.

The face in the picture is unsmiling. The body takes up the whole page, and alongside it is a tiny, solemn-looking child—Mickey. Oh, what a story that picture tells! The mother says, "My husband travels. He's not home much. Mickey adores him, but his father doesn't have too much patience with all his questions. He gets a little mad when Mickey breaks things. Mickey says he wants to know how they're made. Even when his father takes a strap to him, he doesn't stop. He just goes on bothering everybody, asking questions and touching everything."

Poor Mickey! He has curiosity. He wants to know about the world around him. He is driven to seek out and learn. And nobody pays any attention. Mickey can read very well, as he has already demonstrated to the psychologist and as he now shows me by reading a sports story in the newspaper on my "temptation" table.

Like Beth, Mickey has a very high IQ. Unless something is done soon to recognize this ability and give him some attention and encouragement, he can easily become a class discipline problem and may join the long list of learning dropouts, youngsters who stop listening in school and who never have the opportunity to realize their full potential.

Let us meet some famous gifted personalities during their childhood, as they are described by Terman and Cox (68) in their volume *The Early Mental Traits of Three Hundred Geniuses.*

> Desiderius Erasmus (1467–1536)
> Dutch classical and theological scholar and satirist
> Erasmus, from his earliest years, had a passion for learning.... He was checked, threatened, reprimanded. He was refused access to books. But they could not be wholly kept from him, and he devoured all that he could get. And he constantly wrote verses, essays, or anything that came to hand. (p. 400)
>
> Charles Robert Darwin (1809–1882)
> English naturalist
> Darwin's taste for natural history and especially for collecting was well developed by the time he was 8 years old; he tried to make out the names of plants and he collected shells, seals, franks, coins, and minerals with a zeal peculiar to him alone of all the children. He was humane, as a result of the teaching and example of his sisters; he never took more than a single egg out of a bird's nest, and, though fond of angling, killed the bait worms painlessly with salt and water. Love of dogs amounted with him to a passion. He was fond of solitary walks, and on one occasion he became so absorbed in thought while strolling alone that he walked off a wall. (p. 398)
>
> Jakob Ludwig Felix Mendelssohn-Bartholdy (1809–1847)
> German composer and musician
> Aside from music, Felix had many other interests; he was devoted to gymnastics, took great pleasure in riding, swimming, and dancing, and played both billiards and chess with ardor; drawing was like a professional avocation with him and his letter-writing was remarkable for neatness and finish. Whatever he did he thought worth doing well.... In his 11th and 12th years he wrote from fifty to sixty

complete movements, including pieces for the piano, violin, and organ, songs, and a cantata. (p. 589)

George Sand (Aurore Dupin) (1804–1876)
French novelist
Little Aurore learned to walk at ten months; began to talk rather late, but as soon as she had begun to say a few words, she learned many more very quickly. Before she was three, she would amuse herself, while penned in by four chairs, telling interminable stories in which were said to figure few bad people and no serious troubles. (p. 596)

Wolfgang Amadeus Mozart (1756–1791)
Austrian composer
When he was 3 or 4, Mozart began to invent musical ideas; impressed by seeing his sister play, he seated himself at the clavier and picked out thirds, to his great delight. Even at that early age he could retain musical passages that he had heard. On one occasion before his 5th birthday, he learned at half-past nine and in half an hour a minuet and a trio, pieces requiring independence of the two hands and some musical comprehension.... From before his 6th year, Mozart's sole absorbing interest was in music, and even the games he played had some musical element.... Apparently he had few interests unrelated to music.... (p. 592)

Charlotte Brontë (1816–1855)
English novelist
At Roe Head School, although handicapped at her entrance by the irregularity of her earlier studies, she [Charlotte] quickly rose to the first place in the first class. She is described by a school friend as having been "head of the school in all intellectual pursuits." At the close of the first half-year Charlotte won three prizes; and the silver medal "for fulfillment of duties" she retained to the end of her school course.... All four of the little Brontës commenced to write at a very early age. "The History of the Year 1829," a detailed account of family and intellectual activities, was written by Charlotte before she was 13. Her "Catalogue of My Books, with the Period of Their Completion, up to August 3, 1830," includes 22 volumes, all written within a period of 15 months.... A "list of painters whose works I wish to see" indicates (at 13) keen interest in art and a wide and unusual acquaintance with its history on the part of one who had no first-hand acquaintance with pictures. (p. 735)

Johann Wolfgang von Goethe (1749–1832)
German poet
When barely 6 years old Goethe began to examine and read the illustrated *Orbis Pictus,* Merian's illustrated Bible (then and later a favorite), Gottfried's illustrated chronicles of universal history and Heidegger's *Acerra philologica.* A little later he was reading *Robinson Crusoe, Die Insel Felsenburg,* and similar tales. At 8, he was already somewhat acquainted in his father's library with the older

> German poets of the 18th century, the best Latin and Italian poets, Roman antiquities, classic works on jurisprudence, books of travel, historical and philosophical treatises, and encyclopedias of all kinds.... At 8, Goethe learned so readily that he was able to pick up Italian from overhearing his sister and her tutor, while he himself was studying his Latin lesson. (p. 696)

We learned a great deal about what gifted children are like as a result of the Terman studies (67–71). Terman and his colleagues tried to get as complete a picture as possible about each child, so that they could describe gifted children as they really are. As Terman stated in his preface to Volume I (67), first published in 1926, up to the time of his work, major deterrents to understanding such children included:

> (1) the influence of current beliefs, partaking of the nature of superstitions, regarding the essential nature of the Great Man, who has commonly been regarded by the masses as qualitatively set off from the rest of mankind, the product of supernatural causes, and moved by forces which are not to be explained by the natural laws of human behavior; (2) the widespread belief, hardly less superstitious in its origin, that the intellectual precocity is pathological; (3) the vigorous growth of democratic sentiment in Western Europe and America during the last few hundred years, which has necessarily tended to encourage an attitude unfavorable to a just appreciation of native individual differences in human endowment; and (4) the tardy birth of the biological sciences, particularly genetics, psychology, and education. (p. v)

As Terman further observed about his earliest introduction to the field of the gifted, "Child prodigies... were at that time in bad repute because of the prevailing belief that they were usually psychotic or otherwise abnormal and almost sure to burn themselves out quickly or to develop postadolescent stupidity. 'Early ripe, early rot' was a slogan frequently encountered" (24, pp. 34–35).

As a result of Terman's work, we have been provided with descriptions of the gifted and listings of those characteristics by which they differ significantly from their age peers. These conclusions were based on a very well designed longitudinal study which was so successful that Terman (24, p. 37) could justly "take some pride in the fact that not one of the major conclusions we drew in the early 1920's regarding the traits that are typical of gifted children has been overthrown since then." And, the fact is that, even since 1959, when the foregoing statement was written, the Terman observations about the characteristics of gifted children remain unchallenged. If anything, research following upon his original studies has served to confirm this statement.

A CHECKLIST OF TRAITS IN WHICH THE GIFTED EXCEL

In a review of the many characteristics that are usually given to describe gifted children, I found that forty-seven traits were included in one way or another by specialists in the field, but that no one has been able to put together a true syndrome of traits that will serve alone as a way to identify a gifted child. I am currently working on just such research to find characteristics that can be used by parents to identify their very young gifted children. So far the data suggest that there are a few traits which parents cite as clues to giftedness and which are related to IQ levels. (See page 28.)

    Several points must be considered. First, there are degrees of possession of a trait, with varying intensities that cannot easily be measured. Second, many traits by themselves can also be applied to other persons who may or may not be gifted. The fact is that no one trait can be used as a signifier of superior intelligence. It is rather the subtle combination of several key traits, possessed to a certain degree of intensity or with exceptional pervasiveness, that we must look for. Specialists in the field develop a sensitivity to such combinations, but not even they can promote them as sure ways of identifying giftedness. They still must resort to the more objective findings of standardized tests to substantiate their observations. Nevertheless, as a first step, these checklists of traits serve as guides and aids in screening children. Certainly, whether consciously or unconsciously, both teachers and parents use them as descriptors of gifted children.

    Table 2 represents a summary of traits, behaviors, and characteristics that have been used to describe gifted children. Some are more descriptive of one age than of others, although in rare cases they may be observed at any time during the childhood years. The traits are grouped according to broad categories of similarity, but there is no significance to the order of presentation.

    In using this or any other checklist, several critical points must be considered. First, there is the continued lack of information on what constitutes a critical group of characteristics for identifying giftedness. Sometimes, the presence of only one characteristic may be a sufficient indicator of intellectual or talent superiority. At other times, several traits are observable or are required as clues.

    A second factor that must be taken into account is that there are aspects of both talent and intellectual giftedness that are not easily observed by the untrained person. For example, true pitch for potential musicians, color discrimination for potential artists, the capacity for abstract thought or complex reasoning—any of these could and fre-

TABLE 2. A Checklist of Traits in Which the Gifted Excel
(When compared with their age peers)

VOCABULARY	Has a large vocabulary; knows and uses words and terminology that are advanced for his or her years; is interested in words and uses them correctly.
VERBAL FACILITY	Expresses self well; writes clearly; uses longer sentences than most children of own age; uses colorful expressions; learns foreign expressions and languages easily; is fluent in two or more languages.
READING	Enjoys reading; is an avid reader; reads widely; learned to read early; is a self-taught reader; reads more and better books than age peers; reads above grade level by at least two years; selects difficult books for reading; enjoys informative books such as encyclopedias, dictionaries, atlases, and biographies.
WRITING	Writes the alphabet; writes own name; writes words; writes sentences; writes letters, stories, poetry, rhymes.
MEMORY	Has an unusual memory; remembers details; remembers most details of stories; can retell stories almost verbatim; remembers what he or she has heard or read without appearing to need much rote or drill; remembers places, experiences, people, directions; can sing complete songs from memory, remembering both the melody and the words.
LEARNING	Learns quickly and efficiently; learns easily, often without much effort; learns with a minimum of explanation or elaboration.
THINKING	Thinks clearly and logically; reasons, generalizes, deduces, infers; recognizes implied relationships; comprehends meanings; is able to explain reasons for his or her actions; applies learning from one situation to others.
FLEXIBILITY OF THOUGHT	Seeks alternative solutions to problems; adapts to new surroundings and experiences; enjoys new situations; can deal with ambiguity.
ABSTRACT REASONING	Is capable of abstract thought; needs few or no concrete examples to understand difficult concepts; likes to think things out; arrives at mathematical relationships mentally, without visual or concrete stimuli.
SYMBOLIC THOUGHT	Is capable of symbolic thought; works readily with symbols such as words and numbers; enjoys codes; is outstanding in mathematics.
GENERALIZATION— INSIGHT	Recognizes relationships and draws sound generalizations; sees relationships among apparently unrelated ideas; has insight into cause and effect; transfers learning to new situations; looks for similarities and differences in events; perceives trends in the past and projects them into the future.
COMPLEXITY	Is interested in complexity; prefers complex ideas; changes rules of games to increase their complexity; can consider many factors and facets of situations simultaneously; enjoys and understands concepts of large scope, such as geologic time, relativity, origins of

	man; tries to understand complicated material by separating it into its respective parts; is interested in problems that are beyond his or her age experience level, such as religion, politics, sex, and national issues.
PLANNING AND ORGANIZATION	Plans and organizes work; shows forethought in solving problems; thinks before acting; applies scientific research methods to work; thinks about a mechanical problem before trying to solve it physically; selects or creates efficient procedures for work or activities.
CREATIVITY AND IMAGINATION	Is creative, imaginative; creates new games, stories, toys or revises them; tells imaginative stories; generates a large number of solutions to problems and questions; sees unusual relationships and associations; interprets events and experiences in unusual ways; fantasizes; wonders about concepts unusual for his or her age; may have an imaginary playmate during early years; enjoys fantasies, fairy tales, science fiction; envisions new structures and processes and can express them in speaking, writing, art, music, or other art forms.
ORIGINALITY	Produces work that has freshness, vitality, uniqueness; solves problems by ingenious methods; does the unexpected; expresses ideas that are often very original in one or more areas; is resourceful.
CURIOSITY	Is curious and investigative; asks many provocative questions; explores things and situations closely; wants to know how and why things work, will take them apart to find out; is inquisitive; is skeptical about explanations; is curious about meanings; continually asks "Why?"; has a sense of wonder about the world; continually questions the status quo.
SENSE OF WONDER	Expresses awe and is deeply impressed by natural phenomena; has intense feelings about the world; is eager to share discoveries with others.
RANGE OF INFORMATION	Is well informed for age; reads widely and in unusual areas; enjoys reading informative books such as dictionaries, references, and almanacs; seems to be interested in everything; has a highly specialized knowledge in a particular field of interest beyond his or her years.
RANGE OF INTERESTS	Has a wide range of interests; has a strong interest in a specific area; makes collections; has unusual hobbies; pursues interests or hobbies with unusual intensity and attention; seems to have a large storehouse of information on a variety of topics; has interests or hobbies that are beyond his or her years.
AESTHETIC INTERESTS AND/OR TALENTS	Responds to beauty; has aesthetic interests and/or talents in areas such as art, music, rhythm, dancing, writing, and poetry; remembers musical compositions and melodies of songs; responds to variations in colors, hues, and shades; shows grace and precision in response to dance patterns; enjoys hearing, reading, or writing poetry; is responsive to pattern and arrangement; plays a musical instrument with exceptional skill.

(continued)

TABLE 2 (continued)

ATTENTION TO DETAIL	Is impatient with detail and repetition; is easily bored with routine tasks; requires fewer detailed or repeated instructions; often anticipates instructions with a minimum of information; can be accurate and neat, and will attend to details of a topic of intense interest, such as a hobby or special study.
OUTSTANDING PERFORMANCE	Performs with outstanding ability in some area; has received an award in a specific area such as music, art, science, or achievement; has received a scholarship or other academic award; receives consistently high grades in school performance.
SCHOLASTIC ACHIEVEMENT	Attains consistently high grades in schoolwork or in one particular subject area; enjoys excelling in schoolwork; shows exceptional talent in mathematics.
LEADERSHIP	Is a leader; has influence over others; assumes leadership in situations; shows initiative in starting worthwhile activities; usually directs activities; is an organizer; may seem willful; likes to plan and organize; tends to dominate situations.
ATTENTION AND CONCENTRATION	Has a long attention span; is capable of intense concentration; is not easily distracted; has a tendency to lose awareness of time; becomes deeply involved in tasks.
PERSISTENCE	Persists in spite of difficulties; will stay with a task until it is completed; will concentrate on goals that are remote and possibly unattainable in the eyes of others; needs little external motivation to persist in tasks that excite or interest him or her; is tenacious; shows determination in achieving goals.
SELF-CRITICISM	Is self-critical; strives for perfection, is not easily satisfied with own work or product; evaluates own abilities, usually correctly; modifies behavior in terms of own self-evaluation; is modest, not inclined to boast or to overstate own knowledge; is aware of own exceptionality.
RESPONSIVENESS	Is alert; is keenly observant; responds to the environment; is aware.
STRENGTH OF CHARACTER	Is self-disciplined, needs little outside control; is usually well behaved and responsive to moral standards; has more wholesome character preferences and social attitudes than those of peers; is deeply concerned with moral and ethical values, right and wrong, good and bad; is trustworthy; is honest and forthright; is trusting of others; has a forceful, strong character; is pure-minded, tends to shun vulgarity and immorality.
CANDIDNESS	Is uninhibited in expressing opinions; is frank and honest; appraises adults frankly; will not lie to avoid punishment.
DEPENDABILITY	Is reliable, dependable, responsible; can be counted on to carry out assigned tasks; can be counted on to follow instructions.
SOCIAL RESPONSIBILITY	Has a strong sense of social justice; is concerned about the welfare of others; is actively concerned about the rights of others.

COOPERATION	Is cooperative; works well with others; avoids bickering and fighting; is congenial and easy to get along with.
COMMON SENSE	Has common sense; shows good judgment.
SENSITIVITY	Feels criticism deeply; cares about others; is kind on principle; is sensitive to the feelings and needs of others; has both sympathy and empathy for others.
POPULARITY	Is well liked by other children; is sociable and enjoys the company of others; is chosen for leadership roles; is considered a friend by others; is usually of cheerful disposition.
ENTHUSIASM	Likes to try new experiences; expresses delight with unusual developments in science or other fields; frequently interrupts others when they are talking; becomes excited about own and others' discoveries; shows enjoyment in acquiring knowledge.
SENSE OF HUMOR	Has a keen sense of humor; sees humor in situations not readily apparent to others; enjoys humor in intellectual situations; may enjoy benign teasing, but does not like to be teased; dislikes sarcasm or cruel jokes.
SPATIAL RELATIONSHIPS	Likes to do jigsaw puzzles with many pieces; is good at fixing mechanical things; likes games with patterns and designs; is quick to sort blocks of different shapes.
EMOTIONAL STABILITY	Is usually secure emotionally; does not become upset easily; is slow to show anger; has a high frustration tolerance; is patient with people, especially younger and less bright children.
SELF-SUFFICIENCY AND SELF-CONFIDENCE	Is independent, individualistic, self-sufficient, self-confident; needs little direction from teachers or others; is not easily swayed from convictions without reasonable proof; does not accept authoritarian pronouncements without critical examination; does not fear being different; often prefers to work on his or her own; has confidence in own powers and abilities; has definite ideas and preferences.
HEALTH	Has fewer health problems than peers; health history is basically favorable; enjoys generally good health.
ENERGY	Is energetic and active; occasionally may be mislabeled "hyperactive," especially during early years; is well coordinated physically; enjoys athletic games and excels in athletic activities.
EARLY DEVELOPMENT	Sat up, walked, talked early; did everything earlier than expected; seemed to be more advanced than other babies of same age.
COMPARISON WITH SIBLINGS AND OTHERS	Sisters or brothers are also very bright; is different from other children in family; is very bright; is brighter than other children of same age.
PREFERENCE FOR OLDER PLAYMATES	Likes to play with older children; enjoys the company of older persons, including adults.

*Based on a research study by Virginia Z. Ehrlich, parts of which were presented at the Annual Conference of the Council for Exceptional Children, TAG (The Association for the Gifted), April 1981, and at the World Council for the Gifted, held in Montreal, Canada, August 1981.

quently do escape the notice of parents and teachers. It is interesting to note that parents of young children rarely cite such traits as capacity for complex thought, ability to plan and organize, use of common sense, or capacity for self-criticism as descriptors; on the other hand, teachers often will note these characteristics when asked to describe their students. Furthermore, for the very young child, while parents cite characteristics of physiological development such as early talking, walking, social response, or sitting up as clues to possible giftedness, teachers usually are in no position to observe such traits, since they develop prior to the school years.

Another critical consideration is the fact that some traits, though highly significant in identifying both intellectual giftedness and exceptional talent, are not easily observable. These traits are usually revealed with greater precision by objective tests or observation by talent specialists.

In spite of the general tendency to use checklists as guides for identifying giftedness, our data suggest another dimension to the problem. It seems that parents have other, unvoiced criteria for their decisions, criteria which are viewed by them as too vague, too elusive, or even too unimportant to concern the educator, although they may be dominating factors in the parents' estimates of their children's abilities. For example, there are subtle comparisons with siblings, playmates, and other children of their experience that lead parents to think: "Our child is different," although they may never voice the thought. Nor do they mention many of the very traits that are measurable by objective tests and that help to confirm their judgment of the potentialities of their children.

Nevertheless, results from my own research* show that parents of very young children (ages four to five) cite more traits of character and personality that have been found to be typical of gifted children as IQs increase from just below 100 through 164+. Some of the traits they cite discriminate between lower and higher ability children when two groups (IQ 100–131 vs. IQ 132–164+) are compared. These traits are vocabulary, thinking ability, capacity for symbolic thought, insight, early development, and sensitivity. They also cite reading ability, which discriminates between groups with IQs from 100 to 115 versus 116 to 164+.

It is, therefore, advisable for parents who use the foregoing chart or any other checklist brought to their attention to consider carefully the results and trust whatever feelings or intuitive judgments lead

---

*Based on a paper presented at the World Conference on the Gifted, Montreal, Canada, August 1981. "Analysis of Traits Cited by Parents in Identifying Young Gifted Children."

them to believe their child is gifted. Barring the occasional few whose ambitious egos may dominate their motives, parents genuinely concerned for their children should follow through on their beliefs and seek verification of their judgments by objective means. Teachers, too, should listen to such parents and try to substantiate their opinion. Teachers should not be misled by pupil misbehavior or poor achievement in class, as these frequently can be clues to possible giftedness. When a parent says that his or her child is bored in school, it is imperative that the teacher and the administration reexamine the school's teaching methods, curriculum content, and general policies to insure that the needs of potentially gifted children are being met.

PARENTS AS IDENTIFIERS OF YOUNG GIFTED CHILDREN

It has been my experience after many years of answering requests for information that parents are basically good identifiers of their bright or gifted children, even though they may not be able to place their children precisely on a scale of intellectual ability in comparison with other children. They recognize talent, too. Unfortunately, they are sometimes confused by projecting their own unsatisfied dreams or by rushing the development of special abilities.

In fact, parents are more effective than teachers, especially with the very young, preschool, or kindergarten child (14, 38). However, many parents become intimidated by professionals, especially teachers, when their observations are challenged. After all, the convention goes, the teacher (or the principal) must know! In the study by Jacobs (38), kindergarten teachers recognized only 4.3 percent of their gifted children, while parents of children in the same kindergarten group were able to identify correctly 61 percent of their gifted children. In a study conducted in the Rockford, Illinois, public schools, teachers correctly nominated 22 percent of the kindergarten gifted, while parents correctly nominated 67 percent (6). In another study (56), teachers at the junior high school level were no more successful.

I found out how well parents can identify their gifted children primarily as a result of answering hundreds of their requests for aid. As parents wrote letters or telephoned with what seemed to be a universal cry for help, I made notes of what they said in describing their children. The notebooks are filled with comments such as the following, in which the parents themselves describe their gifted children:

My child will be six in three months. He is attending a Montessori School at present. But he reads at the sixth-grade level. Where is there a school that will teach him at his own level?

My five-year-old son reads at fourth- or fifth-grade level. I think kindergarten would bore him. Where can I place him?

My niece is only two and one-half years old, but I know she is more mature than most children of her age. She speaks very well, can carry on an intelligent conversation with adults, remembers things very well. She really is more like a four- or five-year-old child.

My son is two years old. He has a good vocabulary. He dresses himself. He is very fast to adjust to situations. He learns without being taught.

My son knew his alphabet at the age of one and one-half. He is now three and one-half, can read short books. He can also write. He has an excellent memory.

My daughter is three and one-half. She is reading now. She can actually read from the McCall's magazine, and she comprehends what she is reading.

My son has a vocabulary of a ten-year-old. He is not quite five. He can do complicated jigsaw puzzles and has a terrific sense of direction. He remembers everything!

My son is not quite five years old. He plays chess, and has won in championship matches.

My daughter was reading when she was three years old. She is not quite five, but she is now reading books suitable for a child of nine or ten.

My five-year-old writes the alphabet, can spell very well, and she can add two-digit numbers, and sometimes even three. She knows colors and how to mix them to get other colors. She can make change with coins. I don't know how she does it, because I don't teach her, but she really can do it!

My son is three years old. He is very alert and grasps things very quickly. He knows his letters and numbers, and can read the *Jim and Jerry* books and other little books. He taught himself by watching "Sesame Street."

It is of interest to note the dominance of concern with the child's ability to read, which is consistent with our research findings about parent identifiers. A second observation I should like to make in passing is the tendency of parents to identify boys more frequently than girls. In our own work with young gifted children, we had to make a special effort to encourage the nomination of girls.

Parents and nursery/prekindergarten teachers may wish to know these other characteristics that are associated with the early years. Young gifted children may

1. Start to walk, sit up, turn over, or otherwise develop physically at an earlier age than their age peers.

2. Seem to be taller, heavier, healthier than other children.
3. Respond to the environment by giving a social smile, talking, or interacting with others at an earlier age than the average baby.

As these children grow beyond the infant years, they may

1. Learn to read, often without assistance, before going to school.
2. Create imaginary playmates, especially if they are only children or the first-born.
3. Learn easily, requring little or no repetition of instructions or explanations.
4. Play games that are a little more complicated than one would expect for their years.
5. Use money up to one dollar. Know the value of the coins and be able to make change.
6. Learn to tell time in hours and minutes.
7. Ask endless questions, punctuated with frequent "Why's?"
8. Play games that involve organization, classification, and sorting of items.
9. Learn the primary colors and frequently the secondary colors as well.
10. Learn to count well beyond 10 or 20.
11. Make comparisons, such as larger–smaller, taller–shorter, higher–lower.
12. Know number combinations involved in addition and subtraction and frequently solve more complex problems involving two or more digits by methods they themselves have devised.
13. Develop intense interests and pursue them for a long time.
14. Make collections of unusual objects and tend to learn a great deal about their subject.
15. Enjoy playing with older playmates and speaking to adults.
16. Show a delightful sense of humor, without malice.
17. Enjoy "thinking" about things.
18. Show a great deal of concentration and absorption in a task.
19. Display a very good memory for poetry, songs, or other information.
20. Enjoy working with jigsaw puzzles having a comparatively large number of pieces.
21. Use words that are unusual for their age, such as *probably, perhaps,* and *justice*.
22. Enjoy having stories read to them, some over and over again.
23. Know left from right.
24. Dress themselves and fasten buttons and zippers.
25. Compare and contrast items, persons, ideas, and experiences.
26. Know geometric shapes and call them by their proper names.
27. Remember and follow directions.
28. Know their own address and telephone number.
29. Understand gender and be able to identify themselves as boys or girls.

If a child displays at least a fourth of these characteristics before the usual time for such behavior, he or she may be intellectually gifted. It would be desirable to have this suspicion verified by formal testing procedures.

IDENTIFYING THE GIFTED CHILD IN THE CLASSROOM

The view from the teacher's desk is different from that of the parents' living room. Teachers may find the following list, adapted from an early guide prepared by the New York City Board of Education, useful in identifying children for special classes or programs for the gifted. The child should give evidence of at least some of the following characteristics (see also pp. 116–117):

- Creativity in one or more areas
- Interest in many things
- Clarity of thought and language
- Insight and penetration in subject matter
- Emotional stability
- Good character
- Social leadership
- Self-reliance
- Sensitivity to the feelings and needs of others
- Intellectual curiosity frequently shown by asking many questions
- Ability to reason logically
- Ability to plan and organize
- Ability to explain reasons for actions
- Ability to see relationships
- Ability to concentrate and pursue work or interests to an unusual degree despite difficulties
- Ability to put ideas in writing clearly and correctly
- Ability to do work above grade level in several curriculum areas

Combined with these characteristics, any objective evidence of superior ability provided by classroom work or standardized achievement tests, particularly in reading comprehension and arithmetic reasoning, as well as any intelligence test used, will add to the efficiency of the identification process. Teachers should note, however, that any discrepancy between classroom performance and achievement on standardized tests should be checked. If the data are correct, then reliance on the standardized test is to be preferred as a truer indicator of the child's general ability.

WHAT HAPPENS IF WE DO NOT RECOGNIZE GIFTEDNESS OR TALENT?

A study conducted by D. S. Bridgman (3) revealed that large numbers of gifted children who could qualify for college work either do not go to college or, if they do, do not complete their studies. Approximately 55 percent of males and 70 percent of females either do not finish high school, finish high school but do not enter college, or do not complete college work once started. This is an enormous loss of intellectual ability to the work force.

The Marland Report (46), conducted at the request of Congress in 1969, showed that only 4 percent of the national population of gifted children, estimated to be over two and one-half million, are recognized as such and are having their needs met in school. Since 1969, the proportion whose needs are being met has risen to about 35 percent.

Many bright youngsters leave school out of sheer boredom and frustration. Talented children frequently find that formal schools will not make the necessary accommodations to help them meet the demands of their special abilities.

At a conference on education of the gifted (60), Murry Sidlin, conductor of the New Haven Symphony Orchestra, related the incredible experiences he had had in junior high school. One example he gave concerned his guidance counselor, who refused to change his program so that he could take part in orchestra classes on the basis that it was "too much trouble." Another teacher refused to excuse him from classroom attendance so that he could go to a performance where he was the featured soloist. Only the most determined persistence, combined with genuine parental support, helped Sidlin to achieve his goal.

During the early years, unrecognized giftedness can manifest itself in many ways. Among these are inattention, restlessness, mischievous behavior, hyperactivity, withdrawal, imaginary illness, or even outright refusal to go to school. As children grow older, they may become defiant and persist in their earlier behavior or, recognizing their helplessness in the face of stronger forces, they may yield by becoming conforming and compliant, submerging their abilities. Children in environments where intellectual ability is not valued will try to conceal their knowledge and "play the game."

The results are sad for both the child and society. For those who refuse to yield and defy the authorities, there is often conflict and endless heartache. The student may eventually go his own way and create a place for himself in spite of an unappreciative society, even though the price may be one of bitterness and loneliness. For those gifted youngsters who decide to yield and "play the game," the results are even more tragic. They may become misfits in tasks to which they have no real commitment; or they may drift from one job to another in search of an elusive satisfaction that proper identification and training might have provided. Loneliness and frustration become sad aspects of an unfulfilled life. Society, meanwhile, has lost a potentially creative mind that might have helped to solve a critical problem. At this juncture in the history of mankind, we can ill afford to lose the services of the superior gifted and talented persons in our midst. As avowed humanitarians, we are also obligated to recognize the needs of that segment of society to which we owe so much for our personal comforts and satisfactions.

SUGGESTED READINGS

EHRLICH, VIRGINIA Z. "Identifying Giftedness in the Early Years, from Three through Seven." In *Education of the Preschool/Primary Gifted and Talented.* 1980. Edited by Sherri Butterfield. National/State Leadership Training Institute, Ventura County Superintendent of Schools, 535 East Main Street, Ventura, Calif. 93009.

GOWAN, JOHN C., and E. PAUL TORRANCE, eds. *Educating the Ablest: A Book of Readings on the Education of Gifted Children,* Chaps. 4–6, 18. Itasca, Ill.: F. E. Peacock, 1979.

GUILFORD, J. P. *The Nature of Human Intelligence,* Chap. I, Sec. 3. New York: McGraw-Hill, 1967.

HAGEN, ELIZABETH. *Identification of the Gifted.* New York: Teachers College Press, 1980.

"Identification of the Gifted." Exceptional Child Bibliographies. The Council for Exceptional Children, 1920 Association Drive, Reston, Va. 22091.

MARTINSON, RUTH A. *The Identification of the Gifted and Talented.* 1975. The Council for Exceptional Children, 1920 Association Drive, Reston, Va. 22091.

PIAGET, JEAN. *The Psychology of Intelligence.* Totowa, N.J.: Littlefield, Adams, 1976. Reprint of 1947 edition.

TORRANCE, E. PAUL. *Creativity.* Belmont, Calif.: Dimensions Publishing, 1969.

Biographies, Autobiographies

Probably the best way to gain an understanding of the gifted is to read their autobiographies or biographies, particularly those which include extensive coverage of their early years. Some of the personalities whose biographies or autobiographies give significant insight into their early development are

George Washington Carver	Douglas MacArthur
Mary Cassatt	Felix Mendelssohn
Winston Churchill	Yehudi Menuhin
Marie Curie	John Stuart Mill
Charles Darwin	Maria Montessori
Benjamin Disraeli	Wolfgang Amadeus Mozart
Abba Eban	Blaise Pascal
Thomas Alva Edison	Roger Tory Peterson
Albert Einstein	Pablo Picasso
George Eliot	Albert Schweitzer
Margot Fonteyn	Isaac Bashevis Singer
Johann Wolfgang von Goethe	Chaim Weizmann
Helen Keller	Norbert Wiener
Giacomo Leopardi	Virginia Woolf

A most unusual insight into the gifted mind is described in

FYNN (pseudonym). *Mister God, This Is Anna: A True Story.* New York: Holt, Rinehart & Winston, 1974. The story of an abused waif of four who was "adopted" by Fynn's family and who died tragically at the age of eight. Her conversations with Fynn, himself a brilliant scientist and computer expert, reveal a phenomenal mind. The story, though tragic, is told with great tenderness and humor.

Trials and Tribulations of Being Gifted

One of the symbols appropriated by some programs for the gifted is a segment of Michelangelo's Sistine Chapel painting, *The Creation*. The hand of God is extended toward the hand of man, as He bestows the gift of life. But who is the receiver of this rare gift? Is it the individual whom we label *gifted*, or is it the human race on whom the gift is bestowed through the individuals bearing it?

It might be preferable to view the gifted as bearers of gifts to humanity. Like so many gifts, a few of these are received, cherished, and nurtured, while others are rejected, wasted, or lost. So, too, with the intellectually gifted and talented. As the bearers of these gifts, they are occasionally appreciated, but sadly have often been ignored, chastised, ridiculed, and even punished. They have been persecuted as heretics (Galileo), ridiculed (Columbus), crucified (Jesus), exiled (Cicero), ignored (Tesla), poisoned (Socrates), imprisoned (Gandhi), and murdered (Lincoln).

Throughout the animal kingdom, that which is different is not tolerated. Civilization, enlightenment, and religions have only recently instilled in the human a sense of compassion for and understanding of the "different" in the handicapped, the retarded, the negative deviate from the normal. Society at large, however, has not yet learned to accept and understand the positive deviates, the geniuses and intellectual giants, the bearers of gifts to humanity, the "gifted." The lot of the gifted is basically not a happy one. As Norbert Wiener has stated: "We are not wanted by society."

THREE UNFOUNDED BELIEFS ABOUT THE GIFTED

A whole mythology has developed about the gifted, a mythology that persists in whole or in fragments despite the most convincing scientific and experiential evidence to the contrary. The following three myths are among the most common.

MYTH: The Gifted Are Frail, Weak, and Sickly

A persistent notion about the gifted is that they are frail, weak, and sickly. A few names quickly come to mind of persons with whom such associations are made: the sickly writers Keats, Stevenson, Elizabeth Barrett Browning; the crippled Toulouse-Lautrec; the hunchbacked Italian poet Giacomo Leopardi, . . . Other names could be added. However, you may discover quickly enough that the list is not as long as you might expect. Now think of other gifted and talented persons who were basically strong and healthy: Franklin, Jefferson, Schweitzer, Einstein, Michelangelo, da Vinci, Goethe, Picasso, Casals.... Many of these lived very long and healthy lives, and one suspects that their names will come to your mind far more readily than those of the sickly and handicapped. The fact is that the intellectually gifted child is, on the average, healthier, stronger, even handsomer than his average peers. Studies by Terman and his colleagues (67) have demonstrated this quite satisfactorily.

Nevertheless, the bright child who catches a winter cold is told it is because of studying too much, while the rest of his or her classmates go to bed with the seasonal common cold because "everybody has it." The bright child who wears glasses is nicknamed "Four-Eyes" or "Professor," while possibly blinder classmates wear glasses simply because they are nearsighted or farsighted, and not because they "read too much." There seems to be a need to seek compensation for extremes of human traits, causing people to slip easily into such phrases or terms as "beautiful but dumb" or "egghead."

MYTH: The Gifted Are Able to Fend for Themselves

Another notion that is used as an excuse for doing nothing for the gifted is that they will succeed without help or guidance. Add this to your list of unfounded beliefs. No, the gifted cannot fend for themselves any more than other children can. They need guidance, help, good teaching, and nurturing.

If college graduation is used as a criterion of our success with the academically gifted, we are losing a significant proportion of our capable youth. In his study for the National Science Foundation, Donald S. Bridgman (3) reported that only 45 percent of the males who are qualified for college work actually graduate. About 22 percent enter college but do not graduate; 22 percent graduate from high school but do not enter college; and 11 percent do not even graduate from high school. The figures for females are even more disheartening. Only 30 percent finish college and 20 percent enter college but do not graduate. Forty percent finish high school and never enter college, and 10 percent do not finish high school.

When their gifts are not recognized, especially in school, students drop out both physically and psychologically. They learn very early to submerge their abilities, to conform to the preposterous requirements of rigid school systems, and to seek anonymity in mediocrity, since that is what seems to be valued by their peers, their teachers, and others in their child world.

There have been gifted persons who have fought social rejection successfully, but their lives have been sad and lonely, and we have no way of knowing how much more they could have achieved if they had enjoyed more favorable educational and social environments.

MYTH: The Gifted "Burn Out" Early; Their Gifts Don't Last

Another common belief about the gifted is that they "burn out" early, that their precocity is only a childhood phenomenon. This, of course, is said of child prodigies. Nonsense! Child prodigies attract attention because they are young and their divergence from the common experience is so obvious. Actress Helen Hayes made her stage debut at age eight; half a century later she was still "first lady" of the stage. Mozart, Menuhin, Ricci—all were child prodigies, but their talents as adults are no less outstanding. John Stuart Mill was another child prodigy, but the philosophical writings that gave him an eminent place in history were published in adulthood. Although Albert Schweitzer, Johann von Goethe, and Giuseppe Verdi were all brilliant in childhood, each lived to an enviable old age and is known to us primarily because of accomplishments as an adult, many of them produced in the most advanced years. Longfellow put this thought into poetry in commenting on old age:

> It is too late! Ah, nothing is too late
> Till the tired heart shall cease to palpitate.
> Cato learned Greek at eighty; Sophocles
> Wrote his grand Oedipus, and Simonides
> Bore off the prize of verse from his compeers,
> When he had numbered more than fourscore years,
> And Theophrastus, at fourscore and ten,
> Had but begun his "Characters of Men."
> Chaucer, at Woodstock with the nightingales,
> At sixty wrote the Canterbury Tales;
> Goethe at Weimar, toiling to the last,
> Completed Faust when eighty years were past.
> These are indeed exceptions; but they show
> How far the gulf-stream of our youth may flow
> Into the arctic regions of our lives, ...
>
> Lines from *Morituri Salutamus*

Generally, the gifted retain their exceptional superiority throughout life and show evidence of continued growth and expansion of their capacities when properly nurtured. The outstanding work on this aspect of giftedness is, of course, the Terman longitudinal study that has followed the lives of gifted children from their school days right through middle and old age (67–71). The gifted, these studies conclude, fulfill the promise of their youth and make significantly more contributions to society than their peers of lesser abilities.

CHARACTERISTICS RELATED TO GIFTEDNESS THAT MAY LEAD TO PROBLEMS

When we speak about problems related to giftedness, we must realize that the gifted are generally a law-abiding, conforming group that contributes comparatively few offenders to the social order. In Terman's follow-up studies on gifted youth (69–71), in the Hartshorne and May studies on character (31), and in numerous other studies, it has been shown that the gifted are happily endowed with those socially positive traits that do not lead to the life of a criminal. But being gifted can be and often is a trial for the individual.

Students who have had a chance to share their feelings with me or who speak at conferences on the gifted make statements such as these:

> It makes you feel like a real outsider when people turn against you just because they find out you're gifted. It makes you feel like a freak.
> I hate being the best student in the class, mostly because my classmates seem to hate me.
> Doesn't anyone like us?
> You don't mind being gifted, and sometimes you don't even realize you are until you discover that the other kids are jealous of you. Then you want to hide and pretend you don't know anything.
> Sometimes, if you learn quickly or have studied some subject intensively, teachers resent you for knowing more than they do.
> Just when you think you may be finding someone who understands what you're all about, you get a teacher who seems to be your worst enemy—just because you know too much!
> If you're gifted, you seem to be a ready target for a teacher's sarcastic barbs. They seem to be always at war with you, just because you're smart.
> Beginning with the first years of elementary school, the gifted child is pressured by his peers not to reveal either his intelligence or his intellectual curiosity. If he chooses to do so, he is made an object of ridicule and finds himself excluded from social groups within his class.

It is not only the very young, in the throes of trying to understand an unfriendly society, who tell us about the unhappiness their giftedness imposes on them. Those who have finally achieved public approval and acclamation have the same sad tales to tell about their early years.

Versatility of Interests

Usually, gifted children are a versatile group. They have a wide variety of interests and an endless thirst for knowledge in all areas. As one of our high school youngsters put it, "You know, I'm not smart . . . I'm not great. I just have this burning desire to learn!" When we asked very young gifted children in the Astor Program what they liked about school, these five-, six-, and seven-year-olds said the same thing: "I love to learn."

People who work with the gifted will tell you that they want to learn about *everything*. Given the time and the opportunity, they will take courses in topics covering a wide range of fields and, of course, they read everything in sight. Since they tend to be quite proficient in almost everything they find interesting, it is difficult for them to focus their attention on one area and make a satisfactory career choice. These are the people who double up on careers, relying on one for income and on the other for the added pleasure. Thus, we have doctors who are writers, teachers who are professional artists, businessmen who are teachers, and so on. The great achievers of the past are excellent examples of this versatility. Benjamin Franklin was an acute businessman, a diplomat, scientist, inventor, and writer; Thomas Jefferson was an architect, farmer, lawyer, statesman, and U.S. president; Leonardo da Vinci was a scientist, inventor, and painter; Johann Wolfgang von Goethe was a statesman and poet; Albert Schweitzer was a doctor, organist, specialist on Bach, theologian, and philosopher.

Although this versatility is a valuable trait that helps the gifted person to understand and cope with a wide range of knowledge, it must be tempered with some practical considerations. It is too easy for such talent to be dissipated in tinkering with many temporarily interesting activities, with no well-developed skills and capabilities in a concentrated area for productive work. Parents should encourage their gifted children's wide variety of interests, while helping them to focus on one or two specific areas for lifelong attention. This is best achieved by encouraging the early activities and hobbies that hold more than a passing interest for the child, so that they may become the basis of a career choice. This is particularly true for those talented in the performing arts, since it takes long years of practice to achieve ultimate mastery. It is also equally worthwhile in the intellectual areas if the child shows an early propensity for a particular topic.

There are many well-known personalities whose careers were based on a childhood interest. Michael Kahn, director of the New York Shakespeare Festival, related to an enthralled audience how he had decided, while still in kindergarten, that he was going to be a director. With the aid of truly understanding teachers, the young Michael was allowed to "direct" the class plays and to write one of his own in the third or fourth grade. At the time he told this story, Kahn's plays were enjoying a great success on New York's Broadway.

Giacomo Puccini was "chosen" by his mother from among her children to be the musician of the family, and she directed all her efforts toward achieving that goal. Ludwig van Beethoven had written four sonatas by the time he was four years old. George Washington Carver was known as the "plant doctor" while he was still a child. Pablo Picasso was so talented as a child that his father gave up his own painting ambitions in order to further his son's talent. Guglielmo Marconi, inventor of the wireless telegraphy, had been fascinated by the wonders of electricity as a child and carried out many experiments in the attic of his home. Thomas Alva Edison's insatiable curiosity annoyed his teachers so much that by the time he was seven, his mother took him out of school and taught him herself.

Parents should also direct the attention of the child to the great variety of occupations that are available and that are still developing, so that some curiosity and interest can be stimulated in worthwhile projects with potential for future growth. (See Chapter 8.)

Impatience with Detail

The following is a scene that must be familiar to many parents of gifted children.

Tommy catches Daddy in a rare moment of leisure. With no prelude or introductory explanation, he asks: "Dad, do you know why a royal flush is a better hand in poker than four of a kind? I mean, who decided that one was better than the other?" Aha! Now Dad can show off a little of his own genius. After all, he was always good in mathematics and he knows his probability theory. He begins a careful explanation of the number of cards in the deck and the various possibilities involved in permutations and combinations, and he elaborates carefully on the odds of getting a card of each suit. He becomes entranced with his subject and goes deeper and deeper into details. Even though Tommy is intrigued by the theory, he becomes more and more impatient as his father repeats what he thinks are difficult concepts and uses example after example to illustrate his point.

Tommy really understood what his father said the first time around, and all the repetition makes him restless. He tries to interrupt the lecture: "But, Dad, ..." And Dad says, "Now just listen carefully. This is tricky," and goes on and on. Tommy's attentive look becomes somewhat glazed, and he doesn't respond when his father suddenly stops and asks him a question. It is evident that he has not been listening. "Tommy, haven't you been listening? Why am I wasting my time?" the father exclaims, and picks up his newspaper to conceal his disappointment in not having mesmerized his son with his own brilliance.

But Tommy *was* interested. He just did not want to have to listen to the same thing being said over and over again. It is difficult for those of us who have special knowledge of a subject to accept the fact that an inexperienced young child could possibly grasp a difficult concept with a minimum of explanation. Intellectually gifted children face this problem constantly. Schools insist on repetitious assignments, drills, and overelaboration of explanations the gifted child doesn't need. Gifted children have a quick grasp of ideas, can foresee results and consequences, and frequently are far ahead of the teacher in seeing the answer to a problem. They do not have to pay too much attention in classrooms because they can leapfrog over a good many of the intermediate steps toward the solution to a problem or the answer to a question.

This happens often in elementary school when children are learning simple arithmetic processes. Many gifted children do most of the reasoning in their heads, come up with the correct answer, and have no way of explaining how they got it. Teachers, bound by the rigidities of methods courses, insist on breaking everything down into fine analytic bits, which gifted children find unnecessary. However, since they do not arrive at the answer along the prescribed route, they are told they are wrong for not knowing the "right" way to do it.

It is probably true that gifted persons tend to have poor handwriting. This is not so surprising when one considers how slow the process of putting words on paper can be when your mind is racing ahead in a turmoil of ideas. For the very young child, this disparity between the flow of ideas and the physical coordination required by handwriting can be a very frustrating experience. It is not likely that gifted children will spend time to develop a Palmer-perfect handwriting when they are more engrossed with thinking and ideas than with the minor need to make a perfect letter *a*.

Gifted children should be encouraged to understand the need for precision and detail. This is best attained by allowing them to develop and pursue special interests that will hold their attention by their very attractiveness. For example, Roger Tory Peterson became interested in birdwatching at a very early age. At the age of eight, he would eagerly arise before sunrise in order to catch some species of bird he wanted to see. To classify and differentiate among all the different kinds of birds, he had to keep records and notes of special characteristics and markings. Detail was required by the task itself and not superimposed by arbitrary regulation. As a painter, he needed to note each marking very carefully if he was to make a fairly representative picture. As we now know, Peterson field guides and bird paintings are the joy of serious nature lovers and students.

The gifted resent detail when it seems irrelevant, but they are capable of the most painstaking work when attention to such detail is needed to resolve a problem. It is not essential to the resolution of a problem for these children to know the school-book procedures for adding, subtracting, dividing, and multiplying numbers, because very often they have an intuitive understanding of these relationships and can do it all mentally or by their own unique and ingenious methods. We need to keep these facts in mind when teaching such children, and to let them focus on those specifics that are essential to further their knowledge. We will then not find them unwilling. The detail and specifics that are required will command the child's attention simply because they are truly relevant to the solution of the problem.

Repetition and rote learning are usually anathema to the gifted. They need to be taught that there is a place for this in their learning. For example, rote learning of number combinations is essential to efficient work in mathematics. There is no way but the rote technique for learning the alphabet, a necessary tool in using a dictionary, filing important papers, keeping things in some arbitrary order. No would-be doctor can attain that coveted diploma without memorizing the elaborate enumeration of bones in the body, the technical vocabulary of the field, the complex and numerous syndromes that identify and differentiate diseases. These may seem like impossible chores, but they must be done; giftedness alone will not accomplish the task. Application is required, fortunately enhanced by the gifted person's usually phenomenal memory. This characteristic, the superior memory, can sometimes lead gifted children to deceive themselves into believing that all learning comes easily and with practically no effort. It is only after the bitter experience of the first failure to perform that a gifted child comes to the realization that some effort must be expended in order to master certain subjects.

Parents can help their gifted children by trying to explain the long-term necessity for some detail, some rote learning, and some repetition of activities, while at the same time supporting their children in their complaints against the unjustified waste of their time by unnecessary schoolwork. Long homework assignments that require a student to repeat spelling words, solve the same type of mathematics problems, or copy endless notes from encyclopedias for useless reports—all are justifiable causes for complaints to the teacher. The child's time can be spent much better in thinking activities.

A young man of about twenty-two years of age wrote a letter to the columnist Ann Landers in which he complained of the careless education he had received. Because he was so bright, all learning was effortless, and he never learned the disciplines of organization, application, and attention. He found himself now, he said, at loose ends, with no purpose or organization in his life, unable to tackle any task that required these traits. It was a pathetic commentary on school systems that permit this unchallenging approach to the education of the very gifted child.

Those who are talented in the performing and visual arts know the importance of attention to detail and the necessity for repetitious activities. No matter how talented the child may be, he or she will never become a virtuoso violinist, a great dancer, a polished actor, or a skilled painter without practice, practice, practice... and attention to the many little details that are required for the best performance. Parents of talented children need to impress on them the necessity of such concentrated effort in these professions before encouraging them to become too deeply involved. Young children see only the end product of a beautiful ballet or a great concert; they may be enchanted with the finished product without realizing all that is required. The truly gifted usually reveal their giftedness by the fact that they are capable of the kind of concentrated effort that is required for ultimate success. As Edison put it, "Genius is one per cent inspiration and ninety-nine per cent perspiration."

Dyssynchrony

In a talk before the Second World Conference on the Gifted, held in San Francisco in 1977, Professor Terrassier of France (72) introduced a term into our vocabulary for the gifted which is singularly appropriate for describing the inconsistency between the child's intellectual maturity and his social, emotional, and physical development. He used the word *dyssynchrony*. There is a normal, or average, pace at which the body grows, such as in height and weight. Estimates can be made of the average ages at which certain aspects of social and emotional maturity can be expected. In the same way, there is a pattern of intellectual growth associated with chronological age that can usually be predicted.

On the average, these several developmental tracks proceed in approximate harmony with each other, so that we can expect a child to begin walking at about the fourteenth month, to say a few words at that time, to be of a certain height and weight for his age. The developmental clock of such a child may be said to be *synchronized*.

In the gifted child, the developmental clocks frequently are not synchronized. There is a *dyssynchrony*, so that we may have a child whose intellectual growth may be comparable to that of a ten-year-old boy, while he is chronologically, physically, socially, and emotionally only five years old. This dyssynchrony can lead to many complications for the gifted child. There would be no problem if society were not conscious of the apparent discrepancy and if it did not insist on expecting behavior that is consistent, not with the younger age, but with the older age represented by the child's intellectual ability.

Leta Hollingworth, in describing an exceptionally gifted boy of seven with an IQ of 191, wrote (33, pp. 80–81):

> Motor control is, of course, far behind abstract thinking; writing is slow and feeble, while reading is rapid and fluent; shopwork is poor but arithmetic is excellent; he can surpass 8- and 9-year olds—even those of superior intelligence—in the classroom, but in playing with them he cannot catch a ball and is always the last to be selected when sides 'choose up', because he is a handicap in any playground competitions.... In a test of mechanical ability, he could tell what mechanisms were to be constructed from the materials ... but he was not 'handy' enough to put them together.

The problems this inconsistency creates for the gifted child appear in many forms at home, in school, in the playground, almost everywhere. For example, it is difficult for teachers to accept the fact that a five-year-old can read a book that is usually used for a ten-year-old and yet not be able to write or even form the letters of his or her name. There were many such children in New York City's Astor Program for Gifted Children. Their reading ability was phenomenal but consistent with their very high intelligence, which ranged from IQs of 140 right through the very top of the test scale. Since they were anywhere from four to five and one-half years old, they were truly very, very young. Their bodies had not yet developed the physical eye–hand coordination required in the fine movements of handwriting. Some of them did not develop any notable handwriting skill for almost a year, even though almost all progressed a minimum of two years in reading ability beyond the point where they started, and some up to the ninth-grade reading level. Trained teachers accommodated to this phenomenon, but generally teachers do not recognize the discrepancy.

Another problem is associated with the emotional needs of the child. A five-year-old has not yet learned the social inhibitions required to conceal tears or fears, and will cry and pout just like all children, regardless of his or her intellectual ability. A child who is hurt or frightened will react according to his or her chronological age. Then society commits the ultimate insult by asking: "How can such a smart little boy or little girl cry for such a silly reason?" Perhaps because there is no justice in the world and society can be awfully stupid! The child cries because he or she is unhappy, and brainpower has nothing to do with it. A child can be hurt just as much with a high IQ as with a low IQ, and the same medicine applies in both cases—tenderness, love, and understanding.

Children who are accelerated in grade face a different kind of situation. Their classmates are older than they are and therefore are likely to be larger; depending on their ages, they may be at a different stage of emotional and social development. In this situation, on the playground or in the gym, gifted children can become misfits. They can't match their classmates' physical prowess. They can't run as fast or jump as high, even though they may know all the rules of the game better than any of their friends. If a boy is in the middle school years, he is still a "kid" while the others may have reached puberty. Girls find that they are still "little girls" with flat chests, while their classmates have become "young ladies" with blossoming bosoms. Boys are still chirping in their soprano voices while their playmates are beginning to boom as their voices mature. In high school, when the dating game becomes a serious matter, the age discrepancies become more accentuated.

All the brains in the world will not undo the feelings of isolation and alienation that these disparities create. A group of high school seniors, chatting about problems of acceleration through school at too fast a clip, observed that one boy they knew, who was about eleven to their average of sixteen or seventeen, was treated like a "pet"; he was well-liked and respected for his ability but could not be included in their social activities. Accelerated students, in retrospect, view acceleration as a mixed blessing. It is one way, they say, of meeting their intellectual needs and, from that point of view, it may be desirable. However, they do have some negative feelings about the effects of *grade* acceleration on their social and emotional lives, and believe that these factors should be considered carefully by those who make the decisions during their early years.

Power of Concentration

A characteristic of intellectually gifted and artistically talented children is their power of concentration, a total involvement in the task at hand. When they are very young, this power of concentration can lead them into difficulties with their parents if they do not respond or carry out an instruction given while they are deeply involved in some activity. If they are reading, they will lose themselves in their books and shut out all interruptions. Mother ducks her head in the door, looks at the golden curls cascading around and concealing her darling's face, and says, "Come into the living room, dear. I need your help in there." She turns and goes into the living room, expecting someone to follow her. Nothing happens. If she calls out: "Merrie, are you coming?" there is no answer. Oh, my! Trouble is brewing. But it need not, if only Mother will keep in mind that this child is blessed with a high power of concentration that will help her to retain almost everything she reads. Parents and teachers should cherish this trait in children and work with it, not against it. Try to get the child's attention before making a request or giving an instruction. Give the child a few seconds to move from the area of concentration and focus on your interest or request. It isn't a fault; it's a blessing, and we should not penalize the child for having it.

There must also be a certain justice in the interruption of children's activities, even when they are very young. Building a tower of cubes as high as it will go without toppling over is very serious business and requires deep concentration. Let the child finish the task, or wait until the tower inevitably falls, before taking the child off for lunch or to another activity. Give children extended periods of time in which they can work or play without fear of interruption. If they are in the middle of a story, try to let them finish it, or tell them how much more time is left so that they can pace their thinking. Provide a quiet environment for them. Loud music, blaring television sets or radios, and noisy conversation are not conducive to the kind of contemplative thinking gifted children like to do. Yes, gifted children like to think. Others teach them that it is painful and a chore, but that is not their own feeling. Classrooms, too, should be conducted in a manner that respects the child's right to pursue an activity to its logical conclusion. The piecemeal pursuit of knowledge that is prevalent in many classrooms is destructive to good study and work habits.

Love of Truth

Intellectually gifted children are lovers of knowledge, seekers of truth. They want to know the how, what, why, when, and where of everything. They want to know the cause for every effect. They probe and probe for answers. Parents are initiated into this ritual as they face the endless barrage of "Whys" issuing from their children, frequently with no answer for the questions asked. "Who made God?" "What's outside of space?" "Where does time begin?" "What does nothing look like?" Of course, it is this love of truth, this desire to know, this pursuit of knowledge that defines the quality of these children's gift—the gift they bear to expand and improve the world of their fellow human beings. They have been endowed with the capacity to wonder and question, to recognize questions and problems that elude the attention of less gifted peers.

Like so many aspects of giftedness, this love of truth often leads these children into difficulties. They cannot accept an illogical argument. If they hear something in class that seems to be self-contradictory, they do not have the sophistication or, perhaps, the hypocrisy to conceal their doubts. They will often just blurt out: "That's wrong." Neither teachers nor parents are prepared to be corrected by a child. In their own minds, they may justify their misstatements, being unwilling to believe that this younger being can really know enough to correct them. Fortunately, more and more teachers are becoming enlightened to the fact that the gifted have an enormous capacity for acquiring information, sometimes far beyond the teacher's experience, and are learning to accept it and work with it. Parents, too, need to develop this insight into their gifted children's mentality. They must realize that the child is not being "fresh," "argumentative," or "disrespectful." All the child is trying to do is to find out the truth, whatever it may be, and there is absolutely no personal judgment involved in the seeking.

Norbert Wiener describes his own experience thus:

> My experience leads me to believe that the prodigy is desperately unsure of himself and underrates himself. Every child, in gaining emotional security, believes in the values of the world around him and thus starts by being, not a revolutionary, but an utter conservative. He wishes to believe that his elders, on whom he is dependent for the arrangement and control of the world in which he lives, are all wise and good. When he discovers that they are not, he faces the necessity of loneliness and of forming his own judgment of a world that he can no longer fully trust. The prodigy shares this experience with every child, but added to it is the suffering which grows from belonging half to the adult world and half to the world of the children about him. Hence, he goes through a stage when his mass of conflicts is greater than that of most other children, and he is rarely a pretty picture. (78, pp. 117–118)

Parents would do well to keep this in mind, particularly in matters of religion, which relies strongly on faith, tradition, and dogma. The gifted child who questions a religious custom usually is not trying to reject the faith, but rather is seeking explanations that will coincide with his or her sense of logic and orderliness. This is a delicate area in which the guidance of persons trained in the respective faiths, such as ministers, priests, and rabbis, may be helpful to the parents. It would also be helpful to the child to have a serious discussion, in which his or her concerns were treated with adult dignity, with someone who could reply to questions with appropriate authority, and who would recognize the high level of thinking that the child is bringing to the problem.

Sensitivity, Empathy, Sympathy for Others

The lives of eminent personalities, as well as research studies, have shown that the gifted have a deep concern for others. They have a keen sense of justice and tend to be protective of those less fortunate than themselves. In classes for exceptionally gifted children at the prekindergarten and kindergarten level, where the children's spontaneity was still functioning out of reach of adult interference, it was found that the children were very caring of each other. The child who forgot to bring lunch never had to worry. He or she inevitably had a larger lunch than anyone else, because the others gave freely from their own portions. The child who wept quietly in a corner for some reason soon had two or three attentive, loving peers who came to the rescue. As a group, they were eager and ready to give help and assistance to any cause. These were traits that were being encouraged by the teachers in their concern with good character development. It is only as society begins to discourage this caring and cooperative spirit that children become inhibited and may begin to hold back. I have found, however, that gifted children of all ages are deeply concerned about the welfare of others and will give most generously of themselves.

This is where trouble can begin for them. The gifted will espouse causes that others, more cautious and self-defensive, will not touch. They will become involved in social movements, action groups, or other activities whose apparent mission in life may seem to be a just and generous one. Being somewhat naïve and gullible, the gifted find it hard to be persuaded to look for ulterior motives. They see a need and want to take care of it. They cannot believe that people can be unkind to each other, because they tend to be guileless and generous in their own feelings.

In one class, a little boy showed up with a black eye. When asked how he got it, he would not tell and never did. He said that he wasn't going to get anybody into trouble. We learned later that a little girl had given it to him in a moment of pique. In another instance, a bright little girl of three was bitten by another child. When her mother asked, "What did you do? Didn't you hit back?" the child replied, "Why should I? I might hurt her."

Note how artists who are in public life turn out to raise funds for the needy and oppressed. They have an exceedingly generous spirit. Note also how scientists will jeopardize their public image in order to protect the human race from its own follies, such as the atomic bomb, pollution, and wars. At their best, the gifted exemplify the goodness of humanity, and since there is also much that is not good in humans, the gifted suffer for their concern.

Great Expectations, Unfair Demands

The gift of the child is so impressive that we come to expect superior performance at all times—and in all aspects of life. Sad stories are told about the heavy burdens of responsibility placed on very young shoulders, often unintentionally, simply because a child was bright and able. The gifted suffer from excessive pressure to perform imposed by parents, teachers, peers, and others. Just because they are gifted, they are expected to maintain a uniformly high standard of achievement. If they get less than an *A*, or 95 percent, or even a perfect score, they are challenged. "Surely, you could have done better!" "I'm disappointed in you. I was sure you could do better!" "Have you been doing *all* your work? You can do better than that!" "A hundred percent! It must have been an easy exam!" Parents join with teachers in this cruel demand for consistently high performance. Classmates seem to take a special glee in any mistakes the gifted child may make. "I thought you had all the answers," they taunt.

Gifted children are subject to the same variable behavior all children have. They will usually perform better than most in their areas of competence, but they will also have good and bad days, as well as varying degrees of mastery in even their best subjects.

Parents need to learn to accept their child's performance and to make it clear that the child will be loved and valued regardless of the level of his or her achievement. If children receive praise and approval only by bringing home gold stars and top grades, they will begin to feel that their brainpower is all that matters. If their parents tell relatives and friends only about their intellectual accomplishments or magnificent artistic performance, and never mention a thoughtful act, a kind deed, a generous gesture, these children will be justly resentful.

The classic case of tragedy arising out of such treatment is the life story of Henry Sidis. Sidis was a child prodigy, a contemporary of Norbert Wiener. Unfortunately, Sidis's parents used the boy as an "intellectual showpiece," expecting him to be always at his best. Although he received his Ph.D. from Harvard at the age of nineteen and became a colleague of Wiener at the Massachusetts Institute of Technology, Sidis suddenly disappeared. When he was finally found working as a truck-driver, he could not be persuaded to do any of the complex scientific work in which he had excelled.

Social Aloofness: Spectators vs. Participants

Are the gifted truly socially aloof or do their experiences with society force them into that role? If you were to enter a class of gifted fifth-graders grouped on the basis of their intellectual ability, you would be most unlikely to say that gifted children are aloof and withdrawn. If you were to walk through the halls of The Bronx High School of Science and observe the friendliness and congeniality of the students, all of whom are selected on the basis of superior ability, you would not be likely to draw such a conclusion. However, if you were to observe a gifted child in an *unselected* environment in which there is a very broad range of intellectual abilities, you might then note that the child has a detachment, a spectator quality rather than participant behavior. The clue, of course, lies in the possibility for easy communication which each situation presents. The brighter the child, the more difficult it is to find congenial companions and the more likely the child is to withdraw into the spectator role.

In his later years, Einstein referred to his loneliness as a young man. He said, "I live in that solitude which is painful in youth, but delicious in the years of maturity (20)." In the following words, Einstein gives us clues to the reasons underlying some of this withdrawal.

> My passionate sense of social justice and social responsibility has always contrasted oddly with my pronounced freedom from the need for contact with other human beings and human communities. I "gang my own gait" and have never belonged to my country, my home, my friends, or even my immediate family, with my whole heart; in the face of all these ties I have never lost an obstinate sense of detachment, of the need for solitude—a feeling which increases with the years. One is sharply conscious, yet without regret, of the limits to the possibility of mutual understanding and sympathy with one's fellow-creatures. Such a person no doubt loses something in the way of geniality and lightheartedness; on the other hand, he is largely independent of the opinions, habits, and judgments of his fellows and avoids the temptation to take his stand on such insecure foundations. (21, p. 3)

Gifted youngsters have many and diverse interests and enjoy being able to talk about them. If adults reject them or listen only in a condescending manner, this is not communication. Their age peers do not share their depth and range of knowledge and can only listen but cannot discuss. Gifted high school youngsters, given the opportunity to talk about their personal desires, likes, and dislikes, express this need. One, acting as their spokeswoman, said: "We love to talk and we need to talk. Independent study is all right. But we don't like to be isolated. We like to share and exchange ideas, to talk about our work with others who care and understand."

The problem created by this need to communicate and the difficulty of finding people with whom to communicate is a serious one among the gifted and one of the strongest arguments for ability grouping in schools. Parents should make every effort to provide companions with comparable intellectual abilities or similar talent interests for their children, even if it means a certain amount of traveling and "chauffeuring" back and forth between congenial homes. The need begins early in life and persists throughout. One of the most valued aspects of school life for the Astor Program children, who were only four to five and one-half when they started in the program, was the opportunity to meet and be with their intellectual peers (14).

Boredom: Knowing Too Much

For gifted children, especially in the early years, the greatest problem can be the fact that they know too much for their age. In school, they find that other children are just beginning to learn to read, to do mathematical operations, to know about any number of things for the very first time, while they are way past this stage. The teacher introduces a new book about whales and discovers that the gifted child has read, not only this book, but any number of books on whales and knows more about the subject than he does. The teacher proceeds to explain in laborious fashion how to multiply two-digit numbers, and the "brainy one back there" has already shouted out the answer, plucked out of the air, it seems. The social studies teacher has just delivered a long lecture on the causes of the American Revolution, and the quiet lass in the corner of the room, who usually spends all her time staring out the window, rises to deliver her own dissertation on the European developments that preceded and coincided with the Revolution. The high school teacher explains in oversimplified language the application of relativity theory to a physics problem, and the class brain rises to expound on the implications of the theory for the time factors involved, then collapses in his seat to resume what seems to be a deep reverie. The fact is that these gifted children have read widely. Frequently they are self-taught in many areas and understand causes and effects, the implications of scientific concepts, and much, much more, so that usually most of what goes on in school is simply repetition for them. Knowing too much becomes a handicap that may begin with boredom and may end with their becoming nuisances to the class and the teacher. It really doesn't pay to know too much in an unfriendly world!

Of all the complaints one hears from parents about the difficulties their gifted children face, probably the most frequent one is that the child is bored in school. The boredom either can be a general complaint or can be associated with such consequences as disruptive behavior, loss of interest in learning, unwillingness to go to school, frequent early morning "tummy-aches" that vanish as the time for going to school passes, "dropping out" by excessive cutting or by actually leaving school, deterioration in performance, and the inevitable complaints from the teacher and the school.

There are several steps that parents can take to prevent their gifted children from suffering simply because they are gifted and "know too much, too soon."

1. Recognize the fact that the child is genuinely bored, that the schoolwork is not challenging his or her abilities.

2. Discuss the matter with the teacher. You may be fortunate enough to find an understanding person who will accept the challenge and try to help the child with a better school program.

3. Try to have the child placed in the appropriate learning group, class, or school.

4. Don't wait too long to make inquiries about appropriate schooling for your child. Start early and keep ahead of the educational process so that you can be active in making changes take place.

5. If you are faced with an uncooperative school situation, try to help your child understand the difficulties involved. Discuss the matter with him or her and explain the importance of conforming with the basic rules and regulations. At the same time, give your frank support and provide out-of-school opportunities for the child to develop interests and meet with congenial friends.

6. Do not teach your child from the same books that are used in school or try to anticipate what the teacher will be covering. "The world is so full of a number of things..." as the poet Robert Louis Stevenson said, that it is not necessary to duplicate what will happen in school. Introduce your child to special interests. Encourage the child to develop hobbies. Let the child read from a wide variety of books. Use the public libraries. Books suitable for young children are among the most fascinating and are frequently works of art in themselves.

7. For older children especially, some lessons in tact, diplomacy, and common courtesy are helpful. Help them to understand that showing up the teacher's errors and embarrassing the teacher before the class or visitors is, at the very least, rude. There is no way you can relieve the children's boredom in school, but you can help them to cope by explaining the realities of life.

8. Children who cut classes or who take the final step of dropping out of school rarely do it only because they are bored. They quite evidently have poor motivation and no direction for their lives. Children have been known to carry out the most tedious tasks when they had purpose in what they were doing and when they received support from people who mattered to them. Children need to learn early that life can be a garden of roses only when we learn to deal with the thorns. A child can balance boring school sessions with interesting and purposeful activities at home and should be encouraged to do so.

9. Do not overlook the advantages of discussing the problems with the proper authorities in school, beginning with the teacher, guidance counselor, chairperson of a division, or principal. Sometimes a change of teacher is possible. Above all, always support and back up your children, and do not expose them to the wrath of officials who are not sympathetic to their cause. On the other hand, the overly ambitious parent who does not heed the advice of cooperative school personnel can become a major contributor to a child's failure.

Understanding Too Much Too Soon

I walked into a prekindergarten/kindergarten class one day, and was delighted with the atmosphere of the room. The children were cheerfully going about their business, each engaged in what seemed to be an absorbing activity. A few were sitting around a table drawing pictures. I sat next to a little girl, whom I will call Sandy. I admired her picture and asked her whether drawing was a favorite activity, since she did it so well. She snatched her paper away from me and said: "Don't you bother me!" Later, the teacher gathered the children around her to tell them a story. Sandy went to a far corner of the room, sat on the floor, and sucked her thumb. When the teacher called her over, Sandy ignored her and turned her head away. Puzzled by this behavior, I inquired further and learned that this was quite characteristic. Sandy frequently withdrew from class activities and rejected any overtures from anyone. Other behaviors began to worry the teacher and I decided to speak to Sandy's parents. The mother came to my office alone. I explained that some of Sandy's behavior was symptomatic of possible serious mental illness in its earliest stages and suggested that perhaps she needed special help. The mother then told me that she and her husband quarreled bitterly in Sandy's presence, that the father refused to postpone arguments for more private moments, but would scold the child and tell her to get out of the room. The difficulties were so serious that the parents were considering separation. When things got too bad between them, they would send Sandy off to her grandmother. As a matter of fact, the mother told me, they were considering sending Sandy away to camp for the summer, so that she would not be present to witness their extended battle scenes. I asked whether anyone had ever explained to Sandy what was happening. No, the mother said, how could a little girl of only four understand? Understand, indeed! Sandy understood well enough that her world was crumbling around her, that her father and mother hated each other, and that somehow she must be at fault since every time they quarreled they angrily sent her back to her room. They were so mad at her, she thought, that they were even sending her away to camp. She was frightened, miserable, and terribly alone. She just wasn't going to love anybody anymore and wasn't going to let anyone come near enough to hurt her.

Unfortunately, children have some understanding of situations, but it is limited by their experience. Sandy could only interpret what was happening in the light of her own very limited knowledge. She took steps to protect herself in the only way she knew. She withdrew from any contacts that might mean a betrayal of her trust in their caring.

Another child in first grade began to lose interest in his schoolwork and his performance deteriorated drastically. Since he was a brilliant child, this would not have been noticed in an ordinary class, since he still did exceedingly well in comparison with the average child. But those of us who knew his capabilities noticed the loss of sparkle in his work and began to question it. A private interview with the father revealed the fact that the mother was terminally ill. No, the little boy had not been told anything, so why should there be any problem with his schoolwork, the father asked. Of course, the answer was really quite simple. Eddie's problem was that he understood a great deal of what was going on at home, but he was too miserable with what he thought was happening to want to accept it. Someone had to let him talk about what he guessed was happening and express his fears, then help him to understand. If his mother was dying and he knew it, the very least that he needed was comforting and reassurance. Furthermore, his father's expectation that the child should continue to perform at his usual high level was unreasonable. Dealing with a gifted child in such circumstances requires an acceptance of the fact that the child's understanding will extend beyond what he or she is told, that it will be compounded by a very vivid imagination, and that it will be limited by the child's inexperience in coping with such situations. Both teachers and parents need to realize that children, like adults, cannot perform at their very best when they are emotionally disturbed.

Parents need to balance very carefully the child's age and experience with the gifted child's unusual capacity to understand situations. They must also bear in mind that gifted children, because of the wide interests they have and the extensive reading they do, may imagine consequences to situations that are far worse than the facts justify. It is only fair to try to explain as much as possible, answer questions reasonably, and allow opportunities for talking things out. Above all, do not be misled into thinking that the child cannot possibly know what is going on. The brighter the child is, the more likely he or she is to know and understand, within limits.

As Leta Hollingworth observed, the problems of the gifted "are those of the child, not those of society, as ordinarily understood. That this is so is sufficiently proved by the scant attention that organized society has bestowed upon the study of gifted children." (33, p. 267) But the fact remains that being gifted, with all its blessings, can create situations that cause much unhappiness for the child. It is up to parents and teachers to try to understand these traits and to try to work within the framework of their limitations on the child (34).

SUGGESTED READINGS

COLANGELO, NICHOLAS, and RONALD T. ZAFFRANN, eds. *New Voices in Counseling the Gifted.* Dubuque, Iowa: Kendall/Hunt, 1979.

GOERTZEL, VICTOR, and MILDRED GOERTZEL. *Cradles of Eminence.* Boston: Little, Brown, 1962.

GROST, AUDREY. *Genius in Residence.* Englewood Cliffs, N.J.: Prentice-Hall, 1970.

HOLLINGWORTH, LETA S. *Children above 180 IQ: Origin and Development.* New York: Arno, 1975. Reprint of 1942 edition.

KRUEGER, MARK L., ed. *On Being Gifted.* National Student Symposium on the Education of the Gifted and Talented. New York: Walker, 1978.

National Education Association. *Guidance for the Academically Talented Student.* Washington, D.C.: National Education Association, 1961.

See also the biographies and autobiographies of the eminent personalities listed on page 35.

Schooling: When, Where, Why?

Judging from the questions I am asked some parents are prepared to send their gifted children to school from infancy. I have actually received calls from parents of children under one year (as early as four months, in fact) asking whether there is a school for gifted babies. Their fear is that, unless something is done very early in life, the wonderful gifts they suspect are there will be lost. The calls increase in frequency as the children enter the enchanting period after two years, and the trend rises sharply until they finally reach kindergarten or elementary school age.

Parents are justly concerned with encouraging the manifestations of giftedness in their young children. They are uneasy about social pressures that urge them to send their children to nursery school. The current trend that promotes day care centers, using arguments about the benefits that accrue to children from such activities, creates doubts in the minds of conscientious and conflicted parents. Added to these forces is the impact of educational developments that seem to imply that the only worthwhile education takes place in school buildings. A few sturdy souls have countered this notion and are attempting home schooling, but they receive little encouragement from the professionals. John Holt, for example, suggested that almost 500,000 U.S. families would be schooling their children at home by 1988 (35). Holt publishes a newsletter, *Growing without Schooling*, and is a strong advocate of home teaching.

A reasonable course of action should be determined by what seems to work best with an individual child and what the special circumstances in the child's family may be.

At this point we need to make a distinction between "schooling," as in "attending school," and education. Actually, a child's education begins at birth, and possibly even before that. All the experiences the child has are part of his or her education. Parents who wish to maximize their children's abilities, to develop whatever skill, talent, or intellectual prowess they may have been endowed with, need to be concerned with the educational process in its many aspects.

HOME VS. SCHOOL EDUCATION: LEGAL REQUIREMENTS

The decision as to whether parents should or should not send a gifted child to school is one that may cover all the years of compulsory education or only part of that period. Parents have to consider the quality of the education available at every level as they go along. For example, education that is geared specifically to gifted children begins in most

U.S. communities at grades 4, 5, and 6.* For this reason, parents may consider an alternative to public school for the prekindergarten/primary years, yet may wish to participate in the existing programs for the intermediate grades. The same may be said about the higher levels. Local practices vary so greatly that few useful generalizations can be made about what is or is not available throughout the country. Generally, attention to academic or intellectual giftedness increases with grade level. On the other hand, response to a display of talent may occur at any time and occasionally is even forced at too early an age. There are few Mozarts or Beethovens whose abilities are apparent in early childhood. Yet when the talent is there, parents usually respond if they can by encouragement and training. Schools are less inclined to do this during the early years, primarily because they are not prepared to do anything about it even if they do recognize talent.

The compulsory education laws of the states usually cover the elementary school years and at least part of the secondary school levels, from a minimum age of six through a maximum age of eighteen or graduation from high school (65). The great majority require compulsory attendance beginning at age seven, while a few use age six and others age eight as the beginning age. Most set age sixteen as the maximum age, and again a few vary this by setting seventeen or eighteen as the maximum. Exceptions are permitted under certain conditions which vary from state to state. Sources for the most recent legislation are the individual state education departments and publications of the U.S. Department of Education.

The Kindergarten Years

In most states, attendance in kindergarten is optional beginning at about age five; if there are prekindergartens, they may be limited to a special population, such as those requiring day care, or they may also be available on an optional basis. Parents of gifted children, then, still have a choice, under law, about what they will do concerning attendance.

Alternatives

There are alternatives under law to compulsory school attendance, but these vary from state to state and within localities. Parents choosing to

---

*Replication of concepts promulgated by the Astor Program for gifted children in prekindergarten through grade three will probably change this condition; but, as frequently happens with educational innovation, the process is slow and may take several years (14).

educate their children at home, by tutors or other means, should be prepared to demonstrate a *legally qualified* alternative.

HOME VS. SCHOOL EDUCATION: GENERAL CONSIDERATIONS

In deciding between home and school education, parents should consider the advantages and disadvantages at each level in the light of their own circumstances. Many factors operate in this choice, including financial status, availability of teaching services and materials, geographic location, parents' educational preparation, and the school's offerings.

However, it is imperative that parents consider very carefully their motivations for whatever choice they make, as well as the advantages and disadvantages of their choice. Mrs. Edison took her son Thomas out of school to protect him from the negative attitude taken toward him by his teachers. She was not going to permit her son to be considered retarded or "addled," as the school put it. Norbert Wiener's father was totally dissatisfied with the education his son was receiving in elementary school, so he decided to teach him himself. Of this decision, Wiener comments (78, p. 292):

> From him I learned the standards of scholarship which belong to the real scholar, and the degree of manliness, devotion, and honesty which a scholarly career requires. I learned that scholarship is a calling and a consecration, not a job. I learned a fierce hatred of all bluff and intellectual pretense, as well as a pride in not being baffled by any problem which I could possibly solve. These are worth a price in suffering, yet I would ask this price to be exacted of no man who has not the strength to stand up to it physically and morally. This price cannot be paid by a weakling, and it can kill. That I was a boy not only endowed with a certain intellectual vigor, but also physically strong, made it possible for me to bear the wounds of this Spartan nurture. Before I should even think of subjecting any child, boy or girl, to such a training I should have to be convinced not only of the intelligence of the child, but of its physical, mental and moral stamina.

While the decision for home teaching may have served Edison and Wiener well, it does not seem to have been as socially and psychologically beneficial for John Stuart Mill. His father began the education of his son at the tender age of two. By the time he was eight years old, Mill reports that he was able to read *Aesop's Fables,* Herodotus, *Memorials of Socrates,* the first six dialogues of Plato, and others, all in Greek (50, p. 13). These achievements may seem admirable, but Mill paid a high price for their attainment. His father would not permit him to play with other children, lest his intellectual progress be corrupted by them. At about the age of twenty, Mill was a social misfit and had a period of serious depression from which he had great difficulty in recovering.

HOME VS. SCHOOL EDUCATION: ADVANTAGES AND DISADVANTAGES

Nursery Schools

Whether a child attends nursery school during these early years or is educated at home depends in large measure on the child's needs and how well they can be met in either situation. We must grant that, barring unusual circumstances, the best place for any child is at home and preferably with a nurturant, caring mother. The security such early nurturing provides lays a groundwork for learning that is beneficial for all children, and especially for the gifted child.

These are years of physical and emotional dependence, years during which Urie Bronfenbrenner's (4) description of the child's need for an "irrational" commitment by a significant person is especially apt. A child needs the security of love, unqualified, unthreatened, and "irrational," that only a parent, and especially the mother, can give. The security such love engenders enables the child to take the countless physical and emotional risks required in growing up. A secure child can dare anything—letting go to walk, going out of a room where the loved one remains, jumping down from a one-step stool—all are possible because the loved one is on hand to "rescue" the child from disaster. The presence of such a person creates a climate of emotional security in which learning can take place successfully.

Frequently, the exceptional abilities of a gifted child and his or her advanced understanding of complex ideas lead parents and others to believe that the child's emotional and physical needs are equally advanced, causing them to withhold the attention essential to the child's development. Most studies of early childhood development stress the importance for the child of individual attention, sensory and motor stimulation, and body contact and fondling (10, 62). Regardless of the stand anyone may take on the nature–nurture controversy, the fact remains that lack of nurture and lack of experience in a rich and stimulating environment can affect the child's mental development. For example, in a special study of institutionalized orphans, children who suffered from sensory deprivation and a lack of social and emotional interchange became apathetic, cried very little, became intellectually retarded, and actually died at an early age from no known physical cause (63). On the other hand, a gifted child who grows up in a warm and attentive environment that is responsive to his or her intellectual needs has the opportunity to attain maximum intellectual growth. This, of course, would be true of any child.

For those who, for valid reasons, find that they must use the facilities of nursery schools and day care centers, it is important to select only schools staffed by persons prepared to give the child the kind of attention that is required during this period. Teachers in such centers must be well trained and knowledgeable about the developmental, emotional, and social needs of their charges. They need to recognize the importance of the role they are playing in the life of the very young child. There is no substitute for actual observation in the school environment of the interaction between teachers and children, and parents are well advised to take advantage of such opportunities before registering their children. The realities of life are such that many parents, eager to do their very best, have to avail themselves of these facilities. Knowing what is best for their children, they can demand and expect appropriate services and make the necessary accommodations in their daily planning.

Between the extremes of total neglect and excessive attention, there is a desirable path that concerned parents can follow in helping the very young child achieve his or her maximum potential. It is a significant role for the parents in their child's education.

Kindergarten

At the kindergarten level, the following advantages and disadvantages of formal schooling are worthy of note.

The advantages of the kindergarten experience are recognized by both parents and teachers. It serves as an introduction to formal education, provides companionship and socializing experiences for the child, encourages independence, and initiates the separation process from the parent and home. Educationally, teachers of regular kindergartens begin the "readiness" processes for reading and other learning and introduce the children to a wide variety of experiences that lay the groundwork for the later school years.

The single greatest disadvantage of regular kindergartens as one finds them throughout the country is that they are not geared to the needs of children of high ability levels. For gifted children who often can read, know numbers and elementary combinations, and are generally past most of the readiness activities presented, there is little to excite them in this alien world. The books are too easy. The games do not challenge them and their classmates do not understand or respond to their need for more complex activities and more advanced work. They have barely started school and already they are tasting the boredom, frustration, and isolation that will become worse and worse as they pass through the grades. Where most parents take attendance in such kindergartens for granted, parents of gifted children are frequently forced to consider other possible options open to them. If the children have attended a nursery school or day care center, parents may be faced with the possibility that their gifted children have already been "turned off" by school. Even parents whose children have not had such experiences are concerned, because they fear that kindergarten will prove to be a boring and frustrating experience.

Except for a few isolated examples of enlightened teaching and management, the lot of a gifted child in kindergarten is not a happy one. Fortunately, the tide is turning and gradually more and more schools throughout the country are following the lead established by the Astor Program, which was introduced in New York City in 1973 (14). In this program, children receive a prekindergarten/kindergarten education that is related directly to their abilities as well as to their social and psychological needs, so that there is none of the boredom or frustration so commonly encountered in the usual school.

Formal Schooling

Beyond the kindergarten years, of course, the need for formal schooling assumes a different aspect. Between the ages of five and seven or thereabouts, children become ready for greater independence and for an expanded social world of significant persons. The school becomes a socializing agent where children can test their independence and begin the formal education that is intended to prepare them for the responsibilities of adulthood. The school represents a new world, with rules and regulations that are more impersonal yet necessary for functioning in a group situation. The children are now no longer the central figures in their universe as they learn the necessity for accommodation to the needs and desires of others. Although the family can and does require many accommodations, by its very nature the school environment is a more varied and demanding socializer.

Parents who hesitate to send their gifted children to school should consider the many advantages of the socializing aspect of the experience for the child. Regardless of a child's intellectual ability, the craving for peer companionship must be satisfied. Schools provide much more than education in basic skills and knowledge. The passage from the safe shelter of the home to the somewhat unprotected world "out there" is probably taken most effectively through the supervised and less personal portals of the school building. Except in the very rare cases of children who are so highly gifted that they do need special attention, the advantages of formal schooling far outweigh its disadvantages.

OTHER ISSUES

Two questions arise with respect to gifted children and formal schooling. (1) Does every gifted child have to go to college? (2) Should a gifted student be allowed to take time out from attending formal schooling somewhere along the way before completing the customary course of studies?

1. *Does every gifted child have to go to college?*

The answer to this question very simply is "No." We have acquired a notion that the only worthwhile education is one that is capped by a college degree. This belief has grown partly from the awareness that many employers demand a college degree. Nevertheless, there are situations where college training is not necessarily the best route. I recall an episode when a highly successful merchandising executive, the owner of a chain of well-known department stores, spoke before a group of very gifted high school students. The gist of his talk was: "If you want to become a doctor, or lawyer, or scientist, or anything like that, go on to college. But if you want to succeed in the business world where I am involved, come to me, and I will train you with on-the-job experience. With your brains, you're bound to succeed."

With the increasing attention being given to in-service education by many large industrial firms, the road to success may well be through on-the-job experience, with a view to supplementing industrial training with a college education obtained on a part-time basis. (See Table 4, page 145.) Students talented in the visual and performing arts may find that in order to achieve professional success they must place their talent practice first and pursue the culturally satisfying experience of college second.

Current trends in college education that stress the possibilities of part-time attendance may change our ideas about the need to follow an unbroken sequence through the educational experience. This leads us to a consideration of whether a "vacation" from formal schooling may be desirable for the intellectually gifted child.

2. *Should a gifted student be allowed to take time out from attending formal schooling somewhere along the way before completing the customary course of studies?*

Several factors should be considered in weighing the desirability of such a plan. For youngsters who have been accelerated through school at too rapid a pace, a break may be very desirable. In their book *Cradles of Eminence*, Victor and Mildred Goertzel tell of several renowned personalities who did just this (27, p. 255).

> Charles Evans Hughes was graduated from high school twice before he was twelve and could not enter college because of his youth. At the Newark High School he had lost two front teeth when larger boys flung him against the wall while playing a whipcracker game. For six months he wandered the streets of New York, benefiting from the enrichment the city offered, enjoying his freedom and getting used to his changed appearance. Randolph Hearst and John LaFarge also had profitable "time-out" periods during which they wandered in New York City. Richard Byrd went around the world alone at thirteen. Norman Angell, at seventeen, went off to America to be a cowboy. Louis Brandeis never forgot the free summer when he tramped about Europe with his father and brother. Marie Curie had a free year in the country at fifteen.

As the Goertzels report, ten percent of the four hundred eminent personalities whose lives they studied had taken a period of time-out "which significantly influenced their later development."

Apparently, the intellectually gifted child as well as the talented child may sometimes be in need of a reprieve from the intensity of learning and achieving in order to reorganize his or her lifework. Under positive and supportive conditions, this would probably be a valuable experience. For parents who may be concerned that the break would become permanent and therefore damaging to the youngster's career, it would be wise to discuss the matter with the child first, frankly and without prejudice, and then, if there is still doubt, to enlist the aid of a counselor or person in whom both parents and child have confidence.

SELECTING THE RIGHT SCHOOL

Once the parents have made the decision to send a child to school, the next step is to decide "Which one?" or "Is what is available appropriate for our child?" Besides the suggestions that have already been given, there are some other general questions and issues that must be explored.

1. Does the administration (district, superintendent, principal, supervisor) look favorably upon education for the gifted? Without such support, most programs will be of short duration and may be doomed to failure.

2. Does the district or school have a policy concerning gifted children? To insure continued funding and general support, an official policy is of the utmost importance. It should be in writing and reflect community support (18).

3. How are the teachers for the gifted selected? What are their qualifications? Teachers of the gifted and talented should have special training. They must know the psychology, needs, and nature of children with superior abilities. They must be sympathetic to these children and secure about the children's exceptionalities. They must themselves be of superior ability or talented in the area of special concern. They need a broad educational background and should be alert to current developments. Educators of the gifted feel that these children need teachers who are experienced and who will be able to empathize with them. Students ask for teachers who are flexible, well grounded in their subject matter, and endowed with a good sense of humor. The task of teaching superior students is a difficult one and only those teachers who are energetic, dynamic, and willing to work very hard should be chosen.

4. How are classes or programs for the gifted organized? Within the limitations of local budgets and resources, homogeneous groupings are the best. However, an extremely well managed program can meet the needs by other methods if such grouping is not possible. Schools may use part-time programs, pull-out programs, limited-subject-area study, and in-building or out-of-building activities. Methods used vary with locality, funding, and availability of personnel. Each situation must be judged individually.

5. How many hours each week is education for the gifted practiced? Full-time programs have been found to be the most satisfactory and successful. Pull-out programs which do not involve the regular classroom teacher tend to create more problems than they solve, whereas those that do involve the regular teacher in a coordinated plan have greater promise. A program of one or two hours per week is better than nothing, but it is minimal and both schools and parents should strive to do better.

6. What materials, books, and supplies are available that are specifically useful for the gifted? Classes for the gifted require more specialized materials than average classrooms. These should cover a wide span of abilities at *each* grade level, especially textbooks. Resources such as games, dictionaries, encyclopedias, reference books, and audiovisual equipment should cover several levels of complexity and should help children to reach upward in their achievement. There should be a rich class library and the school library should be accessible for use throughout the school day.

7. Is there continuity in the program from kindergarten through grade twelve? It is important that there be coordinated planning specifically for the gifted throughout the school years. A well-planned program will allow continuous progress in work without the barriers of grade or age. Children should be able to move along at their own pace without facing the boredom of repeated lessons from one level to another.

8. How are the children selected for the program? This is a highly technical procedure, requiring the skills of trained personnel. The method used should be equitable, making it possible for children to move in and out of the program from year to year. An open-door policy insures against the dangers of permanent tracking. The selection procedure should rely on multiple measures and should use the most reliable techniques available. The system should be one in which children are screened and identified at various levels, so that results can be checked and so that all qualified children may have access to the program from one year to the next. Parents should not hesitate to question results that contradict their own experiences with the child, and teachers should assume the responsibility for verifying test data against their own classroom observations.

The Prekindergarten and Kindergarten Levels

Schools have a clear responsibility to reorganize their planning and curricula so that the needs of the very young gifted child will be met. Within the average prekindergarten and kindergarten it is possible to make accommodations for these exceptional children. Some steps schools can take are to

1. Provide books and games at more advanced reading levels for the children to use.
2. Permit the children to read and at their own level of achievement. Schools should not deny this pleasure simply because they have not yet put the children through what they consider to be the required readiness paces.
3. Let the children read stories to the class from their favorite books.

4. Allow the children the freedom to play the more elaborate games they prefer. These should be provided in the classroom.
5. Let children plan, organize, and direct activities within small groups.
6. Let the children have special, worthwhile responsibilities, such as taking attendance, collecting milk money, or taking care of the library books.
7. Let children follow a special interest or carry on with a hobby, and try to integrate it into the class activities.
8. Investigate those programs that are directed to this age level for the gifted, in order to adapt ideas to their own classrooms.

MODEL PROGRAMS AT PREKINDERGARTEN AND KINDERGARTEN LEVELS

COEUR d'ALENE RURAL PROGRAM, COEUR d'ALENE, IDAHO

Three two-and-one-half-hour sessions weekly.

Enriched experiences, stressing skills in communication, social development, self-awareness, curiosity and problem solving, and academic activities.

Classrooms staffed by a teacher, a part-time aide, and a parent volunteer.

Eighteen children per class

Write to 418 Coeur d'Alene Avenue, Coeur d'Alene, Idaho 83814.

THE ASTOR PROGRAM MODEL, NEW YORK, NEW YORK

A full-time program at prekindergarten and kindergarten levels, usually four hours per day, integrated within the regular public school system. Formerly privately funded, now part of the regular school budgets. The program extends through the elementary grades as well.

Classes of twenty-five to thirty pupils are subdivided into units of six to ten, organized by interests and compatibility rather than ability. These rotate through modules of twenty to forty minutes through the day, so that all children have equal exposure to the individualized attention of the teacher(s) in developing special basic and thinking skills while other children engage in individual activities or pursue studies in special-interest topics.

Each class may have one or two teachers plus an aide. Where possible and available, specialist teachers join the staff in teaching art, music, foreign language, science, or other subjects.

The basic philosophy of the program is carried out by a specially developed curriculum which stresses acquisition of basic and thinking skills but also concerns itself with academic subjects, character development, moral and ethical values, and the social and psychological needs of the child.

There is continuous in-service teacher training.

Write to Dr. Virginia Z. Ehrlich, Teachers College, Box 223, New York, New York 10027.

The NOVA PROGRAM in St. Paul, Minnesota, is a replication of the Astor Program. Other communities in the United States, Canada, and several foreign countries are also replicating the model in whole or in part, or are using their curriculum materials. For the NOVA Program, write to Mrs. Lorraine Hertz, Coordinator of the Gifted, Capitol Square Building, 550 Cedar Street, St. Paul, Minnesota 55101.

Grades One through Twelve

One should expect schools to have a definite commitment to education for gifted children that reflects a long-range plan and that is supported by the principal, the district superintendent or supervisor, and the local school board (18).

Good planning at the elementary level avoids pull-out programs, which take the child out of the regular classroom for one or two hours a week with little or no coordination with the regular classroom teacher. Full-time grouping by ability levels is the most satisfactory way of teaching such children, but this sometimes cannot be achieved in small communities. Some schools accommodate by scheduling a part of each day for group teaching, as in the Cleveland Public Schools (30). The major advantage of such grouping, of course, is the opportunity provided for intellectual peer group contact, which is so necessary for the gifted child.

Occasionally, schools plan an accelerated program during which the students cover two years' work in one. This may occur once during grades one through six, once in the junior high school (grades seven through nine), and preferably not at all in the last three grades, ten through twelve. With few exceptions, two years of acceleration is the maximum recommended between grades one and twelve.*

Honors classes are often used in specific subject matter, sometimes in grades four through six, but more frequently in grades seven through twelve.

There are many opportunities to meet the needs of the gifted at the high school level. In addition to the honors classes previously mentioned, schools offer advanced placement courses, mentorships, work apprenticeships, special training in the talents (visual and performing arts), summer sessions, residential programs, and sometimes courses given in conjunction with a local college or university. Large cities such as New York and Philadelphia have public high schools that

---

*For information on rapid grade acceleration for mathematically precocious youth, see the works of Julian Stanley and others at the Johns Hopkins University (64).

specialize in programs for the gifted. All of these schools have high admission requirements and are for gifted children only. Such specialized high schools, however, are possible only in areas with large pupil populations. (See the references at the end of this chapter for sources of information.)

College

At the college level, parents must start early to make inquiries about opportunities for fellowships and scholarships. They should lead their youngsters to the college guides that are available (often through school counselors and in the local libraries). Start inquiries when the student is about to finish the tenth grade. That will give ample time to write for and study college catalogs and offerings. The best colleges for gifted students are those that respond to their particular fields of interest and whose standards of performance will demand their best efforts. These are years of decision that will set the student on the path of a satisfying and rewarding work and life experience. Selection of a college should be made from the viewpoint of the student's needs, interests, and ambitions, and by how well these requirements will be met in the institution.

SUGGESTED READINGS AND REFERENCES

AXFORD, LAVONNE B. *Directory of Educational Programs for the Gifted.* Metuchen, N.J.: Scarecrow, 1971. Based on data provided by 34 states, plus other sources. Useful as an historical reference, since there have been many changes since 1971.

BRANDT, RONALD S., ed. *Partners: Parents and Schools.* 1979. Association for Supervision and Curriculum Development, 225 N. Washington Street, Alexandria, Va. 22314.

GOERTZEL, VICTOR, and MILDRED GOERTZEL. *Cradles of Eminence,* Chap. 10. Boston: Little, Brown, 1962.

Growing without Schooling. Holt Associates, 308 Boylston Street, Boston, Mass. 02116. Newsletter. Six issues per year.

JENKINS, REVA C. W. *A Resource Guide to Preschool and Primary Programs for the Gifted and Talented.* 1979. Creative Learning Press, P.O. Box 320, Mansfield Center, Conn. 06250. A concise summary of programs in progress, with descriptive information on grade levels, patterns of organization, identification methods, enrichment activities and experiences, personnel, and contact persons.

KARNES, FRANCES A., and HERSCHEL Q. PEDDICORD, JR. *Programs, Leaders, Con-*

sultants, and Other Resources in Gifted and Talented Education. Springfield, Ill.: Chas. C. Thomas, 1980.

MCCOY, ELIN. "Home Schooling, an Issue for Parents." *New York Times*, February 26, 1981, p. C1. Lists several newsletters and correspondence schools that specialize in home schooling for pupils in general. Not specific to the gifted.

The What and Where of Gifted Programs: A Report to the New Jersey Gifted Consortium, Theodore J. Gourley, Project Director. 1975. Educational Improvement Center, Pitman, N.J. 08071. Data on 130 programs, K–12, from the fifty states are summarized and include information on overview, identification methods, curriculum, in-service training, written information, program characteristics appropriate to the gifted, program exportability, objectives, evaluation, outcomes. An excellent summary.

WOODBURY, MARDA. *A Guide to Sources of Educational Information.* Washington, D.C.: Information Resources Press, 1976.

SUGGESTED MATERIALS FOR HOME TEACHING

Although some of the following materials are not designed specifically for the gifted, they do contain suggestions that are sufficiently complex to challenge such children.

BECKER, WESLEY C. *Parents Are Teachers: A Child Management Program.* Champaign, Ill.: Research Press, 1971.

BLACKWELDER, SHEILA KYSER. *Science for All Seasons: Science Experiences for Young Children.* Englewood Cliffs, N.J.: Prentice-Hall, 1980.

BRAGA, JOSEPH, and LAURIE BRAGA. *Children and Adults: Activities for Growing Together.* Englewood Cliffs, N.J.: Prentice-Hall, 1976.

CARR, RACHEL, *See and Be: Yoga and Creative Movement for Children.* Englewood Cliffs, N.J.: Prentice-Hall, 1980.

COFFEY, KAY, et al. *Parentspeak on Gifted and Talented Children.* 1976. Ventura County Superintendent of Schools, 535 East Main Street, Ventura, Calif. 93009.

DELP, JEANNE A., and RUTH A. MARTINSON. *The Gifted and Talented: A Handbook for Parents.* 1975. Ventura County Superintendent of Schools, 535 East Main Street, Ventura, Calif. 93009.

GOLDSTEIN-JACKSON, KEVIN, NORMAN RUDNICK, and RONALD HYMAN. *Experiments with Everyday Objects: Science Activities for Children, Parents, and Teachers.* Englewood Cliffs, N.J.: Prentice-Hall, 1978.

HOLT, MICHAEL, and ZOLTAN DIENES. *Let's Play Math.* New York: Walker, 1973.

HYMAN, RONALD T. *Paper, Pencils and Pennies: Games for Learning and Having Fun.* Englewood Cliffs, N.J.: Prentice-Hall, 1975.

JENKINS, PEGGY DAVISON. *Art for the Fun of It: A Guide for Teaching Young Children.* Englewood Cliffs, N.J.: Prentice-Hall, 1980.

———. *The Magic of Puppetry: A Guide for Those Working with Young Children*. Englewood Cliffs, N.J.: Prentice-Hall, 1980.

KANIGHER, HERBERT. *Everyday Enrichment for Gifted Children at Home and at School*. 1977. Ventura County Superintendent of Schools, 535 East Main Street, Ventura, Calif. 93009.

LEWIS, CLAUDIA. *A Big Bite of the World: Children's Creative Writing*. Englewood Cliffs, N.J.: Prentice-Hall, 1979.

MITCHELL, JOHN, and THE MASSACHUSETTS AUDUBON SOCIETY. *The Curious Naturalist: A Handbook of Crafts, Games, Activities, and Ideas for Teaching Children about the Magical World of Nature*. Englewood Cliffs, N.J.: Prentice-Hall, 1980.

Pennsylvania Department of Education. *Mentally Gifted Children and Youth: A Guide for Parents*. 1973. Pennsylvania Department of Education, Box 911, Harrisburg, Pa. 17126.

RENZULLI, MARY JO, BARBARA GAY FORD, LINDA SMITH, and JOSEPH S. RENZULLI. *New Directions in Creativity*. New York: Harper & Row, Pub., 1976.

RIGGS, MAIDA L. *Jump to Joy: Helping Children Grow through Active Play*. Englewood Cliffs, N.J.: Prentice Hall, 1980.

In addition, write for catalogs from publishers of educational materials and children's books, games, and toys. A few who specialize in products for the gifted are

Creative Learning Press
P.O. Box 320
Mansfield Center, Connecticut 06250

Creative Teaching Press
5305 Production Drive
Huntington Beach, California 92649

DOK Publishers
71 Radcliffe Road
Buffalo, New York 14214

Trillium Press
Box 921
Madison Square Station
New York NY 10150

Also:

FELDHUSEN, JOHN F., and DONALD J. TREFFINGER. *Creative Thinking and Problem Solving in Gifted Education*. Dubuque, Iowa: Kendall/Hunt, 1980. Provides an excellent discussion on the topic as well as reviews of instructional materials, games, and books for teaching the gifted, with addresses of publishers.

School Days: What To Expect

Most parents' expectations of school are related to their own recollections and experiences. Those who enjoyed their school days will hope their children will find a situation similar to the one they had, and those who were unhappy with their experiences will be looking for a change. In most instances, there is little choice about the school a child will attend, since most of them will go to their neighborhood schools. Those parents who seek out parochial or private schools will have choices and can "shop" around more than those whose children attend public schools. What do parents expect of the schools and how does this coincide with what one should reasonably expect? More to the point, what should the parents of a gifted child expect of the school their child attends?

Parents who learned in formal, rigid school patterns and who feel satisfied with what they learned will look for a repetition of those patterns. Others, unhappy with strictness and formality, will look for more openness. Those who read about current trends will wish to see some of the new practices in effect, while others will expect to find the classroom looking and behaving exactly as it did when they went to school. In most cases, disappointment looms, as times change and schools change and patterns of classroom organization and management change. It is a rare school in which everything is just as it was ten, twenty, or thirty years ago, and this is as it should be.

All parents should expect the school to provide an education for their children that is matched to their individual needs. Equal treatment in education is undemocratic, since it denies to children the right to be individuals, with all the variability that term implies. No reasonable person would expect a blind child to read from the standard textbook, a retarded child to understand complex directions, or a crippled child to run with all the other children. Likewise, no thinking person would hobble gifted children by asking them to dawdle along the educational path simply because all the other children must move at a slower pace. A former superintendent of schools in New York City once observed (51, p. 16): "It has often been said that it is manifestly unfair to expect the turtle to fly with the eagles. Conversely, one should not expect the eagle to crawl with the turtles."

However, before the parent can expect special education for the gifted child, the fact must be established that the child is truly gifted. In some school systems there is a general screening of children in which the gifted child may be identified. But there are few of these school systems and, in the case of the gifted, mandating legislation is not common throughout the states. (See Chapter 10, "The Law and Gifted Children.") Such legislation does exist for the handicapped; schools are required to develop IEPs (Individualized Educational Plans) for each handicapped child in cooperation with the parents. The more general practice is to ignore superior ability when children are admitted to school. All too often, one must trust to the good judgment of interested teachers to identify a gifted child and to be interested enough to do something about it.

Where no screening for ability takes place, it is usually up to the parents to provide the evidence concerning their child. What kind of evidence will a school accept? It is an unfortunate fact that few teachers or principals will pay much attention to parents who go to school and announce that they think their child is gifted. The usual response, whether stated or implied, is that all parents think their children are special and gifted. Parents who wish to convince the school that their child is gifted should be prepared to present evidence to support their opinion. Following is a list of behaviors, characteristics, and records that will be helpful in convincing the school of your child's superior capacities:

1. The kindergartener can read consecutive passages in a book and explain the meaning of what he or she has read.
2. The kindergartener shows a real mastery of numbers, not just counting, and can combine numbers in addition or subtraction. Often, the child can make change up to a quarter and sometimes more.
3. The child has an extensive vocabulary.
4. The child has a special interest about which he or she can speak with much detail and at length. For example, a five-year-old boy I know gave me a long talk on the dolphins—their nature, habitats, foods, and communication abilities. His talk was detailed and very well coordinated.
5. The child is curious about everything and asks endless questions. Select samples of the questions.
6. Describe the child in terms of the behaviors and characteristics listed in Chapter 2.
7. Have the child tested by an accredited psychologist or at a testing center. Centers that are associated with colleges or universities are the most reliable, since they serve as training centers for students. At all times, be sure your child is tested by someone who is experienced in the field or is closely supervised by such a person. For those who cannot afford the expense of an individualized test, inquiries at the school or at the test guidance centers may uncover some source of free service. Occasionally, schools seek volunteers for testing to provide experience for students. Psychological and psychiatric clinics associated with hospitals frequently perform this service free for those in financial need.
8. Use school records of achievement.

9. Obtain recommendations from former or present teachers.
10. Consult with the school guidance counselors or psychologists if the child is already in school.
11. Seek the assistance of your local or state coordinator of the gifted if there is one in your area.

WHAT SHOULD YOUR CHILD BE LEARNING IN SCHOOL?

It has been a long time since parents sent their children to school just to learn the three Rs. Now schools teach everything from hairdressing to astrophysics, and the demands upon them grow year by year. Nevertheless, it seems desirable to take stock and review what our expectations are and whether there should not be a clarification of the role of the school in the education of a young child. Before we can list our expectations, we must know what our goal is. Why do we send children to school? What do we really expect the school to do?

Actually, what most parents ask of school systems is that they prepare the child with the skills and knowledge necessary to function in their world. Since schooling is basically a public function in the United States, parents also expect their children to be prepared to take their part in the social and civic structure of the community. An enlightened citizenry insures the survival of democratic institutions. The teaching of moral, ethical, and spiritual values that are consistent with parental attitudes and beliefs has also been viewed as a function of the school. In the early part of the twentieth century, school books actually included lessons in morality. As more progressive philosophies have exerted their influence on the schools, more and more attention has been focused on the area of thinking skills. The Greek philosophers were well aware of this important aspect of education. Although the movement to include the critical thinking skills in the curriculum began in the thirties, it has only recently taken a firm hold in curriculum development.

In sum, what should parents expect of a school for their gifted child? Briefly, it should provide an education that is commensurate with the child's abilities and interests and that includes

1. Mastery of the basic skills.
2. Mastery of the thinking skills.
3. Acquisition of a core of information essential for existence in this society.
4. Exposure to a broad range of knowledge.

5. Exposure to a wide variety of occupations and fields of work.
6. Development of social and civic responsibility.
7. Awareness of moral, ethical, and spiritual values.
8. Development of positive traits associated with giftedness.

Mastery of the Basic Skills

All children, whether gifted or not, must acquire certain basic skills in order to carry out the routine functions of living in our society. These are the skills that were known as the three Rs, and they are as essential today as ever. However, our understanding of them has become far more sophisticated. As the skills increase in complexity, children's abilities to master them begin to vary, and we find that the gifted need to acquire more difficult techniques in order to carry out the more advanced work they are likely to undertake in later life. They also need to acquire these skills as early as possible, usually months and years ahead of their peers.

Like it or not, the gifted must master all the number combinations of addition and subtraction, the multiplication tables, and the division tables. They have to learn how to spell. They have to learn rules of grammar and punctuation. The list of basic skills that they and their peers have to learn is a long one. Reading involves a variety of skills that have to be carefully developed if the process is to be truly successful. Many gifted youngsters learn how to read and even decode complex words, but they do not always know the important skills that underlie the reading process, such as identifying the main idea, drawing conclusions from the facts presented, summarizing, outlining materials, and deducing meanings. There is a group of skills associated with graphics and maps that must be mastered. Who today can truly manage without being able to read a road map? An abbreviated listing of the basic skills your child should be mastering in school is shown in Table 3.

The important points about teaching the basic skills to the gifted are that this should be done much sooner than usually occurs in school and should be far more extensive at each level of learning. Gifted children can waste a great deal of valuable learning time if they are not allowed to master the essential skills. A seven-year-old in a gifted program was fascinated by trigonometry. His grandfather helped him by teaching him many of the concepts. However, when Donny wanted to solve a trigonometric problem, he spent long hours in a complicated system he had devised to multiply numbers. The rest of the class was not ready for the subject, but since Donny was determined

TABLE 3. A Brief (and Incomplete) Listing of Basic Skills

HANDWRITING	First printing, then script
VOCABULARY	Understanding the meaning of words
	Techniques of word decoding and recognition
	Uses of the dictionary
	Understanding meanings from context
SPELLING	Learning the alphabet
	Alphabetizing, by more than the initial letter of each word
READING	Understanding the main idea
	Organizing ideas, outlining, abstracting
	Following the time sequences of the text
	Locating specific details
	Distinguishing between significant and insignificant statements
	Deducing meanings of words or phrases from the context
	Generalizing from the context
	Recognizing style, author's bias, moods, purposes
	Reading for different purposes
LANGUAGE USAGE AND RULES OF GRAMMAR	Capitalization
	Punctuation
	Sentence structure
	Agreement between verbs and subjects, pronouns and antecedents
	Correct usage of parts of speech
	Avoidance of common errors, such as redundancies, double negatives
MAP READING	Understanding symbols
	Using the key
	Determining direction, distance
	Locating places—longitude, latitude, parallels, meridians
	Interpreting scales

to work on his trigonometry, the teacher suggested that it was time he learned his multiplication tables. Donny did just that and in a few days was delighted to discover that he could now work out his problems more quickly with this new "tool." Of course, he could have been given a calculator, but that would not have taught him anything about the relationship of numbers, which the multiplication tables do.

Children, and especially the gifted, must acquire skills in using reference materials. From the earliest years, as is done in the Astor Program, children should be expected to be able to find words in the dictionary, seek materials in encyclopedias and reference books, and generally acquire the concepts necessary to track down information. This means, of course, learning the alphabet, knowing sources of information and how to use them, reading for information (and not entertainment), and developing library skills.

	Recognizing topography Comparing data from different kinds of maps Applications to seasons, time, living patterns
UNDERSTANDING GRAPHS AND TABLES	Uses of coordinates Understanding the different types of graphs Obtaining information from graphs and tables Interpreting, generalizing, deducing information from graphs and tables Determining relationships among different elements in a table or graph
USING REFERENCE MATERIALS	Awareness of the many different kinds of reference materials Knowing how to use each kind of reference Knowing where to locate required information Using dictionaries, encyclopedias, tables of contents, indexes, calendars, atlases, magazines, special reference materials, library catalogues
MATHEMATICS	Counting Understanding sequencing Numbers: odd–even, positive–negative, cardinal–ordinal Number systems, such as binary, Roman Fundamental operations: adding, subtracting, multiplying, dividing Shortcuts and check systems Decimals, fractions, and percentages Proportions, ratios, scaling, equations Measurement: time, mass, distance, linear, curvilinear, metrics Geometric properties: plane and solid, recognizing shapes and their properties Problem solving

Parents should expect schools to provide this training at advanced levels and as thoroughly as possible for their gifted children. Parents, too, can help by encouraging their children to do the work needed to acquire such skills.

Some of the homework gifted children bring home should be in the areas of developing basic skills. Workbooks, which should not be busywork to relieve the teacher from responsibilities, should be of the type that will provide the drills necessary to master fundamentals as quickly as possible. Gifted children have been known to work through these books in a few days, devouring them with real pleasure. Unfortunately, neither teachers nor principals are ready to recognize the fact that the gifted child is not going to spend all year on one book, doing one page per day, and that many levels of work and many books per child are required for each grade. This is one of the hardest facts to sell to school systems. Gifted children consume materials at a tremendous rate. They need materials at many levels of difficulty. And they need it all *now*.

Parents who wish to help their children master basic skills can purchase such workbooks. It is important that the books provided in the home do not duplicate the work that is being done in school. This creates opportunities for boredom in the child over which the teacher has no control. Check with the teacher to find out what he or she may suggest in the way of more advanced materials and to assure yourself that you are not interfering with planned classroom activities.

Mastery of the Thinking Skills

What do we mean by the thinking skills? There is an elaborate literature on this subject that explores the many aspects of thinking and levels of difficulty involved in each process. Perhaps the best known to the professional and lay community is Bloom's *Taxonomy of Educational Objectives* (2), which covers both the cognitive and affective domains. The volume on the cognitive domain attempts to classify "a range of possible educational goals or outcomes," where the term *cognitive* is used "to include activities such as remembering and recalling knowledge, thinking, problem solving, creating" (2, p. 2).

Since the use of Bloom's *Taxonomy* has become a rather popular basis for educational programs for the gifted, it will probably be helpful to give a very brief summary of what it includes. There is no space here to discuss in detail the meaning of all the terms, but the interested parent can go directly to Bloom's text for further explanation. The following outline will give you the flavor of the ideas included.

BLOOM'S TAXONOMY OF THE COGNITIVE DOMAIN
KNOWLEDGE
    1.00   Knowledge
         1.10   Knowledge of specifics
              1.11   Knowledge of terminology
              1.12   Knowledge of specific facts
         1.20   Knowledge of ways and means of dealing with specifics
              1.21   Knowledge of conventions
              1.22   Knowledge of trends and sequences
              1.23   Knowledge of classifications and categories
              1.24   Knowledge of criteria
              1.25   Knowledge of methodology
         1.30   Knowledge of the universals and abstractions in a field
              1.31   Knowledge of principles and generalizations
              1.32   Knowledge of theories and structures

INTELLECTUAL ABILITIES AND SKILLS
- 2.00 Comprehension
  - 2.10 Translation
  - 2.20 Interpretation
  - 2.30 Extrapolation
- 3.00 Application
- 4.00 Analysis
  - 4.10 Analysis of elements
  - 4.20 Analysis of relationships
  - 4.30 Analysis of organizational principles
- 5.00 Synthesis
  - 5.10 Production of a unique communication
  - 5.20 Production of a plan or proposed set of operations
  - 5.30 Derivation of a set of abstract relations
- 6.00 Evaluation
  - 6.10 Judgments in terms of internal evidence
  - 6.20 Judgments in terms of external criteria

Other programs for the gifted may not present their concepts in the formal fashion of a taxonomy, but basically they cover similar topics.

There is no question that a sound educational program for the gifted should stress the thinking skills. However, parents should be concerned about the approaches used. For example, if a school inaugurates a program for the gifted which is to last for only one year and which requires that the children be pulled out of their regular classroom to spend one hour per week learning "the thinking skills," then parents should question the long-range planning that underlies such an approach. They should also question curriculum plans that isolate a small segment of the thinking process for targeted teaching.

Thinking is a process that permeates all learning activities at varying levels of difficulty and complexity, depending on the subject matter. When children recite the multiplication tables, they are thinking at a simple level of recall. When doctors ponder an unusual set of symptoms and review in their minds the several diseases that present similar symptoms in order to make a differential diagnosis, they are thinking at a far more complex level, but it is still the same process of recall. Later, when they compare the syndromes of the diseases and differentiate among them to arrive at an ultimate diagnosis, doctors engage in several thinking processes at multiple levels of difficulty. In the same way, children move from recall of the memorized multiplication facts to the stage of analysis and application in which they can use the facts to solve a problem. One cannot block out periods of time in which only one thinking process will be utilized over all others. There has to be a continuous interweaving of activities involving all processes. Exercises in particular modes of thinking, however, can help children to direct their thinking along appropriate channels and to understand the various ways in which information can be processed.

It would be a serious regression on the part of educators and parents alike to go along with the current fad for stressing the basic skills if doing so means sacrificing the real progress that has been made in developing the thinking skills in children. A realistic appraisal of the child's future needs cannot help but lead to the conclusion that one must know how to think, as well as how to acquire information and process it as the times require, in order to live comfortably in a contemporary environment. For our children, that "contemporary environment" is not the present but a date ten to twenty years from now. Today's children need to know how to think about the information they acquire, using the basic skills that are needed to build that storehouse of knowledge.

Acquisition of a Core of Essential Information

One of the ways in which we can judge how successful our own education has been is to note the extent of the knowledge to which we were exposed during our educational careers and the degree to which we put that knowledge to use. For example, my education required that I study Latin for five years. On the other hand, I was never required to study chemistry. Since I deal in language, the study of Latin was useful and I have had frequent opportunities to apply what I learned. I did not, however, have to spend all five years on that subject to carry out my work well. I had acquired more than enough knowledge of the subject after three years; all the rest was intellectual luxury. However, I certainly could have used a year or two of chemistry. (I have chosen this as an example, but I do not mean to exclude other areas of learning.) I knew my education had been remiss in this area when I decided to dispose of a chemistry set given to me by a neighbor. My children had never used it and I had no use for it, so I thought I might just as well flush most of the chemicals away in the bathroom. Somewhere along the line I had learned that one should investigate the consequences of an act. I asked one of my children, who had studied chemistry, whether that would be the best way of disposing of the chemicals. You probably already know what I did not, that the way to dispose of chemicals is not by flushing them away, since some can cause serious burns when moistened and others can actually explode. Somewhere along the educational path, I should have acquired that kind of information. Fortunately, I had learned to make inquiries when not sure of my knowledge.

In order to function in our highly technological world, there is an enormous amount of basic knowledge we all must have. For the gifted, the range of knowledge is even greater. It is, therefore, essential that curricula be streamlined so that the child's time is not wasted in learning nonessentials or data of only transitory importance. Parents should review the subject matter that their children are being asked to learn and should try to relate this to what they estimate will be needed in the future. Hopefully, those who are responsible for curriculum development in their children's schools will have done this in an efficient manner. I am not hopeful. There is still too much unnecessary information being forced upon children, information that will have absolutely no value for them either in the present or in the future. Parents of the gifted should be particularly concerned about this since their children's time is so valuable. It should not be wasted or frittered away by other people's inefficiencies.

Parents should bear in mind that not all knowledge must lead to usefulness in the world of work. Some knowledge lays the foundation for a profitable and satisfying use of the leisure time which is increasing for us. You will note that I referred to the last two years of my study of Latin as a "luxury." There are cultural aspects to education that help to enrich our lives and make our leisure moments more gratifying. Since my fifth year of Latin included the study of Horace and Ovid, I must say that I enjoyed it very much and find my own private life enriched by the experience. It did not help me to earn a living, however.

The study of the fine and applied arts and of music should be encouraged for all gifted children. There are two reasons for this. First, as we have said, these aspects of knowledge enrich our lives and help in the enjoyment of leisure; and second, for the gifted, the experience may open avenues of unsuspected talent which should be encouraged. Few know that Nijinsky, the great Russian ballet dancer, loved mechanical devices and invented a version of the eversharp pencil. Einstein played the violin in order to relax from his scientific studies. Enrico Caruso, the celebrated operatic tenor, used to draw caricatures.

Exposure to a Broad Range of Knowledge

Parents have an intuitive understanding of the importance of exposing their gifted children to a broad range of knowledge. In the Astor Program for very young gifted children, parents observed that a real advantage of this program was the fact that the children were exposed to a great variety of activities and interests. A listing of topics covered in a prekindergarten/kindergarten class of four- to five-and-one-half-year-olds included properties of an isosceles triangle, Roman numerals, negative numbers, the Northwest Indians, the election process, symbols, gravity, magnetism, animal adaptations to their habitats, changes in nature, light and shadows, amphibians and reptiles, skeletal differences between man and other animals, and supermarket shopping. Parents of children in the program, responding to a follow-up questionnaire, stated that the long-lasting benefits of the program were the broadening of interests; exposure to a creative curriculum; introduction to professionals in many career areas; and, as one set of parents stated, an exposure to "things I would never have brought up to a five- or six-year-old."

At all ages, gifted children need to be exposed to the widest range of knowledge that can be achieved. Such exposure makes possible a broadening of interests, an opportunity to understand the range and complexity of knowledge, and an introduction to the important concept of the interrelatedness of all knowledge. Parents should expect the school to provide an enriched curriculum in which the pupils can explore as much of the world's knowledge as they can absorb. Children who spend an unusual amount of time on a school assignment, reading everything available and asking endless questions, frequently far beyond the original scope of the assignment, are savoring the joys of learning. They should be encouraged in their intensity, even while one explains that effort should be in proportion to the merits of the task. For the gifted, the pleasure of pursuing an intense interest may be sufficient reward, requiring a careful balancing of choices in discussing what is and what is not an intelligent use of time and deployment of abilities.

In this context, it is wise to note that specialization of learning should not begin too early, to the exclusion of all other subject areas. If the gifted are to grasp fully the implications of their work for all of society, they need to know a great deal about that society and the impact of their work in many areas other than their field of specialization. One cannot hide in a laboratory or university office and pretend that what is done there will not have an impact on the society in which one lives. Certainly, it occurred to those working on the atomic bomb what their work would mean to the rest of the world, as their subsequent efforts to control its uses demonstrated. Watson and Crick were well aware of the tremendous breakthrough their discovery of the helical structure of the DNA molecule would be in genetics. Responsible workers are usually aware of the long-range impact of their work. As a matter of fact, many researchers have difficulty in persuading funding sources and department heads of the significance of work they wish to undertake, simply because others lack the vision and insight that the workers themselves have. It is an unfortunate reality that the public is far readier to support research that has the possibility of immediate results than studies which provide only a distant promise of usefulness. Yet we had to wait for the proof of Einstein's theory for many years.

Exposure to a Wide Variety of Occupations

Parents and schools share the responsibility for exposing all children to the realities of the work world. In the case of gifted children, this education becomes quite complex, since their skills and abilities may lead them to vocations whose specifications have not yet been detailed. Since many gifted children begin to specialize at an early age in terms of their personal interests, they should begin to learn about the great variety of new opportunities that are developing as they go through school. For children of the last quarter of the twentieth century, the opportunities for exciting new jobs are limitless. They can turn to the space industry and consider the entire range of knowledge that is needed there—astronomy, astrophysics, chemistry, engineering, space medicine, hydroponics for agriculture in space, communications, and so forth. The field of medicine is exploring new techniques in chemotherapy, laser technology, psychosomatic procedures, and genetic management. Human relations is a field of study requiring the most informed minds and persons of strong moral and ethical fiber. School curricula should be so designed that the child will have ample opportunity to learn about the great variety of tasks to be done in the world and the preparation that will be required to perform adequately in a chosen field of work.

Such career guidance should begin in early childhood, and parents should expect schools to make this an active part of the curriculum from the earliest years. (For the role of parents in career guidance, see Chapter 8.)

Development of Social and Civic Responsibility

All children need to develop social and civic responsibility. The gifted, who tend to rise to positions of leadership and social influence, need this training even more than others. It is one of their general characteristics that they have a strong sense of social justice and that they are concerned about the welfare of their fellow beings. Educators should capitalize on this tendency and strengthen the inclination to service. The gifted need to know how they can work toward the improvement of the society in which they live and must be given ample opportunity to understand the processes involved in government and personal interactions. Terman and Oden (71), who followed the careers of gifted children into maturity, found that the gifted do indeed make major contributions to society, far in excess of what one would normally expect of their numbers.

The school curriculum should include the basic information required to understand local, state, and federal government and the role of the individual in determining its course. The curriculum should plan frequent opportunities to exercise awareness of and caring for other people. Such training should not be left to chance developments, but should be prescribed in the general training of the pupils. One of the highest compliments ever received by the Astor Program in New York was a statement by a visitor, repeated by others, that the children actually seemed to care about each other. The visitors noted a spirit of cooperativeness and freedom from aggressive competition. In fact, in one class the children explored ways of changing the game of Monopoly so that there would be an equal distribution of properties and wealth at the end of the game.

Parents should encourage school activities that demonstrate a concern for these areas of learning. They should support trips to local government institutions, services to others inside and outside the school, and cooperative experiences in which the children help each other or those less favored than themselves. When the Bronx High School of Science was first opened, it was housed in a school building that was also occupied by classes for the handicapped. The gifted students adopted protective and cooperative attitudes toward these children and learned to curb their adolescent vigor in halls, on staircases, and in the vicinity of the school. I cannot recall a single incident in which a handicapped child was hurt at that school. In another class, second-grade gifted children invited a young blind child to join them. The child was uncommunicative, rarely speaking or smiling. He seemed to be wrapped in a dark world, untouched by the warmth of human interaction. Within a few hours in the classroom with the very caring gifted children, this blind youngster was happily giggling along with them and chattering away. Within their classrooms, the gifted practice a generosity of spirit that is very heartening. It is a sad fact that parents, teachers, and others encourage competitiveness, self-centeredness, and a "me first" attitude, and discourage the many acts of kindness and concern that their gifted children show. These children bring hom stray children and lost animals. They risk scoldings and disapproval to defend a classmate who is in trouble.

Both parents and teachers would do well to take to heart the words of that lovely song from *South Pacific* (61): "You've got to be taught to fear and hate," and revise them to sing: "You've got to be taught to love and care." Of all the problems that face the human race today, the most significant for its survival is the relationship between human beings. If you want your children to live in a happy world, you must help them to learn about and develop those traits that will lead them along a path of fellowship with humanity. Since the gifted are the most willing learners, parents, teachers, and society in general should find this a rewarding task.

Awareness of Moral, Ethical, and Spiritual Values

Before parents become alarmed at the concept of a public school teaching moral, ethical, and spiritual values, they should bear in mind that the whole educational process is one in which value choices are constantly being made. The parent who overlooks an act of stealing is making a value choice as much as the one who punishes a child for such behavior. The teacher who excuses acts of cheating is making a value judgment that affects the class as much as a teacher who disapproves of cheating and penalizes the child who violated the standard.

The reality is that we live in a society which has a code of universally acceptable standards of behavior to which most parents subscribe and which they like to have the school support. As long as there are no religious implications or overtones to any of the actions taken in a public school, parents should welcome activities that develop and reinforce a strong sense of moral, ethical, and spiritual values in their children. The significance of such teachings for gifted children was hinted at in the foregoing discussion of civic and social responsibility. If they are to be the problem solvers, the scientific explorers, the leaders and molders of public opinion, the policy makers, the government officials and holders of power in our society, they will need all the guidance and reinforcement of positive values they can get. And the time to begin their education is at birth.

Parents should welcome classrooms in which there is a great deal of discussion. Actually, there is much too little of this going on in most classrooms. In classes for the gifted, the children benefit as much from an exchange of ideas with each other as they do from listening to a teacher lecturing to them. Issues of moral and ethical behavior can lend themselves to classroom discussion if the teacher has a clear understanding and appreciation of the society's value system.

An interesting classroom episode demonstrates how many of the factors involved in developing moral behavior, caring, appreciation, and good interpersonal relations can be used by a very skillful teacher. The class was visiting a museum and they had to walk a certain distance along the city streets and cross some major avenues. One child, about seven, was physically very small. Let us call him Bevin. A high gust of wind swept through the street and threw Bevin off balance. The children rushed to help him but were urged to get back on the sidewalk, while the teacher helped Bevin to his feet. Bevin hastily gathered his belongings and resumed the walk. Late that night, his family received a phone call from a woman who explained that she had found his bus pass for free transportation and, since she was passing his way, would deliver it to his home. Please bear in mind that this is in New York City's crowded Manhattan, with its population of 1.4 million. As Bevin later told the story to the class, the following scene developed:

TEACHER: Were you surprised to receive the call, Bevin?
BEVIN: Sure. I didn't even know I had lost the pass.
TEACHER: What do you think about the lady who returned it to you?
BEVIN: That was really nice of her. She had to go to a lot of trouble to find out my telephone number. It's a good thing there are only two families with our name in the phone book.
FIRST PUPIL: Boy, imagine if it was Smith or Jones, in our big fat telephone book!
BEVIN: She said she got us on the first call.
FIRST PUPIL: That was lucky. It was kind of nice of her to try.
SECOND PUPIL: Yeah. She didn't have to bother at all. What's a silly old pass?
BEVIN: Well, if she didn't return it I'd have to pay for my own way, and that's a dollar a day. That's a lot of money.
TEACHER: How would you describe this lady or what she did?
THIRD PUPIL: She was real thoughtful. She must care a lot about people.
FOURTH PUPIL: It was a swell thing to do. Most people wouldn't have bothered.
FIFTH PUPIL: Well, I would! After all, it isn't right to keep something that doesn't belong to you. And anyhow, it would mean that Bevin would have to spend a lot of money he doesn't have. I think the lady was very kind and honest.
TEACHER: Bevin, did you get hurt when you fell?
BEVIN: No, but I think I could use some lead in my shoes on windy days.

Simple episodes can become educational experiences if they are properly handled by the teachers. Parents should look for such teaching and consider it an important part of the curriculum. Furthermore, they need to reinforce the work by their own conscious attempts to develop appropriate behavior in their children. Gifted children love to ask questions and challenge existing ideas. Rather than ignoring such questions or repressing the child's pursuit of clarification, parents should provide positive guidance both by their discussions and by their own example. It can become inconvenient and can test our convictions when a child holds us to our own standards of morality and ethics. You are with your child one day and you find a wallet. It has only four dollars in it and some cards. You are tempted to say: "Oh, it's so little, it's not worth bothering about." The child says: "You said we shouldn't keep things that don't belong to us." It is very well worth the bother to pack it and send it back to the loser, so that your child can be secure in your teachings.

The discussion of values provides gifted children with opportunities to explore their doubts with peers. It helps them to crystallize their thinking and find a rationale for some of the inconsistencies in social behavior they are too perceptive to ignore. Of all children, the intellectually gifted are plagued the most by doubts and criticism. They need to share these doubts and questions with others and they need the guidance of mature and understanding adults to find their way through the maze of contradictions their everyday experiences present to them.

Development of Positive Characteristics Associated with Giftedness

Parents of the gifted have a right to expect their schools to know the many positive traits associated with giftedness and to encourage their development. It may seem to some parents that there is a conspiracy among teachers and administrators to plan their programs and curricular activities in such a way as to discourage the very characteristics that will make giftedness flourish. In the classroom, the excessive inquisitiveness of the children may be discouraged. Their questions remain unanswered or are scorned. Their strong sense of social justice is considered brazenness or "activist" behavior and generous motivations are consistently squelched. These children are thinkers who deliberate carefully before responding, but they may be pushed aside in the interest of speed and the instant, automatic response. Curricula may tend to skim over the surface of learning, with little or no planning for the in-depth understanding and probing that a gifted mind is prepared to do. The gifted love to discuss topics of interest but are rarely given the opportunity to do so. Yet discussion is the road to mutual understanding and broadening of points of view. Although gifted children are often creative and divergent in their solutions to problems, the classroom frequently is not hospitable to such ingenuity.

There is a long list of traits of giftedness which should be encouraged in the school setting but which are frequently ignored, squelched, ridiculed, or even destroyed. (See Chapter 2.) Parents should be on the alert to protect their children from the effects of such actions. They should also give active support to those teachers who have the insight and appreciation to encourage positive behavior patterns. Parents should expect that schools will allow their gifted children to function at their own intellectual level and will cooperate in fostering any talents or skills in which their children excel.

HOMEWORK

To many parents, the evidence that something worthwhile is going on in school is the amount of homework the child is required to do. Many parents actually demand that teachers assign homework, even for children in kindergarten. What is homework? What is its purpose? What are reasonable amounts of homework? How does homework for a gifted child differ, if at all, from that given to other children?

Let us begin with the talents, for they have clear-cut demands that are specific to themselves. If your child takes lessons in a musical instrument or voice, the need to practice daily and for a prescribed amount of time seems quite obvious. No one ever becomes a prima ballerina by taking one lesson a week and loafing between times. Even at the height of their careers, performers know that they must practice daily if they are to retain the high quality of their work. Artists make endless sketches, experimenting continually with their media. Particularly in the performing arts, the demands on the budding artist are difficult and unrelenting. It is only those who are willing to put in the great effort involved who actually achieve the fame to which most performing artists aspire.

Parents must exercise a great deal of restraint in order to assist their children through the early years of preparation for achievement in these arts. They have to provide the child with a careful balance between the demands of the art and the needs of childhood for play and relaxation. Usually, the truly gifted child is driven by a desire to achieve and does not need an excess of prodding by parents or teachers. Those who are infatuated with the idea of becoming great performers but who are unwilling to exert the effort involved learn soon enough that there is no easy path to the perfection demanded; they either drop out early or become second-rate artists. Therefore, for these fields in which the talents are involved, homework is built into immediate feedback of performance. If you don't practice your scales this week, you can't play them at the end of the week for the teacher, and you will have made no progress. If you want to progress, you must go back and practice as required.

This immediate feedback does not exist in the intellectual area. If you don't learn some bits of information today, there is always tomorrow, and you may not even need the information for five, ten, or fifteen years. There is always time. Fortunately, the gifted child is usually protected from this type of procrastination by an inner drive to master information and to achieve. Furthermore, the child is usually aided by another striking characteristic, a phenomenal memory, and sometimes a photographic memory. Once exposed to a bit of knowledge, the gifted child will retain it for an unusual length of time.

The purpose of homework is not to keep the child busy after school or to satisfy a parent that something worthwhile is going on in school, but rather to extend knowledge, to provide additional practice, to reinforce ideas. A great deal that is taught in school does not require a follow-through in homework. Furthermore, if we were to take the time to analyze a child's school day, we might discover that our demands for schooling exceed the demands we put on ourselves for working. For example, the school day usually consumes about six hours, from nine to three. Depending on the child's grade and the location of the school, another two hours may be used in travel to and from school. Of the time that is left, the child must be allowed periods for play and socializing, family activities, dinner, bathing, and household chores.

Since schoolwork takes priority over most other activities in many households, homework that lasts more than an hour or two can cut deeply into what should be a reasonably planned day. Many youngsters in the middle and senior high school years are actually asked to put in an unusually long "work day" of from eight to ten hours, all related to the business of getting an education. Since this is almost always work of an intellectual nature, the demands on the human system are scarcely sensible. Sometimes one wonders whether some of the temperamental flare-ups of adolescents are not due to the unreasonable workload related to schooling that is imposed upon them. Even when they choose to ignore the tasks assigned, they cannot escape the guilt of having ignored an obligation.

Who are the greatest number of victims of these abuses of our distorted notions of what schooling should be like? The gifted, of course. Since they can do so much more and can tackle topics of much greater difficulty than their peers, the workload put on their shoulders surpasses that of their classmates. The phrase "burning the midnight oil" was not created for the average working man. It rose out of the need of scholars to work into the wee hours of the night in order to carry out the tasks assigned to them.

Parents must have a reasonable perspective on what a balanced day should be for their gifted children. They should not permit their children to be victimized by the notion that the only way to teach them is by assigning endless hours of homework. Parents should expect teachers in departmentalized schools (usually in grades seven through twelve) to coordinate their planning so that no child need spend more than one to one and one-half hours on homework per night, with occasional provisions for special assignments of longer duration, in the sixth to eighth grades, and no more than two hours per night in the ninth to twelfth grades. Homework, if one can call it that, may be given to kindergartners and even first-grade children, but it certainly should not require more than fifteen to twenty minutes. In grades two and three, the time may be extended to thirty minutes, and in the fourth and fifth grades, it may take up to one hour. Anything exceeding these amounts should be considered an encroachment on the child's time for other, equally important activities.

The gifted, perhaps even more than other children, need to have time in their day for undirected, physical play, for socializing with friends, for participation in family activities, and for pursuing their own special interests. There is nothing wrong with letting such a child just loaf for a while, apparently doing nothing. It may seem that way to the untutored observer, but anyone who has read about or dealt with gifted persons will tell you that these are extremely profitable occasions during which many a germ of a brilliant idea was born.

What constitutes reasonable homework? Let us take it from the early years onward. We begin at the kindergarten level. The assignment might be to bring a picture of something that begins with the letter b. The children can look in magazines or newspapers, or they may choose to draw a picture. In a class of bright children, the next day may find a collection of ideas on the teacher's desk including a picture of a bear, drawn by a child who went to the zoo recently and will talk about his adventure; colored balloons; a book about brontosaurs and other prehistoric animals, which the teacher will be expected to read or allow the child to read to the class; a piece of bronze; some braided string. Other assignments might include an interview with a parent about his or her work; practice in printing one's name; finding and bringing in some autumn leaves; coloring a picture that was drawn in school during the day; or finding some words in the newspaper headlines. The purpose in the assignments at this level is to help children develop a sense of responsibility; to let them practice writing; to teach them how to follow directions; to encourage a curiosity about their environment; to help them relate to others in conversation; and to develop any of the numerous goals of a well-developed curriculum for children of this age.

At no time is the assignment to exceed the children's ability to do the work by themselves. Parental cooperation would be required in providing the magazines or the time for a little interview. Parental concern, of course, should be shown by demonstrating interest in the children's work, providing opportunities for them to carry out their responsibilities, and avoiding the nagging that implies that they would not do the work unless constantly reminded of it. A well-organized home establishes a pattern that says: This is the time reserved for your homework, if you have any; and you will be able to do it, undisturbed by other requirements.

In the primary grades, a teacher may send home some practice exercises in handwriting, spelling, or arithmetic; a search for information related to a special topic; a small reading assignment; or even an instruction to memorize a short poem or limerick. In the intermediate grades, four through six, assignments may include writing a short composition or letter; more exercises in mathematics, spelling, or handwriting; a search for information (research) in encyclopedias, other reference books, or at the library; or gathering some materials for a special class project. As the children progress to the higher grades and departmental classwork, their assignments become more sophisticated and involve special readings, library research work, writing summaries, or preparing reports.

At all grade levels, good home planning requires that a specific time of day be set aside for doing homework, and that there will be parental assistance and support for the effort. Parents should not expect, and should protest against, homework assignments that are overly long and overly repetitious. One very bright youngster in second grade misspelled a word in a class lesson and the teacher assigned her to write the word one hundred times at home. For such a youngster, nothing but rebellion could be the result. She knew how the spell the word correctly as soon as the error was pointed out to her. If she had written it two or three times correctly after that, that was all she would have needed. Naturally, the youngster rebelled and refused to do the homework. A very bright youngster in third grade was asked to solve twenty problems in mathematics, all of the same type. It was a long assignment and he found it boring, since it was merely a repetition of the same process. Frustration with unimaginative assignments, boredom because of the repetitious quality of the work, resentment against the waste of time involved that could be spent in far more rewarding work—all these lead gifted children to rebellion, whether overt or covert. They finally decide it is all a waste of time and drop out, either physically or psychologically; either way, the results are the same—another wasted mind.

SCHOOL TRANSFERS

Help! This seems to be the constant cry of parents of gifted children. They worry about the schools their children attend; they worry about transferring them to other schools; they worry about business relocations that may take their children from a desirable educational environment to one that does not match it. As concerned parents, they worry and with good cause. These are examples of some of the calls for help I have received:

> This is Mr. Jones. I am calling from Wyoming. I have a ten-year-old girl who is exceptionally talented in music. Since my firm is moving me to a new location, I'm wondering if there is some place where I could have my child placed so that she can develop this wonderful talent she has. Can you help me?
>
> This is Mrs. Smith. I am calling from Florida. We are planning to move to your city. Our son is in a very fine program for the gifted here, and we are wondering if we will be able to find something comparable for him up there. He is eight years old and very advanced for his years. Can you tell us where we should locate in the city to be near a good school for him?
>
> This is Dr. Swanson, calling from Texas. We run a research laboratory here for a large corporation and are planning to send one of our men to our branch in your area. He is concerned, however, about schooling for his two children. They are both exceptionally bright and are attending a very fine school here. We would like to reassure him that the children will not suffer by the transfer. One of the boys is in high school, and the other is just entering the seventh grade. If he were to be relocated in that section of the country, would there be good schooling there for his sons?
>
> I live in this city. My little girl is very bright and she is getting bored in school. She's only in the second grade and I'm afraid she'll get into trouble if she isn't placed in a class where someone will pay attention to her brightness. How can I get a transfer to a school with a program for bright kids?
>
> Can you tell me about schools for bright children? I have three children and they are all very bright, and no one is doing anything about it in the school they are attending. They are eleven, eight, and six. I'd like to transfer them to another school where their needs can really be met.
>
> My daughter's teacher says she is very gifted and that I should try to get her transferred to another school where they can teach her in a class for bright children. Can you help me?

Parents should be concerned about the schools their children have to attend and they should make inquiries. The preceding quotations are selected from my notes of telephone calls I have received over many years, and they all can be summarized in this way. Parents are concerned about their children's education, especially if the children are gifted or talented, and they do everything they can to move into areas where the best possible education will be available to them.

Transfers mean other problems. How will the children adjust to the new environment? How will they make the transition from a school where they are participating in an excellent program for the gifted to one where there are no special provisions to meet their needs? How do the children adjust to a reverse situation? Should the children be transferred at all if there is a choice possible for the parents? What should parents do to insure the best adjustment for their children?

Parents of the gifted can ease the transfer process for their children by making appropriate inquiries in advance and by preparing the children for the change.

If the transfer is necessary because of a job relocation, parents can take several preliminary steps. Call the coordinator of the gifted at the local or state level and find out the name of the person who has a corresponding position in the new location. Then call that person and explain your problem. If the job relocation involves an advance visit to the new area, try to arrange a meeting with personnel in the prospective school. Find out in advance the names of the persons who would be able to help you by calling the Board of Education in the new area. Try, if possible, to visit the school to which your child will be transferred and explain the special circumstances to the principal or his or her designee. Be sure to take some supportive information with you so that he or she will understand why you are concerned about special placement for your child. If you cannot go in person, try the telephone or write a letter of inquiry. Of course, if the transfer is within your immediate locality, you will be able to find out about the new school and its programs much more easily. Try to telephone the appropriate persons, or make an appointment if they have the time to see you. (See Chapter 11 for addresses.)

If the school transfer is caused by your dissatisfaction with the present provisions for your child or inadequate programs for the gifted in the system, you will have to make careful inquiries of the prospective school or schools before you begin the transfer process. You will have to examine any descriptive material that is available or actually visit the school and talk to someone who can answer your questions. You should be prepared to offer some evidence of your child's giftedness or special talents and should bring such data along with you to the interview. (Useful evidence is discussed in Chapter 5.)

Be prepared to ask specific questions, such as: How are the

children grouped for teaching? How much time is devoted to teaching the gifted and talented? What preparation will be expected of your child? How long has the program been in existence? (Obviously, the longer the better.) How are teachers selected for the program? How does the curriculum differ from the regular school curriculum? In other words, a simple "Yes, we can take care of your child's needs" will not suffice to assure you that a worthwhile program is in operation and that a transfer to that school is really desirable. If you can, try to speak to other parents whose children attend that school and are of comparable ages. Try to find out when the PTA meets and attend a meeting. Speak to the parents there and find out what the teaching staff is like and how they handle their work with the gifted.

Besides preparing yourself with information, it is important that you prepare the child for the move. Depending on their ages, children's reactions can be quite different. For the very young child, a move to a new school may be fraught with anxieties. At no age do youngsters happily give up known and cherished friendships for contact with a new world of strangers. In a memorandum to its guidance counselors, the Division of Special Education and Pupil Personnel Services of the New York City Board of Education (52) summarizes the problem of moving from one school to another, as follows:

> As children develop, a change in schools can prove to be a frightening experience. The neighborhood elementary school is a child's immediate family. The move to a junior high school or intermediate school is a move into the unknown. No longer will everybody in school have a familiar face and live in the immediate neighborhood; no longer will the student be staying with one teacher in one room throughout the day. It may no longer be possible to walk to school or to ride on a school bus.
>
> The move from junior to senior high school, from high school to college, can often prove to be just as traumatic and threatening for older children as change is to younger boys and girls. Sudden decisions have to be made that may have lifelong implications. Some choices may result not only in a change of schools, but also in a change of living arrangements. These factors may be part of the reason some high school seniors who have previously experienced academic success and positive school adjustment become involved in behavior which imperils their final grades and graduation. If a child has built up a good reputation and a position of leadership in the present school, he or she may worry about starting all over again. It should always be remembered that children, unlike adults, are still growing and thus have within their makeup the ability to bend to new situations. What usually interferes with this normal adjustment is a fear of the un-

known that pushes children into withdrawal or negative behavior which the child unconsciously or consciously hopes may prevent the change from taking place.

Rather than letting the situation lead to more problems, it is desirable to prevent a crisis by discussing the circumstances frankly with the child, even at the kindergarten level. This is particularly important for the gifted, who have difficulty enough in making friendships and in feeling accepted by the school environment. Explain why the move is being made. Listen to their concerns and try to show them that others have the same insecurities and that you will provide the emotional support needed. Reassure them that you will help them make new friends in the new location. If you can, tell them something about the school system.

In spite of the fact that one would wish to provide the best possible educational environment for a talented or otherwise gifted child, the prime concern should be his or her emotional and psychological well-being. Some children can be utterly miserable when they are removed from a familiar location to an unfamiliar one, especially in the younger years. Parents need to weigh carefully the advantages and disadvantages of such moves before undertaking the final step. Consider the child's makeup. Be aware of his or her dependent needs as well as of intellectual prowess or exceptional talent. Give careful consideration to each factor before making a decision. It may be that postponing a change for a year or two will do little damage intellectually, yet will establish the sense of security and comfort that is essential to the child's well-being.

Discuss the advantages and disadvantages of a possible transfer with the child's present teacher. You may find much assistance in that quarter if you will listen carefully and, of course, if the teacher is sympathetic to your child's needs. Do the same with the school guidance counselors or the school principal. You may find that they are quite eager to help you and your child.

Parents will find that they can obtain the most services from their schools when they enter into a partnership with them and try to work together to attain their mutual goals. Under the best conditions, both share a concern for the welfare of the child and will try to provide the maximum learning environment. When that partnership does not or cannot exist, for whatever reason, it is incumbent on parents to work toward change, so that their children will receive the education to which they are fully entitled.

SUGGESTED READINGS AND RESOURCES

General Philosophy and Curriculum Design

BARBE, WALTER B., and JOSEPH S. RENZULLI, eds. *Psychology and Education of the Gifted.* 2nd ed. Parts IV, V. New York: John Wiley, Halsted Press, 1975.

BRUNER, JEROME. *On Knowing: Essays for the Left Hand.* Cambridge, Mass.: Harvard University Press, 1962.

———. *The Process of Education.* Cambridge, Mass.: Harvard University Press, 1960.

EHRLICH, VIRGINIA Z. *Program Planning for the Gifted.* 1978. AGATE Press, Dingman Point, Alexandria Bay, N.Y. 13607.

GALLAGHER, JAMES J. *Teaching the Gifted Child.* 3rd ed. Boston: Allyn & Bacon, College Division, 1979.

KAPLAN, SANDRA N. *Providing Programs for the Gifted and Talented: A Handbook.* 1974. Ventura County Superintendent of Schools, 535 East Main Street, Ventura, Calif. 93009.

MARTINSON, RUTH A. *Curriculum Enrichment for the Gifted in the Primary Grades.* Englewood Cliffs, N.J.: Prentice-Hall, 1968.

PHENIX, PHILIP. *Realms of Meaning: A Philosophy of the Curriculum for General Education.* New York: McGraw-Hill, 1964.

TORRANCE, E. PAUL, and R. E. MYERS. *Creative Learning and Teaching.* New York: Dodd, Mead, 1970.

WARD, VIRGIL S. *Differential Education for the Gifted.* 1980. Ventura County Superintendent of Schools, 535 East Main Street, Ventura, Calif. 93009. 1980. Reprint of *Education for the Gifted: An Axiomatic Approach.*

Affective and Values Education

BERMAN. LOUISE M., and JESSIE A. RODERICK, eds. *Feeling, Valuing, and the Art of Growing: Insights into the Affective.* 1977. Association for Supervision and Curriculum Development, 1701 K Street, NW, Washington, D.C. 20006.

DE PALMA, DAVID J., and JEANNE M. FOLEY, eds. *Moral Development: Current Theory and Research.* New York: John Wiley, 1975.

"Education of Judgment and Action: Personal and Civic," *Educational Leadership* 35, no. 6 (March 1978). A collection of readings.

FRANKENA, WILLIAM K. *Ethics.* Englewood Cliffs, N.J.: Prentice-Hall, 1963.

LIPMAN, MATTHEW, ANN MARGARET SHARP, and FREDERICK S. OSCANYAN. *Philosophy in the Classroom.* Upper Montclair, N.J.: Institute for the Advancement of Philosophy for Children, Montclair State College, 1977.

National Education Association. *Values, Concepts and Techniques.* National Education Association, 1201 16th Street, NW, Washington, D.C. 20006.

PHENIX, PHILIP. "The Moral Imperative in Contemporary American Education." *Perspectives on Education,* Winter 1969. New York: Teachers College, Columbia University.

SHAFTEL. F., and G. SHAFTEL. *Role Playing for Social Values.* Englewood Cliffs, N.J.: Prentice-Hall, 1967.

SIMON, SIDNEY B., and HOWARD KIRSCHENBAUM. *Readings in Values Clarification.* Minneapolis, Minn.: Winston Press, 1973.

SIMON, SIDNEY B., and ROBERT D. O'ROURKE. *Developing Values with Exceptional Children.* Englewood Cliffs, N.J.: Prentice-Hall, 1977.

WILLIAMS, FRANK E. *Classroom Ideas for Encouraging Thinking and Feeling.* Buffalo, N.Y.: DOK Publishers, 1970.

Creativity

CALLAHAN, CAROLYN M. *Developing Creativity in the Gifted and Talented.* 1978. The Council for Exceptional Children, 1920 Association Drive, Reston, Va. 22091.

FELDHUSEN, JOHN F., and DONALD J. TREFFINGER. *Creative Thinking and Problem Solving in Gifted Education.* Dubuque, Iowa: Kendall/Hunt, 1980.

GETZELS, JACOB W., and PHILIP W. JACKSON. *Creativity and Intelligence.* New York, John Wiley, 1962.

GOWAN, JOHN C. *Development of the Creative Individual.* San Diego, Calif.: Robert Knapp, 1972.

HOPKINS, LEE BENNETT, and ANNETTE FRANK SHAPIRO. *Creative Activities for the Gifted Child.* Palo Alto, Calif.: Fearon, 1969.

KAGAN, JEROME. *Creativity and Learning.* Boston: Houghton-Mifflin, 1967.

PARNES, SIDNEY J. *Programming Creative Behavior.* Buffalo, N.Y.: State University of New York, 1966.

SHALLCROSS, DORIS J. *Teaching Creative Behavior.* Englewood Cliffs, N.J.: Prentice-Hall, 1981.

TORRANCE, E. PAUL. *Creativity.* Belmont, Calif.: Dimensions Publishing, 1969.

_____. *Gifted Children in the Classroom.* New York: Macmillan, 1965.

_____. *Rewarding Creative Behavior.* Englewood Cliffs, N.J.: Prentice-Hall, 1965.

Curriculum Models in Education of the Gifted

EBERLE, BOB. *Classroom Cue Cards for Cultivating Multiple Talent.* Buffalo, N.Y.: DOK Publishers, 1974.

EHRLICH, VIRGINIA Z. *The Astor Program for Gifted Children: PreKindergarten through Grade Three.* 1978. Box 223, Teachers College, Columbia University, New York, N.Y. 10027.

MEEKER, MARY NACOL. *The Structure of Intellect: Its Interpretation and Uses.* Columbus, Ohio: Chas. E. Merrill, 1969.

RENZULLI, JOSEPH S. *The Enrichment Triad Model: A Guide for Developing Defensible Programs for the Gifted and Talented.* Weathersfield, Conn.: Creative Learning Press, 1977.

SORENSON, B., and L. ADDISON, eds. *Model Units for the Gifted.* The Council for Exceptional Children, 1920 Association Drive, Reston, Va. 22091.

TANNENBAUM, ABRAHAM. "Model for Differentiating Education for the Gifted." *Gifted/Talented Education* (November 1978), 1, 7–8.

TAYLOR, CALVIN, *Igniting Creative Potential.* Salt Lake City, Utah: Project Implode, Bella Vista Elementary School, 1971.

WILLIAMS, FRANK E. *Classroom Ideas for Encouraging Thinking and Feeling.* Buffalo, N.Y.: DOK Publishers, 1970.

Reading

BETTELHEIM, BRUNO. *The Uses of Enchantment.* New York: Knopf, 1975.

DURKIN, DOLORES. *Children Who Read Early.* New York: Teachers College Press, 1966.

EHRLICH, VIRGINIA Z. "The Role of Reading in the Astor Program for Intellectually Gifted Preschool/Primary Children." 1979. Paper commissioned by the U.S. Commissioner of Education, AGATE Press, Dingman Point, Alexandria Bay, N.Y. 13607.

"Reading, Language, and Learning." *Harvard Education Review* 47, no. 3 (August 1977). Special Issue.

Self-Concept

AUSUBEL, DAVID P. *Theory and Problems of Child Development*, Chap. 9, "Ego Development." New York: Grune & Stratton, 1958.

BERMAN, LOUISE M., and JESSIE A. RODERICK, eds. *Feeling, Valuing, and the Art of Growing: Insights into the Affective.* 1977. Association for Supervision and Curriculum Development, 1701 K Street, NW, Washington, D.C. 20006.

CANFIELD, JACK, and HAROLD C. WELLS. *100 Ways to Enhance Self-Concept in the Classroom: A Handbook for Teachers and Parents.* Englewood Cliffs, N.J.: Prentice-Hall, 1976.

KRATHWOHL, DAVID R., et al. *Taxonomy of Educational Objectives: Handbook II: Affective Domain.* New York: D. McKay, 1964.

SIME, MARY. *A Child's Eye View: Piaget for Young Parents and Teachers.* New York: Harper & Row, Pub., 1973.

Parents' Roles in Educating Gifted/Talented Children

The role of parents in the lives of their children is multifaceted and incredibly difficult, yet it is a role that is usually undertaken with pleasure. Parents are nurturers and providers, educators and mentors, intellectual models, listeners, social models, disciplinarians, planners and managers, interpreters and buffers, authority figures, partners in schooling, promoters of special interests and talents, career guides. They can be a constructive or destructive influence on the lives of their children, depending on their own perceptions of their roles, the skills, knowledge, and experiences they have, and their own motivations and desires.

RECOGNIZING GIFTEDNESS AND TALENT

In the section on identification (Chapter 2), there are several lists and guides to help in recognizing giftedness. A first responsibility of parents and teachers toward gifted children is that of recognition. These are some suggestions:

1. Acknowledge your children's giftedness to yourself, and let them know that you understand their capacities.
2. Treat them at a level of ability where they are able to function, always remembering to make accommodations for chronological age, experience, physiological development, social and psychological needs, and any other factors that may be appropriate to the individual child.
3. Help your children accept their abilities as desirable traits to be developed rather than hidden.

PARENTS AS SOCIAL MODELS

All children need emotional stability. They thrive best in a home where there is warmth, affection, and understanding. Gifted children, with whom we can more readily reason and discuss serious problems, should not be expected to respond on an abstract, intellectual level to family crises and difficulties. Simply because they may seem to understand and respond with precocious maturity to sickness, separation, divorce, death, and other tragedies does not mean that they are not bruised emotionally. Sometimes they may suffer even more than other children of their own ages because of their vivid imaginations and unusual range of knowledge, which are untempered by real-life experience. As far back as 1926, Terman and others (67) observed what we find even now, as reported for Astor Program children (14), that most gifted children have stable, two-parent homes. It has been suggested that their giftedness can best emerge in such an environment, which is free from the tensions and distractions of less secure, emotionally stressful homes, particularly during the early years.

The home needs to provide *demonstrated* affection for children. They must be valued for themselves as whole persons, and not solely for their brainpower or special talents. Children need to know that they do not have to function constantly at the highest levels of their abilities or talents, and that they have the right to be children like all others of their age. They must feel that they can cry, loaf, play silly games, run, shout, and do all the carefree things children do, without fear of being scolded for being too "babyish" (*for such a smart boy or girl*). Being of superior intelligence does not neutralize one's feelings. If anything, they are sharpened and heightened to an even higher degree than is usually found among the age peers of the bright. As we have said before, the gifted have a higher degree of sensitivity than is usually found among others of the same age.

PARENTS AS DEFENDERS OR BUFFERS AGAINST SOCIETY

Gifted children need to know that they will be defended by their parents against the unfair attacks and injustices meted out to them by outsiders, particularly school personnel and classmates. They need to know that there is someone in the background who has faith in both their ability and their sincerity about learning and the pursuit of knowledge.

Equally important is the protection they need from the teasing and name-calling that others seem to find necessary defenses for their own lack of abilities or intensity of interest in learning and achievement. Parents can act as buffers for their gifted children in providing the protective shield that circumstances require.

PARENTS AS DISCIPLINARIANS

Gifted children should be neither privileged nor denied simply because they are gifted. Home discipline should be one that relies on the child's capacity for self-control and independence of behavior. Heavier-than-usual reliance can be placed on reasoning and discussion, to help the child understand the justice of any action taken. Like all children, the gifted benefit by a reasonable amount of organization and control, provided ample opportunity is given for the full exercise of their mental abilities. Talented children will cooperate if understanding is displayed for their need to practice and enjoy the performance of their art.

Consistency in applying value systems is of the utmost importance. We must not forget that gifted children are good logicians, and inconsistency between parents on standards of behavior or social patterns will arouse the child's rebellion. "Do as I say, and not as I do!" will carry no weight with a child whose capacity to see relationships, infer conclusions, or reason is sometimes superior to that of many adults.

PARENTS AS SOCIAL PLANNERS

Gifted children complain of the gradual isolation that overtakes them in the social world solely because they excel in intellectual ability or a particular talent. Other children leave them out of games; adults ignore their ideas and contributions to discussions; classmates leave them out of social activities. The gifted may be respected for their abilities, but they are not always viewed as fun people to be with or, from an adult's point of view, as sufficiently grown-up to have anything worthwhile to say.

Parents can help to avoid many of these unhappy situations. First of all, they can seek out friends for their children who share the same interests and whose abilities are comparable. This may require some adult socializing that may not be as congenial as one would wish. But the brighter the child, the more difficult it is for him or her to find appropriate companions. Parents can take advantage of the many parent advocate groups that are springing up all over the country. By joining such groups, they can reinforce their work and at the same time meet people who share the same circumstances. Information about such groups can be obtained from statewide or national PTA groups, state coordinators for the gifted, and the Committee on Affiliates in The Association for the Gifted, which is part of the Council for Exceptional Children. (See Chapter 11 for addresses.)

PARENTS AS PLANNERS AND MANAGERS OF TIME

In trying to meet the many needs of their gifted children, parents become time managers. They try to arrange for special lessons in art, dance, music, and foreign language, as well as for other activities. They arrange for attendance at after-school special studies. They try, as suggested earlier, to provide companionship that may require special time arrangements. The task becomes complicated and, to some parents, confusing. How far should one go? How much time must be filled in?

Gifted children have a need to satisfy their eagerness to learn, but more importantly, they need "time space," freedom to relax and do nothing (or so it seems), time to "fool around." Planning a child's day or week or year must take into account his or her age and social needs, carefully balanced against an insatiable hunger to learn everything at once. Parents must manage their children's schedules so that there is a wholesome balance between enrichment of the mind and relaxation of the spirit.

PARENTS, AND OTHERS, AS LISTENERS, CONVERSATIONALISTS

Part of the joy of learning lies in sharing the discoveries made along the way with someone who cares and understands. This sharing becomes an essential part of the child's experience. It provides opportunities for socializing, relaxing, and intellectual growth. Parents, of course, become the prime targets as listeners or conversationalists.

The social interactions of gifted children can also be enhanced by adults in the home and elsewhere who will encourage interesting conversation. Grandparents, older relatives, and big brothers and sisters are all noteworthy as being good listeners who frequently show a genuine appreciation for the child's level of discussion. Family participation in group discussions, at the dinner table or in leisurely get-togethers, can create ideal situations for the gifted to partake in more advanced thinking and talking than is usually possible for them with their age peers.

In sum, what these children need is a good audience, someone who will listen, appreciate, and not mock the ideas they wish to explore. Gifted children, as they themselves tell us, love to talk . . . talk . . . talk . . .

PARENTS AS EDUCATORS

Although parents may be sensitive to the superior abilities of their intellectually gifted children, they frequently fail to provide appropriate educational experiences. A few suggestions may be helpful here.

1. Use language that is natural to you. Do not edit your vocabulary to make it simpler. Bright children will learn long words as easily as short words, technical names as easily as euphemisms. You will be amazed at how rich a vocabulary a gifted child can master, as long as it is in connection with experienced phenomena.

2. Purchase toys that involve what educators call "thinking skills." These are toys that require color, size, or shape discrimination; keeping tallies of "wins"; counting and money transactions. Very young children, five- and six-year-olds, can play complicated card games, checkers, and chess. As the children get older, there are more complex games involving planning, strategy, deduction, inference, and often a broad range of information. Even at the infant or pre-nursery school age, toys should be of mixed levels of difficulty, including easy ones and some that are a little harder than those you would ordinarily buy for such children.

3. Make books accessible to gifted children. When they are very young, read to them on a regular basis. Continue to read to them even after you think they have learned how to read. Do not hesitate to read the same story over and over again, nor should you discourage children who do this on their own. If you can, have a good library of books at home, including dictionaries, encyclopedias, atlases, maps, almanacs, and other reference books. As soon as the child can write his name, he or she should join the public library. Include visits to the library along with your shopping trips or other excursions "to town." Take out books for the child from all sections of the library, and do not let their presumed difficulty stop you. If the child sees a need for it, it should be taken out. Ignore teachers or librarians who may tell you otherwise.

4. Take advantage of cultural facilities in your community such as exhibits, museums, theaters, and festivals. Expose children to many experiences, including any travel you may do. An excavation, building construction, the installation of a machine or a house telephone, the inspection of meters, the docking of a ship, the threshing of wheat—anything and everything is of interest. Do not overlook the wealth of information that can be gleaned from your immediate environment, whether it be rural, suburban, or urban. Each has a history, a culture, and resources that are peculiar to itself and each provides endless opportunities for learning.

The advantages of large cities are fairly obvious, and usually education departments, newspapers, and libraries will have lists of useful resources. Local libraries and papers in suburban areas should have listings of important events. Those living in rural areas may have to travel more to expand their children's experiences, but they should realize the many advantages of their special environment. The lack of distractions provides opportunities for meditation, thinking, and analyzing that the overly busy city life tends to destroy. What is needed is the stimulus to thinking provided by reading matter, television and radio, and the exchange of ideas with others, particularly older members of the community.

5. When it seems appropriate, enrich the child's life by providing opportunities to engage in sports or to develop special talents. The advice of professionals should be sought on when to start certain activities, such as ballet, voice training, or playing an instrument. Provide the child with exposure to fine arts, so that any latent ability can unfold. Gifted children should be exposed to activities that can enhance the use of leisure time. In spite of all we may try to do, for some these activities may become the most important sources of comfort and companionship. A time frequently comes in the lives of the intellectually gifted when the number of persons with whom they can share common interests and ideas becomes more and more limited. They need sources of relaxation that are different from their primary fields of work.

6. The role of parents as home teachers has been discussed in Chapter 4. Whether the child goes to school or not, parents can and should take an active part in his or her education. Parents should not be overwhelmed by their children's brightness to the extent that they become immobilized with respect to educating them. Regardless of the level of the child's ability, parents have the advantage of age and experience, which will serve them in good stead. Some parents become a little uneasy because they have not had a college or graduate school education. Some may not have completed high school. None of these factors should act as deterrents in parents' efforts to help their gifted children.

Following are specific activities that are suitable for the preschool child. Some are repeated from the previous listings, to stress the fact that they are definitely appropriate to such young children.

- Provide books, whether by purchase or from public libraries, in great quantities, varieties, and levels of difficulty.
- Subscribe to or use magazines of special interest, which may or may not be directed specifically to children. Of course, the children's magazines are very good, particularly for those who live in isolated areas.
- Help your child learn to read, but do not force the issue. Respond to requests for help and guidance. Do not bother with spelling and phonics. Just tell the child what he or she wants to know. If the child asks, "What is this word?" or "What does this say?" you answer: "Milk," "Cereal," "Stop," "Go," and so forth. You do not say:

"Mmm—iii—lll—kk." Most bright children learn to read by acquiring a sight vocabulary. Let the school worry about the phonics.

- Let children share in your activities. Involve them in the kitchen, where foods must be measured, weighed, and combined. Take them to the food store and explain why you do or do not reject certain vegetables or packaged goods. Talk to them about anything and everything. If you live on a farm, include them in chores and explain why you cannot skip the milking, why the weather is so important to you, why you add this or that to the soil in your garden. Use correct names for everything, so that the child's vocabulary can grow. Words are not difficult because they are long or short. They are difficult only when they are used with no obvious relationship to what is already known or when they are introduced out of context.
- Help the child develop arithmetic concepts by learning to make change and handle small sums of money. Simple games that involve counting or money transactions are excellent.
- Take advantage of the excellent educational toys and games that are available. If your child is bright, disregard the age boundaries usually given on the packages. Buy toys that include the present age but that also go beyond it by two or three years.
- Read to your children every day, whether or not they know how to read by themselves. Read anything that interests them and read it as many times as they wish. The repetition is partly for enjoyment and partly as a basis for learning to read.
- Encourage the child's interests and hobbies. Many a child's early interest has formed the basis of a vocation or avocation in later life. (See Chapter 8.)
- As a general rule, involve the child in the activities of daily living as fully as possible.
- If you can, even at this age, try to provide playmates who are intellectual peers. If the child is being taught at home, some provision for playmates must be made. So long as they are congenial and your child is happy with them, they should be welcome friends. The important point is to maintain a careful balance between meeting the intellectual needs of the child and fulfilling the equally important social, psychological, and emotional needs.

PARENTS AS PROMOTERS OF TALENT

For children who are talented in the visual or performing arts, parents must make the many adjustments required to help the talent develop. Frequently, a total revision of family scheduling is required. Musicians and dancers require many hours of practice. Painters need special light and supplies. The life styles of those engaged in these professions follow a different time schedule, a different pattern from the usual.

Parents of budding artists must be ready to make the many adaptations necessary if they are going to be helpful to their children. It might be informative for both parents and children to read about the lives of artists who have described the demands of their work and the priority they have had to give to certain aspects of their particular art. Margot Fonteyn, famous ballerina, tells how she had to practice daily even after years and years of giving star performances (22). So, too, do most of the great instrumentalists, singers, and other artists.

PARENTS AS PARTNERS WITH THE SCHOOL

In order to obtain the best educational conditions for a child, it is wise for parents to establish a partnership with the school in a task that should be of mutual concern. Avoid the adversary role. Discuss your child's needs with the appropriate personnel. Become involved with the PTA. Get to know what is going on in the school, the district, the state. (See Chapter 5.) Know your child's rights under the law and any local regulations that may apply. (See Chapter 10.)

In trying to educate your child, don't anticipate school teaching by providing the same readers or workbooks that are being used in the classroom. This will just promote more restlessness and boredom. Instead, supplement or expand on what the school is doing. Buy or provide different materials on a more difficult level or on other subjects. If your child has a special interest, help him or her by using the library to get additional and different material from that provided in school. If you are fortunate enough to have a neighbor or friend who specializes in your child's area of concern, try to arrange for them to meet and talk together. Do not discourage a child from writing to well-known personalities who may have special expertise in some areas. If the child's interest is genuine, a valuable resource may be forthcoming. At all times, try not to push children into doing more than is basically required of them in school or more than they are willing to do. Extracurricular study should originate with the child and should not be imposed by overly ambitious parents.

PARENTS AS CAREER GUIDES

Parents play a significant role in the career choices their children make. For the gifted and talented, this influence is especially important, since the early impact of the home can and does affect the choices made. This subject is discussed at length in Chapter 8. The early history of eminent personalities shows that their parents often were very important forces in determining their career choices. Puccini's mother was determined that the musical history of her family be continued through her children. She selected young Giacomo and exerted all her efforts toward training his talent. We are fortunate, for she chose one whose gift has enriched the world with his now-famous operas, including *La Bohème* and *Madame Butterfly*. Louis Bromfield's mother was determined to have a writer in the family and designated her son Louis to carry out her goal. Such determination on the part of parents can be dangerous. Fortunately, Puccini and Bromfield were talented in the areas chosen for them and liked the choices. Others are not so fortunate.

Parents can and should provide opportunities for their children to learn about the many careers that are available now or that are emerging. (See Chapter 8.) The parents' role should be one of guide, supporter, and educator; however, the ultimate choice must be left to the child.

From the very beginning of life, parents must come to terms with a reality—they cannot, and should not, be the sole influence in their children's rearing. Obviously, they are the most important persons in the child's world, but many others are and should be involved. There are all those who reach the child because of services they perform: the doctors and nurses who attend the birth and later provide medical care; workers in the home such as domestics and repairmen and women; storekeepers and sales help encountered in the normal daily routine. Then there are the friends and relatives who visit or reside in the home, as well as any siblings who precede or follow the child's birth. Certainly, baby-sitters play a crucial role. Later there are playmates, classmates, teachers and all the other school personnel, and endless others who reach and interact with the child. All, in one way or another, affect the child. Besides personal contacts, there are the impersonal effects of radio and television; books, magazines, and newspapers; geographic location and climate; and many, many other factors. Interwoven with all of these influences is the role of the genetic endowment and natural tendencies with which the child was born.

It is an illusion cherished by some parents that they alone can direct and control what happens to their children. Successful parents are actively involved with their total environment and recognize the limits of their influence on their children's growth and development. Wisely, they know the importance of their own roles and capitalize on their strategic position in their children's lives to exert whatever influence they can. Hopefully, the motivations for their behavior will be constructive and in the best interests of the children.

SUGGESTED READINGS

AUSTIN, GLENN. *The Parents' Guide to Child Raising.* Englewood Cliffs, N.J.: Prentice-Hall, 1978.

BETTELHEIM, BRUNO. *The Uses of Enchantment.* New York: Knopf, 1975.

BRANDT, RONALD S., ed. *Partners: Parents and Schools.* 1979. Association for Supervision and Curriculum Development, 225 N. Washington Street, Alexandria, Va. 22314.

BREHM, SHARON. *Help Your Child: A Parents' Guide to Mental Health Services.* Englewood Cliffs, N.J.: Prentice-Hall, 1978.

COFFEY, KAY, et al. *Parentspeak on Gifted and Talented Children.* 1976. Ventura County Superintendent of Schools, 535 East Main Street, Ventura, Calif. 93009.

DELP, JEANNE A., and RUTH A. MARTINSON. *A Handbook for Parents of the Gifted and Talented.* 1974. Ventura County Superintendent of Schools, 535 East Main Street, Ventura, Calif. 93009.

ELKIND, DAVID. *A Sympathetic Understanding of the Child: Birth to Sixteen,* 2nd ed. Boston: Allyn & Bacon, 1978.

ELKINS, DOV PERETZ. *Glad to Be Me: Building Self-Esteem in Yourself and Others.* Englewood Cliffs, N.J.: Prentice-Hall, 1976.

GESELL, A. *Infancy and Human Growth.* New York: Macmillan, 1928.

HERBERT, CINDY. *I See a Child.* Garden City, N.Y.: Doubleday, Anchor Press, 1974.

KNOX, LAURA. *Parents Are People Too.* Englewood Cliffs, N.J.: Prentice-Hall, 1981.

MUSSEN, PAUL HENRY, JOHN JANEWAY CONGER, and JEROME KAGAN. *Child Development and Personality.* New York: Harper & Row, Pub., 1963.

Pennsylvania Department of Education. *Mentally Gifted Children and Youth: A Guide for Parents.* 1973. Pennsylvania Department of Education, Box 911, Harrisburg, Pa. 17126.

WHITE, BURTON L. *The First Three Years of Life.* Englewood Cliffs, N.J.: Prentice-Hall, 1975.

Teachers' Roles in Educating Gifted/Talented Children

Teachers, like parents, are frequently faced with the problem of recognizing gifted children and making provisions for them in the classroom. Unless the identification process has been conducted by the school, often in preparation for implementing a special program, the teacher is faced with the task of evaluating the intellectual abilities of the pupils. This is not necessarily a conscious process, yet it underlies many report card evaluations, such as "This child could do better"; "The student is not working up to capacity"; "This pupil is doing excellent work."

RECOGNIZING GIFTEDNESS IN NEGATIVE BEHAVIOR

The many traits in which gifted children excel have been listed in Chapter 2. Teachers can use these traits as guides, or they can resort to the many checklists that are available (47). For teachers of children aged four through eight, I have described a summary of procedures in a publication called *Education of the Preschool/Primary Gifted and Talented* (15).

Besides identifying gifted children by means of known positive traits, the teacher should reevaluate the child who shows the following negative characteristics that may be clues to unrecognized giftedness:

1. Excessive restlessness or diagnosed hyperactivity.
2. Mischief making, especially if it is associated with a sharp sense of humor.
3. Poor achievement, even though other behavior contradicts this evidence.
4. Leadership as recognized by peers, for example, leading a gang.
5. Withdrawal, indifference, inattention, daydreaming in class.
6. Excessive cutting.
7. Unwillingness to do homework.
8. Persistence in pursuing a discussion or topic beyond the teacher's expressed cutoff point.

Also to be noted is any sign of discrepant achievement between classwork and the results on standardized achievement tests. Usually, if no error has occurred, the standardized achievement test data will produce fairly accurate estimates of the child's ability in comparison with that of his or her peers. Children who read two to three years above their grade level and who are advanced at least one year in mathematical reasoning are likely candidates for gifted programs.

Many of these so-called negative traits are sometimes reflections on the nature of the curriculum. They may actually be saying

1. The curriculum is too easy.
2. The pace of the classwork is too slow.
3. There are insufficient opportunities for in-depth discussions.
4. The classwork is repetitious.
5. The classwork or homework is not challenging enough to sustain interest or attention.
6. The subject matter is uninteresting, too trivial, beneath the child's social maturity level or limited in intellectual scope.

TEACHING THE GIFTED CHILD IN A REGULAR CLASSROOM

Programming for the gifted will not be discussed here, as this topic implies an administrative policy which makes provisions for such children by some form of organizational arrangement. (The desiderata of a good curriculum are discussed on pages 78–95.) However, the teacher of a heterogeneously grouped class has none of the benefits of such planning and has to manage with whatever is on hand or is easily accessible. A few suggestions for classroom practices for teachers in these circumstances follow.

Please Do

1. Ask the gifted the more difficult questions. Stretch their minds by asking for new ideas, different applications of a concept.
2. Let them carry out special research assignments related to classwork.
3. Let them follow through on special projects that interest them, and let them share their work with the class.
4. Let them chair committees, direct plays, be the planners.
5. Let them move on in the basic skills at their own pace and regardless of grade-level barriers.
6. Let them advance in subjects that are clearly hierarchical, such as mathematics and science.
7. Let them be free to follow through on advanced work, while others do necessary, repetitive work.
8. Let them explain topics or procedures to the class. They frequently can meet fellow students at their own levels.
9. Obtain tutorial services for them in special subjects from a volunteer parent, teacher, or local university colleague.
10. Obtain local library cooperation in providing them with books of special interest to them. Let them have access to adult sections as well as to the children's library.
11. Help them to value their abilities and to feel that they, too, are worthwhile people.
12. Let them know you care.

Please Do
(at the prekindergarten/kindergarten levels)

1. Provide books and games of more advanced reading levels for the children to use.
2. Permit the children to read and at their own level of achievement. Do not deny them this pleasure simply because they have not been put through what are considered "required" readiness paces.
3. Let the children read stories to the class from their favorite books.
4. Allow them the freedom to play the more elaborate games they prefer. These should be provided in the classroom.
5. Let such children plan, organize, and direct activities with small groups.
6. Let the children have special, worthwhile responsibilities, such as taking attendance, collecting milk money, taking care of library books, or recording daily weather.
7. Let them follow a special interest or carry on with a hobby, and try to integrate it with the class activities.
8. Investigate those programs that are directed to this age level for the gifted, so that you can adapt ideas from them to your own classroom (14, 57).

Please Do Not

1. Give them longer assignments for the same topics. (They can learn with *fewer* examples.)
2. Crush their enthusiasm by never calling on them. (Obtain the easier responses from the others. Stretch the mind of the gifted by asking for *additional* ideas.)
3. Ask them to do repetitious, rote tasks.
4. Repress their creativity by rejecting unusual ideas whose applicability may not be immediately apparent. (Let them explain.)
5. Waste their time by having them be school monitors, doing menial tasks.
6. Ask them to tutor others for excessive lengths of time. (Their school time is for learning.)

INTRODUCING INNOVATIONS INTO CLASSROOM PRACTICES

It is a rare principal who will not respond to the outstanding performance of a student or to a well-done class project. In visits to many, many schools, I have been impressed by the glowing reports principals have given about the special achievements of students and teachers. They show with great pride the special products on display in their offices or that decorate school corridors or bulletin boards. Of course, any special awards are prominently displayed. Although a disproportionate number of these are related to sports events, there still may be a large number that reflect academic achievement. The teacher who can develop special projects or activities that will elicit this level of pride on the part of the principal, supervisor, district superintendent, or local school board will usually meet with encouragement and acceptance of the ideas he or she presents.

Always involve these supervisors in any innovation. Invite them to see what is being done and let them share the limelight at general functions. One must remember that credit must be given for a management philosophy that permits the freedom to exercise initiative.

It is also most important to involve parents. When parents share in school activities, they are more ready to support requests for funding from local school boards and, where the school budget is dependent on their votes, they are more likely to view this budget with favor if they have been given a chance to learn what is happening.

Teachers should also become acquainted with the many sources of grants and special funding. The teacher who has a good idea for curriculum adaptations for the gifted and who is willing to invest the time and effort to carry it to fruition is usually in a favorable position to generate productive programs. The best sources of information about funding in the public domain are your local, county, and state education departments; state and federal legislators; the U.S. Office of Gifted and Talented; and *The Federal Register*. (See Chapter 11 for addresses.)

Private sources of funding can be located through *The Foundation Directory* (23) and by checking with any large industries in the immediate area. Even smaller businesses and local banks will contribute small amounts for projects they consider worthwhile.

EVALUATING QUALIFICATIONS TO TEACH THE GIFTED

Martinson and Wiener (47, pp. 20–21) have prepared an excellent scale which teachers can use as a method of self-analysis. Gifted children need to be taught by special people. Not everyone can handle a class of brilliant children and do justice to their full potential. Many talented teachers simply do not respond to giftedness in others, and there are some who just prefer not to become involved with a gifted child. Endless lists have been promulgated about the special qualities needed by teachers of the gifted, but there is in fact no ideal teacher, no one complex of traits that will identify a superior teacher of the gifted. Many of the traits suggested are those one would like to find in any teacher. What is required is a matching of teacher and pupils on many levels, particularly on characteristics which in themselves are related to giftedness and are displayed by gifted students. Among these traits are the following:

1. *Talent or Intellectual Superiority.* Given the choice, it is wisest to select from among those teachers who rank in the highest range of intellectual ability. For talent classes such as music or art, one must seek out the specialist. For the gifted, education by a specialist in any curriculum area cannot begin too soon. The efficacy of using teacher specialists even during the elementary years was demonstrated in a special study conducted in the areas of music, science, and foreign language for gifted children in grades four, five, and six (16). There was no question that the children learned more with the specialists and that they were generally more favorably disposed toward the subject matter when a specialist taught them. An important aspect of this study was the fact that the regular teacher remained in the classroom while the specialist's lesson was in progress.

2. *Empathy/Sympathy.* Another very important characteristic one looks for is a genuine liking for and understanding of gifted children. A teacher with this trait will have insight into the way the gifted child thinks and reacts to the environment, and will be able to understand different ways of learning.

3. *Acceptance.* Coupled with the capacity to empathize and sympathize with the gifted child is the need for the teacher to accept the child's superiority or excellence without rancor, resentment, hostility, or jealousy. A readiness to acknowledge the child's ability and an attitude of appreciation and understanding are absolutely essential to creating a productive rapport between teacher and student, particularly during the early years of schooling, but also right through the educational experience.

4. *Preparation.* The teacher of the gifted must always be fully prepared in the subject matter. Gifted students usually have their own resources of knowledge and are very quick to perceive shallowness and certainly misinformation or poor logic. Teaching gifted children is a very challenging, demanding experience.

5. *Versatility.* This applies to interests, abilities, and skills. It requires that the teacher read extensively, be alert to current trends and developments, and have a variety of special skills to enrich and broaden the scope of the curriculum beyond the routine or prescribed topics of school syllabi.

6. *Receptivity.* Teachers of the gifted must be open to new and strange ideas and to the child's individual point of view, while maintaining an evaluative, critical, yet supportive approach.

7. *Self-Insight.* Teachers of the gifted must be ready to acknowledge the limitations of their own knowledge and abilities and be willing to use all resources available in people, materials, and training in order to provide their students with the best education possible.

8. *Perceptiveness.* The teacher must recognize the needs of gifted pupils as individuals, without either favorable or unfavorable prejudice. It is important that no preconceived notions about giftedness be allowed to enter the classroom. There are too many myths abroad about the gifted child; these can often interfere with objective evaluation of the individual's needs or behaviors.

9. *Flexibility.* It is important for teachers of the gifted to be able to modify the day's plans, to make easy changes from one activity to another, to be able to convert or extend a planned lesson to one more relevant or more appropriate to special circumstances. The teacher's outline or weekly plan book must be considered only as a guide and not prescriptive. Gifted children are imaginative, creative, almost volatile in their pursuit of knowledge. The teacher must be ready to move along at their pace and in the many exciting directions toward which they can frequently lead a class. There is no room for rigidity in planning the education of gifted children.

10. *Capacity for Dealing with Complexity.* Because of the very nature of giftedness, it becomes necessary to study subject matter in greater depth and to a greater degree of complexity than is usual in the average classroom. If the teacher is not equal to this task, the education of a gifted child quickly degenerates to unimaginative, unproductive rote learning.

11. *Creativity.* In order to cope with the creativity of the gifted child, teachers also must have the ability to be creative. There is a sense of kinship among creative individuals. They recognize the divergencies in other people's thinking, the validity of novel approaches to solving problems. If the teacher does not have this capacity, it is unlikely that the trait will be fostered among the students.

12. *Patience.* Of course, all teachers need patience, but with the gifted, the need for this trait has a special significance. Gifted children are thinkers but not necessarily risk takers. When called upon to give an answer, they tend to mull things over, to think them through. Thinking takes time, and often teachers expect prompt, instantaneous answers, especially from their brightest pupils. If the teacher is genuinely concerned with teaching the "thinking skills," then it is important to allow the child to exercise his or her natural ability. On the other hand, the teacher must have patience in dealing with the overly enthusiastic child who knows all the answers and wants so much to give them. A little patience will help the teacher to recognize the child's ability without discouraging the enthusiasm. A gentle word or sign of recognition, with a statement of the need to hear from other children, can go a long way toward making a gifted child feel secure and wanted in the classroom. The teacher must bear in mind that this child has a great urgency to communicate and share ideas.

13. *Sense of Humor.* Combined with patience is the need for a sense of humor. Gifted children have a delightful sense of humor, which sometimes is so subtle that only the teacher will be able to "get the point." They usually are not mean or sarcastic, since they are quite sensitive to the feelings of others. They do, however, enjoy the fun in an intellectual or social experience and look for teachers who can share this fun with them. While sarcasm can crush gifted children, the spontaneous enjoyment of learning situations is something they can share quite readily with understanding teachers. Armed with a sense of humor, teachers will be able to cope with the many difficult situations presented by the exceptional abilities and knowledge displayed by a gifted pupil in class. The following episode that occurred in a junior high school may help to illustrate this point. One brilliant student was so good in chemistry that his teacher frankly acknowledged his superiority. But the boy had a tendency to ask significant and often difficult questions, and Parents Day was approaching. Said the teacher with a twinkle in her eye, "Derek, I'll grant that there are times when you know more about a chemistry lesson than I do, but please, when the parents are here, don't ask me any questions to which I might not know the answers." Derek cooperated very nicely and acknowledged in later years that he had learned more chemistry from that one teacher than he had acquired in the more advanced courses of later grades.

14. *Efficiency.* Teachers who wish to cope with educating their gifted pupils must be extremely well organized and must be able to make efficient use of their time and resources. They need to do a great deal of advanced planning in order to be prepared to meet the daily consumption of knowledge and information required by the gifted child, which in most cases will be far greater than that of other children in the class. The gifted child is entitled to the individual attention that is given to others, but it must be of a different nature if it is to satisfy his or her intellectual level. Such demands require a great deal of the conscientious teacher, who is trying to meet the needs of all the pupils in the class and not only those of the gifted few.

15. *Intellectual Integrity.* Above all, the teacher of gifted children must always exercise intellectual integrity and not compromise with standards of achievement or performance. The student must be expected to perform at the peak of his or her capacity, with sensible allowance being made for the performance variance characteristic of all human beings.

PARENTS' EXPECTATIONS OF TEACHERS

Parents have special expectations of the teachers of their gifted children. In a study of their reactions to a program for the gifted through an analysis of spontaneously written letters and a structured questionnaire (14), it was found that parents are very perceptive about what goes on in the school with respect to their gifted children. They notice results in areas where they feel teachers should be working, especially if they have been involved by the teacher in what is going on in class. This can be accomplished by having orientation sessions early in the school year, during which the teacher will explain to the parents what the goals of the school year are and how they may be accomplished. At such sessions, parents can ask questions and come to an understanding of what the school year holds for their child. Another technique used by some schools is to send home a monthly newsletter for the early grades and to involve the children in later grades in preparing a newspaper of class news to share with the parents. However it is done, it is important that there be some level of communication between the school and the home to create a cooperative atmosphere for successful learning.

In the previously mentioned study, parents expressed concerns in the following areas:

1. Are the children happy in school? Are they in a friendly, accepting environment?
2. Does the teacher recognize the children's ability or talent, and what does he or she do about it?
3. Does the teacher challenge the children's ability, making them use it to the fullest extent possible?
4. Are the children being taught the basic skills necessary for efficient learning?
5. Are the children being taught to think clearly and logically?
6. Is the classwork being presented at a pace that is consistent with the children's ability?
7. Is the homework interesting, useful, purposeful?
8. Do the children have opportunities to talk and share ideas with others of similar ability levels?

9. Does the teacher show a concern for the children's emotional, social, and psychological needs?
10. Are the teacher's expectations of the children's performance reasonable for their age and maturity levels?
11. Is the amount of work expected from the children reasonable? In giving assignments, does the teacher make allowances for play, family participation, and other after-school activities?
12. Do the teacher and the school cooperate with the demands of special training for talent development, as in music and the performing arts?
13. Is the work being presented in class of sufficient difficulty and interest for the children? What adaptations is the teacher making?
14. Are parents kept informed of school activities? Are they invited to participate, when possible? Is the teacher receptive to parent concerns?
15. Does the school administration support the teacher's efforts in the classroom?
16. Is there a plan for continuity of work in later grades for gifted children who are permitted to progress at their own pace?

Following are excerpts from letters written spontaneously by the parents of very gifted children, in which some of these expectations and their realization through a specially designed program (14) are voiced:

> SAMARIE'S PARENTS: It needs something more than words to express what the Astor Program has been doing to our daughter. We are just trying to put into words that intangible magic the program has worked on her....
> Her reading skills are growing fast. We are very pleased when she reads, writes and spells the words that are supposed to be beyond a child of 5. She has grown much more inquisitive now than she ever was. This must be the magic wand of the Astor teachers behind this thirst to know more. May their magic grow stronger and stronger!!! ...
> We are often left aghast at the paintings and drawings she does in the school. It sure is the outcome of Astor training. Having seen her growing from finger painting to water colors via crayons, we often wonder, what next. All because of the Astor Program, thanks again!!! ...
> *Elation* is the one word to sum up our feelings when we see all the kids mingling with each other, appreciating each other's work. They have received exposure in the newspapers and some have even hit the T.V. May God grant more power to this program replete with love for each other!!!

> MARY'S PARENTS: My husband and I have witnessed an amazing change in her development over the past months. She has become extremely verbal, self-confident, mature, independent, and *orderly*. She has assigned herself chores at home, loves homework assignments, is speaking French, putting on plays, sings and dances, writes stories, draws, makes exhibits, but most of all she is happy as can be and looks forward to school each day with eager anticipation....

TIMMY'S MOTHER: Timmy has only been enrolled for a short time, but already he's showing tremendous growth in his reading and reasoning abilities....

He brought home his workbooks over the holiday and I was most favorably impressed with the materials used. By taking advantage of the many opportunities the program offers for parental involvement, I have also been able to observe the class as a whole, and I am very pleased. I could not wish for a more stimulating environment nor a more varied exciting peer group....

In addition, the dedication and personal warmth displayed by all the program's teachers before, during, and after regular class hours have made a strong and decidedly favorable impression....

BETH'S PARENTS: The creation of a program for gifted children has been long overdue. Beth's brothers have been faced with boredom, frustration and teacher resentment for most of their elementary school years. Skipping them from first to third grades did not help the problem—they continued to be bored in the higher grade. Acceleration is not the answer; gifted children need a special program with other gifted children to make a challenging environment....

The Astor Program has given us hope that Beth will not have to experience her brothers' frustrations in elementary school. She looks forward to going to school and comes out exuberant. She is delighted with her teacher, her classmates and herself because of the learning experiences and environment to which she is exposed....

TERRY'S AND SARA'S MOTHER: Terry began the Astor Program in February of this year. Within a period of a few weeks I began to see a beautiful change take place. My son became much more articulate. His vocabulary practically tripled in this short span of time. His mind seemed to open up to the world around him. He began "experimenting," as he so aptly expressed it. The knowledge he has gained is particularly noticeable in the areas of the alphabet and numbers....

All of the above is quite remarkable in itself but there is something even more wonderful that must be added to this to complete the picture. Terry has become aware of himself and his own capabilities. He has gained so much confidence that he tackles things which would have, in the past, turned him off. He has come to accept the fact that he is bright and can relate to his sister who is also very bright but has the advantage of being older. He has learned to put his intelligence to work for him and I am sure that this lesson will follow him throughout his life....

SARA AND TERRY TWO YEARS LATER: I cannot praise this program enough. Both of my children have blossomed emotionally as well as intellectually through the curriculum offered by the Astor Program. They have met learning with a new vitality and inspiration. The challenge the work presents keeps them interested and makes them want to learn more. Their minds, like the minds of all young children, are like sponges; the more they are offered, the more they absorb....

JONATHAN'S PARENTS: This program has had such a profound effect upon my son that I am willing to make any sacrifices necessary in order to assure its being continued....

I have only the highest regard for all the teachers, especially Ms. _____. She has aided me in handling my son at home through methods employed in school. My son was not a very happy child before his exposure to the Astor Program. He was bored, frustrated and difficult to control. Other programs he attended catered to the normal child and he felt abandoned. It was *only* this program which has challenged his intellect while proving exciting and worthwhile to him....

The program is diverse enough to have his undivided attention every day. He is anxious to begin each school day without coaxing. His reading has improved and his vocabulary has broadened. Most important of all, he has learned how to function socially and has respect for others and their opinions....

Words are really inadequate in trying to convey the impact this program has had on his life and therefore the lives of his family. All I can say is that the tension under which we lived prior to the program has practically disappeared....

MELINDA'S PARENTS: What I most appreciate is the air of freedom and spontaneity in the classroom, although I know the planning that must go into each day. Given the wide range of interests among these children, their questions never seem to be put aside, but are somehow integrated into the total learning experience. I must also add that the warmth and affection shown the children has probably contributed much to the success of the Astor Program....

Teachers have the opportunity to become significant persons in the lives of gifted and talented children. They are in a position to recognize the existence of ability; they can foster its development; they can lead children into productive and satisfying ways to realize their potential; they can provide the encouragement and stimuli needed for creative expression. Many teachers work in anonymity, little recognized for the important roles they play in the lives of their students. It is only when one of the students, achieving eminence or success in later years, looks back and says: "That teacher set me on this path," that a teacher can fully enjoy the great satisfaction to be derived from this profession. Such occasions may be few and far between, but they give intense meaning to the entire experience of teaching. Every teacher would like to enjoy a re-creation of the scene in Emlyn Williams' play *The Corn Is Green* in which Miss Moffatt hears Morgan, the student she groomed out of the Welsh mines into the sacred halls of Oxford, say (79, pp. 989–90):

Since the day I was born, I have been a prisoner behind a stone wall, and now somebody has given me a leg-up to have a look at the other side.... Starling and I spent three hours one night discussin' the law—Starling, you know, the brilliant one.... I came out of his rooms that night, and I walked down the High. That's their High Street, you know.... I looked up, and there was a moon behind Magd— —Maudlin.... All of a sudden... I saw this room; you and me sitting here studying, and all those books—and everything I have ever learnt from those books, and from you, was lighted up—like a magic lantern: Ancient Rome, Greece, Shakespeare, Carlyle, Milton.... Everything had a meaning, because I was in a new world—my world! And so it came to me why you worked like a slave to make me ready for this scholarship!

SUGGESTED READINGS

See the readings at the end of other chapters as well as among the titles cited in the references (pages 192–196). The following are a mere sampling of what is available. Several have excellent bibliographies that can serve for further study.

BARBE, WALTER B., and JOSEPH S. RENZULLI, eds. *Psychology and Education of the Gifted*, 2nd ed. Part V, "Teaching the Gifted," pp. 435–474. New York: John Wiley, Halsted Press, 1975.

BRUNER, JEROME. *Toward a Theory of Instruction*. Cambridge, Mass.: Harvard University Press, 1966.

CANFIELD, JACK, and HAROLD C. WELLS. *100 Ways to Enhance Self-Concept in the Classroom: A Handbook for Teachers and Parents*. Englewood Cliffs, N.J.: Prentice-Hall, 1976.

COHEN, RONALD D. "Meet the Rechargeable Humanoid Mark III Electric Teacher." *Elementary School Journal* (March 1975), 339–347.

EBERLE, BOB, and ROSIE EMERY HALL. *Affective Education Guidebook: Classroom Activities in the Realm of Feelings*. Buffalo, N.Y.: DOK Publishers, 1975.

EHRLICH, VIRGINIA Z. *The Astor Program for Gifted Children: PreKindergarten through Grade Three*. 1978. Box 223, Teachers College, Columbia University, New York, N.Y. 10027.

_____. *Program Planning for the Gifted*. 1978. AGATE Press, Dingman Point, Alexandria Bay, N.Y. 13607.

FRENCH, JOSEPH L. *Educating the Gifted: A Book of Readings*. 1st ed. New York: Henry Holt, 1959.

- "Teachers for the Gifted," by Nelda Davis, pp. 432–438.
- "The Expressed Attitudes of Teachers toward Special Classes for Intellectually Gifted Children," by Joseph Justman and J. Wayne Wrightstone, pp. 450–456.
- "Preparing Teachers for the Education of the Gifted," by Arthur M. Selvi, pp. 444–450.
- "In-Service and Undergraduate Preparation of Teachers of the Gifted," by Frank T. Wilson, pp. 438–443.

GALLAGHER, JAMES J. *Teaching the Gifted Child.* 3rd ed. Chap. 11, "Training Educational Personnel for the Gifted." Boston: Allyn & Bacon, College Division, 1979.

GOLD, MARVIN J. "Teachers and Mentors." In *The Gifted and the Talented.* Edited by A. Harry Passow. 78th Yearbook of the National Society for the Study of Education. Part I, pp. 218–236. Chicago: University of Chicago Press, 1979.

Ideas for Urban/Rural Gifted/Talented: Case Histories and Program Plans. n.d. Ventura County Superintendent of Schools, 535 East Main Street, Ventura, Calif. 93009. A collection of essays.

KAPLAN, SANDRA N. *Providing Programs for the Gifted and Talented: A Handbook, Including Worksheets and Models.* 1975. The Council for Exceptional Children, 1920 Association Drive, Reston, Va. 22091.

LORCH, MICHAEL. *An Outline for Teacher Performance Objectives for Secondary School Programs for Gifted Students.* San Diego, Calif.: San Diego Schools, 1972.

MAKER, C. JUNE. *Training Teachers for the Gifted and Talented: A Comparison of Models.* 1975. The Council for Exceptional Children, 1920 Association Drive, Reston, Va. 22091.

MARTINSON, RUTH A. *Curriculum Enrichment for the Gifted in the Primary Grades.* Englewood Cliffs, N.J.: Prentice-Hall, 1968.

———. *A Guide toward Better Teaching for the Gifted.* 1976. The Council for Exceptional Children. 1920 Association Drive, Reston, Va. 22091.

MILEY, JAMES F., et al. *Promising Practices: Teaching the Disadvantaged Gifted.* 1975. Ventura County Superintendent of Schools, 535 East Main Street, Ventura, Calif. 93009.

SANDERLIN, OWENITA. *Teaching Gifted Children.* South Brunswick and New York: A. S. Barnes, 1973.

STOVALL, B., and C. TONGUE. *The Itinerant Resource Teacher: A Manual for Programs with Gifted Children.* Raleigh, N.C.: State Department of Public Instruction, 1970.

TORRANCE, E. PAUL. *Encouraging Creativity in the Classroom.* Belmont, Calif.: Dimensions Publishing, 1969.

Careers for the Gifted and Talented

The earliest ambition of one talented young man was to be a "park paper picker-upper." His father, and more insistently his mother, had other ideas. If their son could not become president of the United States, they would settle for his becoming a lawyer. Some thought he should have become an artist, but instead he became a dentist, using his artistic skills to illustrate dental texts. A highly successful movie director left home in his senior year of high school because he could not fulfill his father's ambition that he should become a doctor. He had been a highly gifted and creative child, and his great interest had always been the theater. Parent and child could not reconcile their differences, so the boy ran away. Another highly gifted young man finished college with an excellent education and no idea at all of what he wanted to do with his life. So long as he earned money, which he did fairly easily, no one attempted to guide him into focusing his interests and actually developing a fulfilling career. He drifted from one job to another, not because he was incompetent, but because he became bored very quickly and kept seeking "new worlds to conquer."

Often highly capable girls are deflected from the advanced education of college training because their parents feel that "girls don't need all that education." Other girls who may be particularly talented in the sciences and male-oriented professions are discouraged by schools, teachers, guidance personnel, and parents from following their chosen professions. A gifted young woman was intensely interested in the sciences. Her junior high school science teacher labeled it a passing phase. "She'll grow out of it," he told her mother, and he discouraged the girl's attendance at a scientifically oriented high school. Contrary to her teacher's predictions, the girl became a toxicologist, via degrees in physics, chemistry, civil engineering, and public health.

Other equally talented girls are scorned for giving up "promising careers" for homemaking and child rearing, as if the latter were not noble careers in themselves. In fact, in a forty-year follow-up of the Terman gifted group, Oden (55, p. 29) reports that 45.4 percent of the women chose homemaking as a life style and, of these, more than 80 percent indicated that their marriage and children were their most important sources of life satisfaction. Of the women who were employed and married (neither widowed nor divorced), 84.2 percent considered their marriages the source of greatest life satisfaction and 70.0 percent mentioned their children as a source of such satisfaction. As Oden observes, "in any case the gifted women, for the most part, show neither discontent with their lot nor a marked drive for career achievement. Marriage apparently is an important factor in the lack of career-mindedness." It may be that current changes in social patterns will alter these points of view and particularly the proportions of women who may choose to add careers to their homemaking inclinations. Unfortunately, there is no longitudinal study such as Terman's in process to evaluate the results of such choices forty years hence.

WHAT IS CAREER EDUCATION?

What do we mean by the term *career education*? In *Career Education for Gifted and Talented Students*, Hoyt and Hebeler (36) cite a series of definitions and explanations for the term, again making apparent the fuzziness attached to most terms of this type. Note the following:

> Career education is the infusion into all educational curriculum and student counseling, kindergarten through grade 14, of information and hands-on experience pertinent to real life jobs and world of work experience. (p. 23)
>
> Career education is education for a profession or other occupation demanding special preparation. (p. 23)
>
> This in essence is what the career education approach is all about: to refocus education so that what is taught in the classroom has a clear, demonstrable bearing on the student's future plans—whether these plans be to find a job immediately, go on to college or graduate school... or to enter the world of work for a time and then return to education... to enable the student to go forward secure in the knowledge that he or she is prepared to deal with the world on its own terms (Pierce, 1973). (pp. 25–26)

Based on these and other definitions, our conclusion must be that the concept of career education is a complex one that includes fundamental issues of developing a satisfactory life style that may include the need to earn a living as one of its components. Such a concept, therefore, makes provision for effective uses of leisure time. We are speaking here, then, of a broad concept which includes preparing the child to become an independent, self-sustaining member of society with maximum opportunities for leading a satisfying and fulfilling life.

CAREER EDUCATION: WHEN SHOULD IT START?

When does such training start? And why are we particularly concerned about the gifted child? How do his or her career education needs differ from those of other children?

The education required to manage one's own life actually begins at birth. Parents have the responsibility of helping their children acquire those skills and bodies of information that will lead them toward a successful mastery of life-sustaining skills. The whole goal of schooling is toward this end and parents show justified concern when schools do not deal with the realities their children must face.

For gifted children, both parents and schools must consider the prospects in terms that are dictated by the child's abilities. Adjustments must be made because the child is intellectually capable but totally inexperienced. The child, for example, may understand the concept of traffic hazards and obeying traffic lights but may not be able to anticipate the oddities of human behavior on the road. A playmate of one of my children was an exceptionally brilliant little girl who loved to chatter away about her many interests. She would get so involved in her discussions that she seemed oblivious to all else around her. Her mother was rather casual about this aspect of Tammy's giftedness until one terrifying day when Tammy, chattering away as usual, stopped in the center of a heavily trafficked New York City street to make a point to her companion. Trailer trucks, taxis, delivery trucks, and cars, traveling in both directions, screeched to an outraged halt—and Tammy went dreamily on with her conversation while her companion tugged at her to move on. Tammy was not quite seven at the time. She was perfectly capable of understanding the hazards of crossing a street, but she had an active, creative mind that seemed to be constantly at work.

Such developmental dyssynchronies or inconsistencies create problems for those who wish to prepare gifted children to cope with life experiences. Parents and teachers must begin early to guide their gifted children, and yet they must be careful not to confuse intellectual understanding with life experience. This, of course, carries over to the child's view of the world of work and the focusing of interests on particular vocations or the development of special talents. Gifted children are no different from their age peers in being fascinated by what is, to them, exciting work. Little boys want to be firemen and aviators, and little girls want to be movie stars and nurses. However, if you were to ask, as was done in a special survey (16), "And what else would you like to be when you grow up?" the gifted child will probably give you other goals, such as astronomer, mathematician, biochemist, or linguist. It is not uncommon for a fourth-grade gifted child to offer these vocational choices, at one and the same time: policeman—doctor—veterinarian; fireman—president—lawyer; teacher—nurse—mother; astronaut—wife—space doctor; truck driver—mechanic—engineer.

The environment that is created at home, the interests and concerns of all members, the levels of aspiration of family members, and the realities of socioeconomic status all contribute to the child's understanding and approaches to the world of work. Career education, in its broadest sense, begins in early childhood and persists through the school years and beyond.

ASPECTS OF CAREER EDUCATION

Parents and teachers can help gifted children in many ways if they will consider carefully the various implications of career education.
  One interesting aspect of career education for the gifted is the fact that many such persons place personal fulfillment first and economic independence second with respect to their primary career choice. For example, Albert Schweitzer (59), known as a great doctor in Africa and contributor to research in tropical medicine, considered music as his primary career. He studied medicine as his way to serve humanity, but pursued his love of music with intense interest, becoming known as one of the world's greatest organists and interpreters of Bach. He used his talents in music to give concerts and raise funds for his hospital among the natives of Lambaréné. As is well known, Schweitzer was an intellectual genius of the highest order. His friend and contemporary Albert Einstein worked quite contentedly in a patent office while he indulged his major interest, the study of the physical universe, sending articles to professional journals on his now-famous topic. Jack London worked in a laundry, the agonies of which are so well portrayed in his novel *Martin Eden* (43), while working at his primary love, writing.
  This dual involvement in the world of work is not at all uncommon for the gifted and talented. There are many who are quite willing to forgo economic comfort in the pursuit of more personally fulfilling goals when they choose careers. It is therefore imperative that those responsible for guiding gifted and talented children provide them with work alternatives, recognizing that most will need to earn a living, whether it be in their field of primary interest or as an adjunct to it.

FACTORS OPERATING IN THE CHOICE OF CAREERS

Many factors contribute to the ultimate choice of a career or lifework; these include circumstances of birth, socioeconomic level or social status, location, historical setting, personal inclinations and characteristics, parental directions, experience at school, political developments, scientific observations, and even luck or chance. Examples of these influences are numerous in the history of eminent personalities. Goethe lived in an era of military expansion. His family was wealthy and invading troops were billeted in their home. The family was deeply involved in politics and the child was present to hear their discussions. It was not surprising that, with this background, Goethe should choose the life of the statesman, even though his first love was literature and writing. Roger Tory Peterson lived on a somewhat isolated farm. Early rising was a routine part of his daily life. It was not too difficult to blend this life pattern with the observation of birds in the area. Coupled with his unusual artistic talent and his mother's acceptance of his interest, it was almost inevitable that Peterson would choose the life of a naturalist. The course of John Stuart Mill's life was largely determined by the very strict direction and supervision his father exercised over his education.

Educational experience should be subsumed under the broader concept of life experience in career choices, partly because all experience is educational and partly because formal education is only a fractional part of the total life experience. Within the formal setting of schools, colleges, and universities, all types of learning contribute to preparation for and choice of careers. Characteristics of teachers, curriculum content, the school environment, disciplinary practices, success or failure in schoolwork, peer activities, parental involvement—all play a part in directing a student's interests and preferences for work.

Of course, the schools' courses of study usually form the critical basis for a student's later involvement in one field or another. Preparation for many professions, whether direct or indirect, frequently begins in the high school and sometimes even in the junior high school. Parents, often far more realistically than teachers and guidance personnel, recognize the importance of the basic education their children will receive in different types of schools. Not many delude themselves that attendance at an inferior school with a limited curriculum will open doors for their gifted children in the more prestigious colleges. One can fully understand the parent who calls asking about schools for the gifted, long before the child is ready to attend school. Competition is keen, places are few, and opportunities for the gifted are all too limited. Realistic parents have every reason to be concerned about the kind of educational experience their gifted children are being offered and the kind of preparation for future employment they will receive in the schools they attend.

FACTORS TO BE CONSIDERED IN CAREER PREPARATION

What should a parent, teacher, guidance counselor, or other significant person in the life of a gifted child consider when advising on career choices? A few important points that should enter the counseling process are suggested in the following questions:

1. *What is the level of intellectual ability or the special talent of the child?*

Guidance counselors must consider that those in the lower and middle ranges of giftedness have needs that are different from those at the upper extreme of ability. There are certain strengths and weaknesses associated with the upper extreme of intellectual giftedness that suggest the need for a very special kind of guidance and understanding. For example, regardless of how impractical it may be, the child of very superior intellect will persist in his or her interests and pursue his or her chosen work at almost all costs. The creature comforts that seem essential to others may have no significance for such a person. Einstein was hardly a model of sartorial splendor, nor did he acquire much wealth. Artists have been known to give up the comforts of wealthy homes to follow their particular muse as, for example, in the case of Toulouse-Lautrec.

Certainly, one must be very careful to allow exceptional gifts and talents to flourish, while providing the practical guidance that will permit the gifted person to obtain the means of ordinary survival, such as food, shelter, and clothing.

For all gifted and talented persons, the choice of careers should match their intellectual and talent capacities. There should be ample opportunity for growth and development and for advancement to more demanding and challenging levels of work.

Members of minority groups should avoid being forced to settle for careers that do not recognize their capacities; they should not allow themselves to be deflected to tasks of secondary choice simply because no one of their particular ethnic or racial group has ever been admitted to the inner circle before. Barriers are broken down regularly, and those of superior ability, with the persistence and willingness to do the work required for the task, should aim as high as they can. Everyone should "dare to dream." Certainly, it could not have been easy for Marie Curie to break down the barriers to women in the medical profession of her time; nor for George Washington Carver to achieve an education denied to most black people of his day; nor for Helen Keller to attain the status she did, when all other handicapped people found nothing but closed doors. "Only recently have persons who are both gifted and handicapped begun to be widely noticed by the public...," as Maker has observed (45, p. 8). The handicapped gifted are not a paradox, she states. Rather they are persons who have "*both* strengths and weaknesses that are very pronounced" (45, p. 7). The gifted, by the very nature of their gifts and talents, have been known to ignore all barriers in their pursuit of truth and knowledge, and the walls have inevitably yielded to the onslaught of the power of knowledge and ability.

2. *What is important in the child's life and to what extent is he or she willing to pursue the interest or talents displayed?*

An interest in the physical sciences may be fine, but if the student is unwilling to acquire the mathematics concepts required to pursue scientific studies, no amount of interest will lead to success. A fine sense of rhythm, excellent body control, a supreme grace, and exquisite interpretation of music may all indicate the potentialities for a great ballerina, but unless the child is willing to submit to the discipline of grueling and uninterrupted practice, there is no point in encouraging the choice of a career in the dance. Certainly, as Margot Fonteyn has revealed in her autobiography, once the choice has been made, the demands of the art must take priority over all else. Whether one likes it or not, success in any field is dependent on the degree of application and industry one is willing to apply. Since the gifted find at an early age that most things come to them quite easily, it is important for those who advise them to point out the demands of any lifework that is chosen. A doctor's life may sound glamorous, but success comes only as a result of many years of dedication and little compensation during a time when young people might rather be enjoying the lighter side of life.

3. *What are the child's priorities, motives, beliefs, and values, and to what extent will they influence success in the choice of a career?*

The route the gifted child will follow is closely interwoven with his or her personal philosophy of life as it slowly emerges from the child's developing priorities, beliefs, values, and motives in engaging in any activity. Certainly the child who is determined to be an ardent pacifist would scarcely be encouraged to enter military life voluntarily. Winston Churchill, on the other hand, enjoyed all aspects of military planning and was able to engage in strategy planning during World War II as a consequence of his intense interest in the military. Again, one would not advise or encourage a child who had no facility with words to become a writer, no matter how superior the child's ability for abstract reasoning might be. Louis Bromfield's mother was fortunate that her son loved reading and was happy to follow the literary profession she chose for him. Arthur and Karl Compton were reared in a very stimulating environment where it was easy to accept the scientific life as a priority. If they achieved eminence in their field of science, it was in part because they were pursuing interests that were closely tied to their basic values and beliefs.

4. *What have been the child's experiences with the career areas under consideration?*

Occasionally, youngsters select fields of specialization on the basis of misinformation, glamorized stories, or other inadequate reasons. During the period of the space explorations of the moon, many children wanted to become astronauts, with no awareness of all of the requirements of the task. Many children dream of becoming great doctors, but have little knowledge of the years of study and intensive application required for the field. Others, who dream of producing great music on an instrument, are unaware of the demands of the music profession.

Those responsible for guiding gifted children in their choice of professions or careers should be aware of the great diversity of opportunities available and of the constant change in demands for particular specialties. For a while, shortly after Sputnik was launched into space, physical scientists were in great demand. In the seventies, many people with doctorates found themselves unable to locate jobs that were in any way related to their specialty. In the eighties, it seems that the engineering fields have great promise, but this can change quickly as the field becomes glutted with graduates pursuing this muse to the neglect of other areas of study. Parents, teachers, guidance counselors, and others should keep in close touch with the flux of occupational opportunities, always looking a few years ahead to the ways in which needs will change in response to new demands. A frequent review of the classified sections of newspapers, especially those reserved for professional and technical skills, should be a prerequisite for anyone advising the gifted on what lines of work to investigate.

Gifted children should have many opportunities to meet and talk to people in a great variety of jobs. Schools should invite such persons to talk about their work. Whenever possible, students should be allowed to visit the locations where people actually work at their careers. It is not sufficient for schools to introduce young children to community helpers such as the mail carrier, the custodian, the firefighter, or the police officer. Even at an early age, young children begin to make their career choices and, if they are gifted, are not likely to follow the role models of such helpers. Schools should draw on the variety of tasks represented by parents, local businesses, and other community resources, always bearing in mind that the job choices should be consistent with the children's ability levels. Although role models in the visual and performing arts are generally more visible to young people through the communications media, it is not usual for them to be able to meet and talk with persons who engage in such pursuits. Early in their school life, children should visit an office or location where engineers, architects, doctors, scientists, and others are actually at work. Apprenticeships should be provided for those youngsters in the higher grades, so that they can become better acquainted with the milieu in which they will be expected to work. Parents can take their own children to their places of work, if it is permitted, so that the child will obtain a realistic view of that mysterious place: "the office," "the plant," "the laboratory," or "the hospital." The view of a hospital as a patient is far different from the perspective obtained by seeing it as a place where people of many different skills work.

5. *How does one deal with an "embarrassment of riches"?*

Many gifted and talented persons suffer from what has been called an "embarrassment of riches." They find mastery of many subjects easy. They have a wide range of interests. To them, the world is an exciting place in which many fields of endeavor are challenging and tempting. They may want to pursue not one, but several careers. Frequently, one finds youngsters who are about to leave college and still have no idea of what they would like to do as a lifework; having no particular plans, they drift from one activity to another, or they continue going to school indefinitely, absorbing knowledge and never reaching the point where they contribute to it.

Gifted children need to be taught early how to make choices and arrive at reasonable decisions in the face of many alternatives. This requires a clear evaluation and understanding of oneself, an awareness of one's own strengths and weaknesses, likes and dislikes. Although one would not encourage the forcing of career choices too early in life, certainly not in the elementary or secondary school years, it becomes a necessity somewhere along the way in the college years. Students should not be faced with either/or situations in making a career choice. It is possible and practical to have several choices and to plan accordingly. There are those who have become doctors and writers, scientists and writers, athletes and scientists, musicians and teachers, performers and businesspeople. Some have combined several careers. Classic examples of these are Edward Lear, painter and writer of limericks; Maria Montessori, educator and physician; and Lewis Carroll, mathematician and writer.

The important point that must be made is that whatever careers are chosen, education must be planned so that it will provide the competence required for successful pursuit of the choice. It is sometimes possible to plan an educational program that touches on several areas, so that the student can prepare himself simultaneously for more than one field of work. Sometimes the training must be taken in stages, completing one before the next can be started. Whatever the choices, it is important to help the student make wise and practical decisions in the direction that will lead to maximum satisfaction with life and utilization of whatever talents or abilities he or she may have. What gifted students need more than anything else is encouragement to fulfill as much of their potential as possible, while trying to meet the practicalities of daily existence. Parents need to recognize the forces that may tend to dissipate the child's abilities and must be aware of how difficult it is to make the seemingly final decisions that are implied in a career choice. Understanding the multiplicity of interests gifted children have becomes of the utmost importance at such times.

THE ROLE OF SCHOOLS AND OF PARENTS

The role of schooling in career education is clearly important. For many children, schooling is the key to preparation for their lifework. If educators are interpreting their roles properly, they know that a well-planned curriculum includes career education as a major objective.

Educators are involved with four phases of career education: *awareness, orientation, exploration,* and *preparation.* The last two are usually classified as vocational training. *Career awareness* is developed by helping students understand their own needs, evaluate themselves as future workers, and recognize their role in society. *Career orientation* refers to activities that help students to understand worker roles and the nature of related jobs, and to determine their ability to meet the demands of particular roles in the world of work. *Career exploration* permits students actually to participate in the working world and understand the requirements of a task through first-hand experience, and to find out for themselves how well they are matched to the task. Exploration can also come about by observation and discussion of the various job categories, and by way of apprenticeships, work-study programs, and volunteer work. *Career preparation* is usually related to specific training in a chosen career area.

Career education is an integral part of the entire school curriculum, as pupils relate the fields of knowledge to particular jobs and find out what knowledge and skills are needed for those jobs. Well-planned career education will recognize the possibility that the skills and knowledge acquired in preparation for one vocation must be sufficiently flexible to permit switches and transfers to allied fields of work.

Parents have the right to expect schools to provide a well-designed career education program for their gifted children beginning in the earliest years. It is reasonable for parents to expect and for teachers to provide the kind of education that will make it possible for gifted children, as well as all others, to make wise decisions in career preparation and choices.

Among the career-related activities schooling should provide for the student are the following:

1. The fundamental body of information that is basic to the broad fields of knowledge such as mathematics, the social sciences, the physical sciences, and the language and communication arts.
2. Thorough mastery of the basic skills required to deal with these broad fields of knowledge.
3. Opportunities for relating the fields of knowledge to requirements for workers in the field.
4. Exposure to workers in a wide variety of occupations that are *consistent with the child's ability levels or special talents.*
5. Information about a variety of career opportunities, provided through readings, films, and other communications media.

Parents, in turn, have special responsibilities toward their gifted and talented children with respect to career choices. Besides assuring themselves that the schools are carrying out their side of the contract, parents can do many things that will help the children to make wise choices.

To begin, parents can encourage the special interests displayed by their children. Gifted and talented children usually develop intense interests in particular subjects and pursue them with incredible persistence. Whereas other children may be satisfied with a cursory reading about some topic, a gifted child will read many books, ask endless questions, request trips to areas where the topic is available for further study, make related collections, create scrapbooks, write stories, and so on.

For example, in a class for gifted prekindergartners, the teacher announced that a specialist on whales would be visiting the following week. With no prompting by the teacher, the children requested books about whales at home and read about the subject or asked to be told about it by the teacher, their parents, or anyone who would listen. When the specialist arrived in the class, he began by asking whether the children knew how many different kinds of whales there were, assuming that their lack of knowledge would prove to be a good opening for his presentation. Within a few minutes after he posed the question, the children had listed the ten major kinds of whales for him. Taken aback, he asked if they knew how these whales could be distinguished from one another. Once again, to his utter amazement, the children gave him the key points of difference among the ten different types. Since he was an authority on how whales communicate with each other, he was able to retrieve his authoritative state by sharing with them how he and his fellow explorers had recorded the songs of the whales and by relating some of their experiences in the Arctic waters. Later, several of the children asked if they could talk to him longer. Obligingly, he sat with these few children for over an hour, answering their eager questions. One child whose interest had been thoroughly aroused, finally prepared a small volume on the subject.

Interests begin very early and frequently are maintained over a long period of time. For some children, these early interests may become lifelong ones that gradually lead to a choice of vocation. This was true of Roger Tory Peterson, whose birdwatching began when he was only eight or nine years old; of Virginia Woolf, who used to make up stories to entertain her friends and family and eventually became a writer; of Pablo Picasso, who showed his talent as a young boy and whose father gave up his own career in order to foster his son's development; of Guglielmo Marconi, whose parents provided a laboratory within their home so that he could carry on his experiments while he was still in his preteens.

On the other hand, parents must bear in mind that the intense interest displayed by a child may not last. Once the child has exhausted all the pathways of personal curiosity about a subject, he or she may quite easily abandon the old interest for an entirely new one. Parents must be cautious and permit this shifting of interest from one topic to another. The child is exploring the world, frequently in much greater depth than age peers would, but still can be diverted by other, newer interests with the passage of time.

As children begin to express interest in particular vocations, parents must be careful to separate glamour from reality. The fact that Watson and Crick announced a tremendous breakthrough in genetic research with their discovery of the helical nature of the gene is not reason enough for all the youngsters in the current biology class to suddenly decide they will become geneticists. Nor should the conquest of another killer disease lead youngsters to want to become research scientists in medicine. The beauty of ballerinas in their tulle tutus hardly provides a reason to encourage a child who wants to become a ballet dancer after seeing her first *Nutcracker Suite*. The realities of careers should be made clear to children so that they will not set their paths along unrealistic routes.

In guiding their children, parents must look ahead to the years of their adult life. This means projecting plans about twenty years ahead of the child's birthdate. Parents must always keep in mind that the world community is in a constant state of flux, with new developments and relationships constantly emerging. The demands of the work world change continuously. By considering carefully what the societal trends may be, parents will be better able to advise their children. They should also seek the advice of agencies that are involved in vocational planning and career guidance, since these agencies will be likely to have information on the latest developments in the world of work, such as where shortages are contemplated and where there may be an oversupply; what new jobs are developing; and what skills new industries may require. There are several texts on the status of occupations in the United States and elsewhere, and these too can be of service (77, and supplements).

A further consideration for parents is the need to avoid saddling their children with their own unfulfilled ambitions. Too often, children are urged to pursue careers that are more in line with parental ambitions than they are with the child's training, interests, and abilities. I recall a young man who had won numerous coveted prizes by the time he graduated from high school. His father insisted that he become involved in a premedical program at an outstanding university, even though the young man had absolutely no interest in the field of medicine. After two years of misery in college, the son sought advice. As a result, it was possible to convince the father that his son would probably become a rather mediocre physician if he were forced to do something in which he had no interest whatsoever, whereas if he were permitted to follow his own bent, he would probably become an excellent mathematician and actuarial statistician, which was where his real interests lay. Fortunately, the father relented and the young man was able to follow his chosen career, which he did with great success.

Parents must realize that there is a difficult component to the pursuit of the visual or performing arts by a talented child—the requirement for constant practice. They must be realistic in helping their child understand the importance of commitment in the arts and the need for the highly specialized daily training that is required. Both the parents and the child then need to be willing to make the necessary sacrifices if true success is the goal. It might be wise for such parents and their children to read the biographies of personalities who have become very successful in their chosen arts and learn about the constant sacrifice in application and time that these careers require. Teachers of such children need to help parents realize these points. They also need to evaluate the actual degree of commitment both parents and children show before encouraging a student to follow through on what could become a most distressing and disappointing life, with only mediocrity as the reward for years of haphazard application.

In addition, both parents and teachers must bear in mind that not all careers lead to paid employment. There must be a provision in their practical planning for the possibility that the gifted child will have to prepare in two areas: one for paid employment to establish economic independence and one for employment in a favored area of activity in which the sole compensation would be the satisfaction and fulfillment of a talent.

Parents and teachers should also remember that the gifted do not all need to go to college and postgraduate school in order to realize their gifts. For some, the route may be an entirely different one. They may choose to become involved in the business world, gaining experience in preparation for relevant education in the field most appropriate to the industry of their choice. Others may wish to travel or just withdraw from intellectual activity for a while in order to reassess their interests and desires. Still others may need freedom from routine to follow through on a private project that requires freedom of action and mobility. There are as many possibilities as there are creative opportunities in a rapidly changing society; therefore, both parents and teachers should retain a flexibility in their approaches to guiding the young toward the world of the future.

A frequently neglected aspect of education for the gifted child who is headed for a career in the professions is the importance of mechanical skills in the exercise of many professional activities. Many engineers, chemists, and doctors are required to have a good deal of mechanical ability in order to carry out their work. It is therefore important that such students be given the opportunity to develop whatever latent talents they may have in these areas by taking the appropriate courses. For example, Stuyvesant High School in New York City, which prepares gifted youngsters in the fields of science and mathematics, has excellent shop and mechanical drawing courses, even though almost all the students, over 99 percent, will eventually go into the professions by way of college and graduate school.

CAREERS FOR THE FUTURE

When talking about career education for a child, the phrase "for the future" is actually a redundancy. All career education for children is future oriented. What we are really trying to say is that there has been a marked change in the nature of work and that what we, as parents or teachers, have viewed as the conventional preparation for many fields of work is changing rapidly. Our understanding of the work world needs careful review, particularly as we apply it to gifted and talented children.

Several developments contribute to this need. First, we must recognize the increased interlocking of many fields of knowledge in current applications. Although this has always been true, the links were more apparent before the recent period of mushrooming expansion in our knowledge of the universe. Now, more than ever, we should recultivate the philosophy of the Renaissance man (or woman).

In a discussion quoted in the New York Times (54) about what it takes to be an educated person today, John G. Kemeny, president of Dartmouth, said:

> The greatest need is still for breadth of education and it is much greater today than it was 10 or 20 years ago. In particular, we desperately need individuals who can pull together knowledge from a wide variety of fields and integrate it in one mind. We are in an age when we are facing problems that no one discipline can solve. I suspect that 20 years from now there'll be entire new disciplines with new names. But we haven't invented them yet, so we call them interdisciplinary programs.

To which George Miller, professor of psychology at Princeton University, added, apropos of the relative importance of being expert in one subject area:

> Interesting ideas spring up at the boundaries between disciplines where people can work on the same thing from different points of view without realizing they have common interests. Like when an engineer suddenly discovers that all the time he was studying transistors he was really solving a psychological problem.

There is a growing feeling that education today must stress these aspects of learning:

1. Thorough mastery of the basic skills needed to *acquire* knowledge until they become automatic responses, thus freeing the mind for coping with more complex problems.
2. Acquisition of a relevant body of knowledge that is considered basic to specific fields and necessary for functioning in society.
3. Flexibility in the applications one makes of knowledge.
4. Awareness of the interdependence of all knowledge, no matter how remote the relationships may seem to be.
5. Capacity for intensive study in special areas when necessary.

As one studies the career market, one cannot escape the realization that (1) careers are far more complex now than they ever were; and (2) the need for trained minds is growing at a dramatic pace.

In a special issue entitled "Careers in the '80's," the *New York Times* (53) reported on a survey of job prospects based on data gathered by the U.S. Department of Labor Statistics. According to their survey, significant numbers of opportunities would be available in fields directly related to the abilities usually associated with the gifted child. All require a minimum of college graduation and most indicate a need for graduate study. For example, in the same survey Kodak published Table 4, showing the relationship between college degrees and job opportunities in their firm.

Among the jobs with good prospects listed by the *New York*

TABLE 4. Educational Requirements for Job Titles

B.S. or M.S. in Ch.E., M.E., I.E., E.E., or possibly other engineering disciplines	B.S. or M.S. in chemistry	B.S. in computer science, applied mathematics, economics, or other quantitative business studies	B.S. in marketing or general business or B.A. in liberal arts	Strong on-the-job performance and appropriate career interest can lead to positions ordinarily filled from within the company
Design	Development Product Processes	Programming and systems technology	Sales assignments require individuals responsive to the challenges of selling. Must be willing to travel and, when necessary, to relocate.	Administration
Manufacturing services				Advertising
Development Product Processes	Marketing Technical sales Customer services	Sales		Industrial Relations
		Forecasting and planning		Market Research
Marketing Technical sales Customer services	Research			Public Relations
	Manufacturing Organic synthesis			Supervision and management
Research	Analysis Production operations	M.B.A. following technical undergraduate major	Forecasting and planning or Cost Engineering	
	Nearly all Ph.D.s start in research assigments			

Personnel Resources, Kodak, Rochester, N.Y. 14650. In "Careers in the 80's," *National Recruitment Survey, New York Times,* Section 12, Sunday, October 14, 1979, p. 68. © 1980 by The New York Times Company. Reprinted by permission.

Times survey, the following are those that require training suitable for gifted children (53, p. 9):

- Engineers—Particularly in mining, petroleum, metallurgical fields. Note the relationship to contemporary concerns with fuel and energy shortages.
- Biologists—Especially marine and agricultural. Although prospects for farmers as laborers were poor, management in farming had excellent prospects. Food as a resource was a continuing critical area.
- Mathematicians—An area of continuing and growing need, for which only the gifted can qualify. Theoreticians are essential to many fields of study, especially in space exploration and science technology, and in applications to financial management.
- Architects—Prospects were among the best, not necessarily for housing, but rather for large-scale industrial planning and as urban and regional planners in cooperation with sociologists. Bell Laboratories, for example, advertised for specialists in "Systems Architecture—applied research on multi-processor and multi-computer architecture. Assess [note engineering/mathematical aspects] cost/performance of distributed microprocessor arrangements."
- Social Scientists—Including particularly economists, psychologists, sociologists, and urban and regional planners (see *Architects*).
- Computer Specialists—Especially programmers and systems analysts.

This listing is not intended to exhaust the possibilities, but merely to suggest a few trends and the increasing complexity of the tasks.

In this section, note that the source is a newspaper. Career needs change so rapidly that one should resort to the most current and up-to-date information. For example, a major discovery in sources of energy could completely revolutionize the emphases in engineering specialties.

What is evident from all of this is that one can only provide ample opportunity for a broad-based education and information about new fields as they come into existence. As John C. Crystal, career consultant, advises the job hunter in an interview with Dan Hulbert (37):

> The prudent thing, before specializing in anything, is to find out what you really want to do. Don't be misled about projections that X years from now there's going to be a shortage of accountants or whatever, because nobody knows. Our economy is changing so quickly that no one can say who will be in demand 10 or 15 years from now, or even in the four years you're in college. Many people discover they have been trapped in their specialty when that specialty became a dead end or obsolete. Specialists may move quickly within their own organization, but for the top positions, companies look for the person with breadth. Technical or business degrees are extremely helpful when one is starting out. But the person with the broad, solid liberal-arts education, if he can land that entry-level position, has greater possibilities to explore.

Advisors to gifted students thus have a difficult task before them, but there is no doubt that the opportunities for successful careers for these students will undoubtedly increase in the years ahead.

SUGGESTED READINGS

BOLLES, RICHARD. *What Color Is Your Parachute? A Practical Manual for Job-Hunters and Career Changers.* Berkeley, Calif: Ten Speed Press, 1980. Excellent resources and bibliography. Useful for teachers.

COLANGELO, NICHOLAS, and RONALD T. ZAFFRANN, eds. *New Voices in Counseling the Gifted.* Chap. V, "Career Development and the Gifted," pp. 247–300. Dubuque, Iowa: Kendall/Hunt, 1979.

HOLLAND, JOHN L. *Making Vocational Choices: A Theory of Careers.* Englewood Cliffs, N.J.: Prentice-Hall, 1973.

HOYT, KENNETH B., and JEAN R. HEBELER. *Career Education for Gifted and Talented Students.* Salt Lake City, Utah: Olympus, 1974.

NASH, WILLIAM R., CHRISTOPHER BORMAN, and SHARON COLSON. "Career Education for Gifted and Talented Students: A Senior High School Model." *Exceptional Children* 46, no. 5 (1980), 404–405.

RODENSTEIN, JUDITH, L. R. PFLIEGER, and NICHOLAS COLANGELO. "Career Development of Gifted Women." *Gifted Child Quarterly* 21, no. 3 (Fall 1977), 340–358.

SEARS, ROBERT R. "Sources of Life Satisfactions of the Terman Gifted Men." *American Psychologist* 32, no. 2 (February 1977), 119–128.

TORRANCE, E. PAUL. "Future Careers for Gifted and Talented Students." *Gifted Child Quarterly* 20, no. 2 (Summer 1976), 142–156.

WHARTON, CLIFTON R. "Education and the Job Market." *Science* 185, no. 4151 (August 16, 1974). Editorial.

Tests: Intelligence, Achievement, Aptitude

"We're having a *test* on Friday," your child announces in a voice filled with horror, insecurity, and outrage. "I've got to *study!*" The word *test* somehow conjures up memories of many anxious hours for the parents and, for the child, an element of fear and foreboding. "What if I fail!" For the next few days, the dominating word of the child's and family's life is *test*.

The reality is that, in whatever form, we are required to take and, hopefully, pass many tests throughout our lives. Just crossing a street is a test of many skills: estimating the speed of approaching cars, accommodating one's pace to their speed, estimating the distance of the car in relation to the amount of pavement or road to be traversed, and so on. The problem with tests in a formal educational situation is that the final judgment as to our passing rests upon an external authority. If we estimate poorly in crossing a street or road and have to make a sudden dash to the safety of a sidewalk, our only judge is within ourselves. But when the judgment of our performance lies outside ourselves, our egos and vanities are threatened. For the school child even more may be at stake: the approval or disapproval of one or more significant persons, such as teachers, parents, classmates, or relatives.

School children are beset with many tests on which their progress is rated. For gifted children, tests play an even larger role, since they are frequently required to compete with others for places in special classes or programs or, as they get older, for the few awards available that may help them gain admission to the schools or colleges of their choice.

In spite of all the adverse publicity tests have received in recent years, they do serve a function for which as yet there seems to be no adequate substitute. They provide an impersonal, objective evaluation of capacities in a way that no amount of observation or interviewing can do. Parents and teachers can and should avail themselves of the positive benefits such tests provide.

Tests can help to answer such questions as the following:

1. Is my child intellectually gifted?
2. How well is my child performing in school subjects in comparison with his or her grade peers? With respect to his or her ability level?
3. Does my child have a special aptitude for mathematics, science, mechanics, language?
4. Is my child talented in one of the visual or performing arts?
5. Is my child performing at a level high enough to insure acceptance to and success in college?
6. What are my child's special interests and how do they relate to a choice of careers?

Actually, it is possible to design tests to measure achievement, aptitude, or performance in an endless variety of subjects and fields of work. The *Mental Measurements Yearbooks*, edited by Oscar Buros (5), describe hundreds of these tests. For anyone interested, these are excellent source books of information about tests, including evaluations of each by specialists in the field. They are usually to be found in the education section of libraries on the reference shelves. These volumes are quite technical and require a certain amount of background training. For more readable information on tests, textbooks by Anastasi (1), Thorndike and Hagen (73), and Cronbach (9) offer excellent discussions of their good and bad points.

TEACHER-MADE TESTS VS. STANDARDIZED TESTS

Tests have certain general characteristics that are helpful to know if we are to make the best use of them. The usual classroom test devised by a teacher is useful for a limited situation, most often to determine whether students have mastered a specific content area, such as addition facts or the causes of the American Revolution. Such tests are usually limited to one-time use and have no general applicability. On the other hand, standardized tests are constructed deliberately so that their results can be generalized to a specific population. They may be marked by objective or subjective means. They may be limited to classroom use or standardized on a much larger population, often a school system or a national sample of pupils. They may take the form of true–false or multiple-choice answers; or they may be open-ended, requiring the examinee to respond in his or her own language. They may be given in any number of areas, such as intelligence, achievement, aptitude, critical thinking, personality, attitudes and beliefs, or performance. They may take the form of scales, questionnaires, questions and answers, or essays; or they may be nonverbal in that the response required is that of pointing or performing some physical act.

Standardized tests have the advantage of being developed on a large student sample which, under the best conditions, reflects the population to which the tests will be applied. Usually thousands of children are involved in the norming procedure.

For the gifted child, certain tests have special significance; parents and teachers should be familiar with their general characteristics.

INTELLIGENCE TESTS

There are two types of intelligence tests: those that are administered on an individual basis and those that are used for groups. Since group tests can vary from the more thorough individual tests by as many as thirty points, they should be used for screening purposes only, followed by an individual test. (See Chapter 1.)

Individual Tests

The two best-known individual tests are the Stanford-Binet (S-B) and the Wechsler scales (WISC, WAIS, WPPSI). The Stanford-Binet yields a single IQ score, while the Wechsler scales yield a score that combines performance and verbal scores. There are advantages and disadvantages associated with both tests, but they do yield useful information about a child's intellectual ability and *capacity for academic performance.* Both have been analyzed extensively, the Stanford-Binet much more than the Wechsler scales, and a great deal of corroborative evidence about their effectiveness is available, for example in Buros (5), Anastasi (1), Thorndike and Hagen (73), and Cronbach (9). These tests will help answer the questions: "Is this child intellectually gifted?" "What can we expect about this child's ability to perform in an academic situation?" "What is this child's learning potential?"

Both tests must be administered by qualified psychologists. The Stanford-Binet can be used for children as young as two years of age, while the Wechsler scales apply to children four or five years of age and older. Both tests can be used through age sixteen. The decision as to which test should be used is best left to a qualified examiner, who may even prefer to use some of the other tests that are available for special circumstances.

For gifted children, the IQ scores derived from the tests are not directly comparable. Children of all backgrounds achieve higher scores on the Stanford-Binet than on the Wechsler scales and adjustments must be made for this in interpreting the results. Furthermore, the Stanford-Binet tends to be more reliable at higher levels of ability than are the Wechsler scales (5, 73).

Individual tests of intelligence must be administered by qualified persons with specific training in the use of the tests and, preferably, with experience in dealing with gifted children. In many states, such trained persons are licensed. Parents and teachers should be cautious in accepting information that is provided by sources whose qualifications are in doubt.

Group Intelligence Tests

Group intelligence tests are so called because they do not require one-to-one administration. They can usually be used for whole classes at once or, at earlier levels, for small groups of children. They have objective scoring systems, making them free from personal judgment.

Many of the group tests in use have long histories of development and application. For the most part, they have been developed under high standards of test construction, involving a great deal of research and item analysis as well as participation by large numbers of pupils representing a variety of communities and origins. They are very good instruments for screening large numbers of pupils, provided the follow-up takes into account any discrepancies between observation and knowledge about the student and the test score. Parents and teachers can feel secure with the results of such tests if they are satisfied that they are consistent with what they know about the child. That security can be reinforced if they know that pupils are retested at regular intervals. No gifted child should be denied participation in a special program on the basis of a single test score without supporting evidence.

Regardless of how elaborate the initial process may be, neither parents nor teachers should be satisfied with test data that are more than two or three years old. During the early years, evaluations should be repeated annually up to and including age six, then every two or three years up to the high school years. Although individual IQs show good stability from year to year, particularly on the Stanford-Binet, they do vary and may be quite different after five or six years. It is urgent for both parents and teachers to bear in mind that the IQ is a measure of behaviors which are strongly influenced by environmental factors. To the extent that intelligence is genetic, its true range can only be inferred from overt behaviors. The statement that special treatment has raised an IQ by twenty or thirty points is startling only because the observers are disregarding the essential fact that intelligence as native endowment is an elusive trait, subject to all the environmental influences affecting other human behavior as well.

ACHIEVEMENT TESTS

The usual achievement test is given in the classroom; however, most children in the United States as well as in other parts of the world are also given standardized achievement tests. These tests make it possible to compare the performance of children with others of the same grade (rarely age) over a large population, most frequently a national sample.

There are many well-known tests in this area. A few of these are the Metropolitan Achievement Tests, Iowa Tests of Basic Skills, California Achievement Tests, SRA Scholastic Series, Stanford Achievement Tests, Wide Range Achievement Tests, and Sequential Tests of Educational Progress. Some are batteries of tests while others may cover individual subject areas only. Most have been developed by complex statistical procedures. They are usually written with the advice of curriculum experts who make a survey of textbooks and school practices throughout the country to determine the most representative information, skills, and abilities that are being taught.

The results of standardized achievement tests are usually reported by grade equivalents or percentiles, telling us how well the child is performing in a given area *in comparison with children of the same grade level.* Just because a second-grader achieves at a sixth-grade level on an achievement test, there is no reason to believe that he or she can perform the work of the sixth grade. For this reason, the percentile is a less confusing record. It merely states that the child is performing better than x percent of his or her grade peers.

Gifted children usually perform better than their grade peers on standardized achievement tests regardless of how they perform on school-made tests. This is partly due to the more universal knowledge that is required for such tests. Parents and teachers should take these results into careful account in evaluating a gifted child, as they are a truer reflection of the child's level of performance.

Another important point teachers and schools should bear in mind is that, although gifted children usually do well on such standardized tests, the results are not a true picture of how well they could perform if their education were actually challenging their abilities. There is too much complacency about responding to the needs of gifted children simply because, with no help at all, they achieve higher scores on these tests than their classmates.

Still another aspect of achievement testing as it applies to gifted children is the limited reliability of the higher scores. Most tests are geared to pupils in the average range of abilities. The test items reflect these average abilities. The number of items that reach the abilities of brighter students is limited, and therefore growth from year to year is not measured accurately at these higher levels. In other words, if an average child moves one grade in reading ability each year, estimates of his or her progress may be fairly accurate. For a gifted child, a gain of two grades over a one-year period may actually *underestimate* his or her progress. Few teachers and school systems ever take these facts into account, since they are not easily understood. However, it is important for parents to know that test results for their gifted children are not as reliable as those reported for other children.

TESTS OF SPECIAL APTITUDES

Tests of special aptitudes are used to estimate abilities in particular areas, such as mechanics, music, language, or creativity. While achievement tests are designed to measure or evaluate exposure to a particular curriculum or course of study, aptitude tests are most often designed to *predict* performance in a given area. Special statistical techniques are used to find out how well the tests work in these areas. Like achievement tests, aptitude tests are not independent of all the experience and learning the child has acquired prior to testing. Achievement tests in themselves also serve as estimators of aptitude in particular areas.

Creativity Tests

A few comments about creativity tests are in order here. There has been a growing tendency to include such tests among the criteria used to select students for classes or special programs for the gifted. In some cases, they have been used in lieu of intelligence tests. These tests measure the ability to solve problems in unique, unusual ways, using divergent thinking. A common sample item is: "Name as many different ways of using a brick as you can." The tests are not necessarily related to the fine arts, since the thinking processes involved are used in most human endeavors.

Like so many other areas of research, more errors are committed in the application and interpretation of data than in the actual development or research basic to acquiring the data. As in all other testing, one must bear in mind the purposes for which creativity tests are used. In programs where activities specifically related to creativity will be stressed, these tests may be useful. However, it is important that those using the tests be familiar with their technical manuals and that they be fully aware of the limitations on predictive validity for academic success.

Parents presented with the results of such tests should ask for a careful explanation of their purpose. They should be aware that a "low creativity" score on one test does not preclude the pursuit of a career in the arts.

Teachers, on the other hand, should know that scores on these tests are merely indicators of an ability that may or may not reflect the true creative potential of their students; therefore, they should not discount the efforts of a student whose behavior is contradicted by the scores. Generally, teachers should be skeptical of any test score that is not consistent with pupil performance.

OTHER TESTS

Other tests may relate to interests, attitudes and beliefs, personality traits, and so on. However, these tests are usually used in special studies rather than in school placement.

TESTING AND COLLEGE WORK

There are two major testing programs that affect high school students: (1) those required for admission to the college of their choice, and (2) those that will allow the students to enter college with advanced standing in selected curriculum areas.

In general, it is wise to prepare a calendar of important test or competition dates during the student's second year of high school. Knowing at what time of year an important opportunity will take place will help parents, teachers, and students to make the best preparations for the occasion.

The most intensive and extensive work done in the area of testing for college admissions and program guidance is carried out by the College Entrance Examination Board (CEEB). The College Board is a "nonprofit membership organization that provides tests and other educational services for students, schools and colleges." It conducts the ATP or *Admissions Testing Program*—a broad term that covers the services performed by the CEEB. The ATP is "designed to assist students, high schools, colleges, universities, and scholarship agencies with postsecondary educational planning and decision making and to provide a channel of communication between the schools and colleges." The Educational Testing Service (ETS) at Princeton, New Jersey, develops and administers the tests for the CEEB.

TESTS GIVEN BY THE CEEB UNDER THE ATP

SAT

The SAT (*Scholastic Aptitude Test*) is a multiple-choice test that measures verbal and mathematics reasoning abilities "that are related to successful performance in college" (7). Many colleges request SAT scores along with other data about students for admission. The CEEB prepares a manual which describes the purposes of the test, provides sample questions, and explains how to interpret the scores (8).

PSAT/NMSQT

The PSAT/NMSQT, or *Preliminary Scholarship Aptitude Test/National Merit Scholarship Qualifying Test,* is sponsored jointly by the CEEB and the National Merit Scholarship Corporation. It is similar in nature to the SAT and usually is taken during the student's junior year in high school. Students who achieve high scores in the test are eligible for about one thousand National Merit Scholarships of one thousand dollars each. Other students take advantage of the opportunity to take the test as a tryout for the SAT to be taken in their senior year. Details about this test are provided in *The Student Bulletin,* available through the CEEB. The *Bulletin* includes all necessary, up-to-date information about application forms, sample questions, suggestions on how to take the test, special provisions for black or needy students, interpretation of test scores, and so on.

ACH

In addition to the PSAT/SAT series, the CEEB administers an extensive program of Achievement Tests (ACH) in many areas such as English composition, literature, American and European history, mathematics, foreign languages, biology, chemistry, and physics. Many colleges require data from these tests as part of their admissions or placement procedures. For details about this part of the CEEB testing program, obtain a copy of their *ATP Guide for High Schools and Colleges* (7).

TSWE

The TSWE (Test of Standard of Written English) is designed to aid colleges in selecting appropriate English courses for students. It is not intended to be used for admissions purposes.

School guidance counselors have access to the carefully prepared brochures published by the CEEB for their use. Parents and teachers can obtain additional information by writing or calling the CEEB office in their own locality, or they can write for a list of pamphlets and order them from:

College Board Publication Orders
Department C50
Box 2815
Princeton, N.J. 08541

APP

The APP, or *Advanced Placement Program*, is another of the services provided by the CEEB. Many colleges will give credit or advanced placement to students who show satisfactory performance in the tests for these college-level courses given in high school. This is an excellent way to enrich the high school years, while at the same time opening up greater opportunities at the college level. Courses given in this program vary from school to school and may include several choices, such as English, American and European history, calculus, biology, chemistry, physics, music, art, and foreign language. By taking these courses in addition to their regular schoolwork, exceptional high school students can enter some colleges with a year's advancement. Most are permitted to take advanced standing in special areas.

In addition to the College Board program, there are tests that are given by some colleges on their own that also offer advanced placement.

Information about advanced placement programs is available from the CEEB and from colleges.

Whatever the test, parents and teachers can use the results as guides. They serve as objective evidence of a student's ability, achievement, or aptitude and as clues to what one can expect in future work.

DOES COACHING HELP?

The goal of test writers is to create a novel situation so that an independent, objective judgment can be made about the child's abilities. Most standardized tests are designed to be "secure," and it is considered unethical to reveal specific items. Of course, if you were to discuss in advance the specific items of an individual intelligence test with a child who had a good memory, his score would be altered. This would serve no purpose, however, since a false score would create inappropriate expectations for the child, thus doing only harm and no good.

On the other hand, if students are prepared by discussion and example on the types of questions they may encounter and good procedures for test taking, they will certainly have an advantage over those without this experience. Studying sample problems in advance adds to one's store of knowledge; therefore, the student's score still is an estimate of achievement.

It would be a foolish person indeed who did not explore the many guides to tests of all kinds that are becoming more and more available. Every bit of information helps, especially when a few points can make all the difference in acceptance to a special program. However, coaching courses, which may be quite expensive, should be recognized for what they really do, which is to provide a systematic review of the subject matter covered in school curricula. To the extent that such reviews are true learning experiences, they are beneficial. At the same time, the public should be aware that test publishers are aiming for generalized abilities and are rarely concerned with specific information, except where the subject calls for it. This means that they present items that require the student to pull together many skills, for which there is no "instant" preparation possible.

COMMENTS

It is obvious that today's school children, especially the gifted, must be prepared to take many tests as they progress through the educational system. The process does not end there. It continues through many other experiences, including employment requiring special skills. Parents and teachers should be familiar with the goals and scope of testing programs and should be prepared to make maximum use of the guidance such tests can furnish. Usually college admissions personnel are especially careful to consider many aspects of the student's background, using the test data only as an indicator and objective aid in making final decisions. The impersonal, unbiased evaluation of progress and possible future achievement that tests give, combined with personal observations and other data concerning the student, can be used as a sound basis for advice, guidance, and selection. A caution stated earlier is worth repeating. Any discrepancies between test data and other relevant information should be investigated thoroughly in order to insure an accurate evaluation of the student.

    Test taking should be viewed as just one more skill (or combination of skills) that is required for success in the current educational scene. Children should be encouraged to approach the process with confidence and, most importantly, with thorough preparation in their subject matter.

SUGGESTED READINGS

See references cited in this chapter.

The Law and Gifted Children

10

There is probably no area in which parents of the gifted feel more helpless than in discovering what their children's rights are in the educational process. As soon as they consider sending their child to school, parents begin to feel frustrated and overwhelmed by administrative evasion and secrecy.

Parents send their children to school in the hope that all the forces in their particular school system are motivated to do the very best for the children. They are keenly disappointed when they approach a school with a gifted child in tow and learn that there really is no special provision for this child in the system. They talk to their friends and neighbors and learn quickly enough that little differentiation is made between the bright child and others in the routines of their local school.

Over and over again, one hears cries such as these:

> Susan will be bored to tears in kindergarten. What can I do for her?
>
> Jonathan is getting into trouble in school. He doesn't pay attention and the teacher says he's a "smart aleck." I know he gets restless. After all, he already knows everything she is teaching him. What do I do?
>
> My teenager is completely turned off from school. She was a very good reader, had a keen interest in science, but now she is getting poor marks and has absolutely no interest in her classwork.
>
> My son is very much interested in mathematics. He has taught himself a lot of geometry and trigonometry, yet the teacher insists on teaching him simple addition and subtraction. He's only nine. What am I supposed to do?
>
> I am the principal of a private school. We have an eight-year-old girl here who is extremely intelligent. We are not equipped to handle such children, especially with our very large class sizes. Is there somewhere in the public school system where this child's needs can be met?

A distraught mother wrote the following letter, which seems to sum up the plight of many parents.

> Please help me find a school for my gifted son. His IQ is over 175. He is going to be 7 years old in October. The public school in the area admits to having no facilities for handling him. There are no private schools for gifted children that I know of. Some private schools that I have contacted have told me it would be too much trouble to have such a child in their schools. Why should the ability of a bright child be ignored? Such children surely deserve as much attention as the retarded. It would almost seem as if high intelligence has become a handicap since no one is willing to extend himself in behalf of the child. We need help before the child's potential is completely wasted and atrophied through lack of stimulation.
>
> Thank you for any advice you may give me.

Parents should know far more than they usually do about the law and their children, especially with regard to education. They tend to rely on the school to keep them informed about local regulations and their children's rights. Actually, there is a whole body of rules and regulations, including town, city, state, and federal laws, that have a direct impact on your child. If you are a parent of a gifted child, you need to know what is and is not possible and what you can justly expect from your particular school system.

Parents who may never have been interested in the legislative process will certainly become involved when they begin to realize how much power they have to bring about changes in educational provisions for their children. The best example one can offer of parent power is legislation concerning the handicapped. In 1978, the federal government appropriated close to one billion dollars for the education of handicapped children. It is estimated that there are about 3.4 million handicapped children in the country. These include the mentally retarded, hard of hearing. deaf, speech impaired, visually handicapped, emotionally disturbed, orthopedically impaired, and learning disabled. This comes to an authorization of about $295 for each handicapped child in the United States, which does not include state and local provisions. Almost all of the federal legislation, as well as that at state levels, came about because of parental pressure, strengthened by organizational support. The lobby for the handicapped is a most powerful one.

Interestingly enough, it was recognition of these facts about the handicapped that led a small but deeply concerned group of educators and parents to initiate legislation for the gifted that led to an Office for the Gifted and Talented housed—where else?—in the Bureau for the Handicapped in the U.S. Office of Education.

A little history might help parents understand the legislative process and how much power rests in their hands.

HISTORY OF LEGISLATION FOR THE GIFTED AND TALENTED

Although President Lyndon Johnson authorized a task force to prepare a report on the education of the gifted in 1967, it remained unknown until 1974, when the Johnson Library was opened. In 1969, amendments to the Elementary and Secondary Education Act (ESEA) reached the gifted in three categories: one for state leadership training; a second for development of innovative programs; and the third and most important to direct the Commissioner of Education to make a national survey on the status of education of the gifted. This came to be known as the Marland Report (46), and it proved to be a major impetus toward further action on behalf of the gifted.

The first legislative action for the gifted and talented came in 1974, with an allocation of 2.56 million dollars. Since it had been estimated in the Marland Report that there were about 2.6 million gifted and talented children in the country, this amount represented the magnificent sum of one dollar per child. That this niggardly allocation was converted into a major effort nationally on behalf of these children is a credit to the small but devoted number of professionals, aided and supported by eager parents, who generously gave themselves to the very complex task before them. For three years, the allocation remained fixed at 2.56 million. For 1979, it rose to about 3.78 million dollars, and in 1981 it was set at 5.6 million.

These figures represent allocations. Allocations are monies that can actually be spent and must be passed on by Congress. Authorizations are merely statements of legislative intent. The authorizations for the gifted are much more satisfying than the allocations, but they are the kinds of imaginary figures that look good on paper but never pay for anything. From 1974 to 1978, the authorization was for 12.6 million, while the allocation never changed from 2.56 million. In the Education Amendments of 1978 "there are authorized to be appropriated $25,000,000 for fiscal year 1979, $30,000,000 for fiscal year 1980, $35,000,000 for fiscal year 1981, $40,000,000 for fiscal year 1982, and $50,000,000 for fiscal year 1983." [Section 903.(a).]

Congress passed the amendments to the Education Act known as the "Gifted and Talented Children's Education Act of 1978" as Title IX, Part A, of the Education Amendments of 1978 under pressure from a growing group of active and very concerned educators and parents.

The Act begins with this declaration:

Sec. 901. (b) The Congress hereby finds and declares that—
(1) the Nation's greatest resource for solving critical national problems in areas of national concern is its gifted and talented children.
(2) unless the special abilities of gifted and talented children are developed during their elementary and secondary school years, their special potentials for assisting the Nation may be lost, and
(3) gifted and talented children from economically disadvantaged families and areas often are not afforded the opportunity to fulfill their special and valuable potentials, due to inadequate or inappropriate educational services.

And in Section 901. (c), the purpose of the Act was stated as follows:

(c) It is the purpose of this part to provide financial assistance to State and local educational agencies, institutions of higher education, and other public and private agencies and organizations, to assist such agencies, institutions and organizations to plan, develop, operate, and improve programs designed to meet the special educational needs of gifted and talented children.

The text of the complete act is given in the Appendix.

HOW SOME LAWS ARE BORN

How does legislation like this come into being? Interested persons call, write, or visit those senators and congressmen who are on education committees or who have shown an interest or concern for this topic. Usually, an aide of the legislator follows through with a letter or telephone call. If the legislator is sympathetic to the cause, he may assign aides to draw up a tentative bill. People familiar with the field are usually called upon to offer advice and information. Professional organizations specializing in the field offer their services as resources.

For example, when Congress asked the U.S. Commissioner of Education, Sidney Marland, to inquire into the status of education for the gifted in the United States, the commissioner's aides sought help from specialists in the field who had expressed an interest. I had appeared before the committee which held regional hearings on this subject and had summarized what I felt were important needs of the gifted; this list was circularized throughout the country by a volunteer group. Such hearings are open to anyone who wishes to attend, but they usually are not publicized in major headlines. Later, I was asked to cooperate in the development of the questionnaire that formed the basis of the commissioner's report. Others in various parts of the country were also asked.

On the basis of the commissioner's report to the U.S. Congress, former Senator Jacob Javits and his colleagues drew up legislation in 1974 to fund programs for the gifted. This legislation also created the Office of the Gifted and Talented, to be housed in the Bureau of the Handicapped. This legislation came into being and was passed because hundreds of interested persons made their needs known and were willing to give their time and services. Personal letters (not form letters or petitions) and telegrams were sent to Senator Javits and other senators by parents, citing personal circumstances and urging passage of the bill. Parents should tell legislators what their concerns are. They should write asking questions such as:

- What bills are there before the legislature in education for the gifted?
- What is your position on these bills?
- Are you willing to sponsor a bill on education of the gifted?

They should write letters in which they describe the special characteristics of their own children, detailing unusual performance or behavior, so that the legislator will develop an understanding of the special requirements of such children. It is important that legislators hear from their constituents over and over again about their children's needs for special educational programming.

The process at the state level is no different. In New York, I invited an interested senator to visit a program for the gifted that I had created for the city. He came with two other senators and an assemblyman. Parents who were present asked them: "What are you doing in the legislature for our gifted children?" The senators replied, in essence, "This is the first time anyone has mentioned anything about gifted children to us. What's the problem?" As a consequence of these parents' expression of concern, one senator obtained special funds for the gifted for his constituents and another prepared a bill for consideration by the legislature.

In another community, I was honored with a testimonial luncheon that included a state senator among the honorees. He came, was impressed by the parent turnout, and went back to his office to prepare a bill on behalf of their gifted children. I spent more than a week preparing an analysis of the bill he and his colleagues had drafted so that I could make a proper presentation at the hearings that were held in my area. Yet when the day of the hearings arrived, I was disappointed to note that, of the thousands of parents in the metropolitan area who had gifted children with needs that were not being met, only four appeared before the legislative committee to express their concerns or show their support.

Few bills reach legislative floors and still fewer pass into law. But writing the bill is the first step in a long and tedious process. Continuous, active signs of interest that reach the legislature can eventually bring about success. Parent power and people power are realities, but few take advantage of them. In 1978, there were four bills concerning the gifted in the N.Y. State legislative hopper, all stimulated by parental and professional concern. In 1981, a bill was finally passed by the Senate, after years of unrelenting pressure by concerned citizens, but it failed to pass in the Assembly. However, more funding was added to the state budget to encourage local school districts in programming for the gifted.

PARENTS' ROLE IN LEGISLATION FOR THE GIFTED

Parents of the gifted must take an active role, and they must fight harder on the legislative battleground. They yield all too readily to other pressures, accepting meekly the excuses that other problems are more urgent. Parents of the gifted are particularly intimidated by the expressed needs of the disadvantaged and the handicapped. Apparently we are determined to use larger and larger bandages to help unfortunate children, but will not train the one group that has the capacity to solve their problems.

It was not because he was a member of a minority group and economically disadvantaged that Jonas Salk discovered the vaccine against poliomyelitis. It was because he was gifted and had had a good education to enhance his gifts. It was not because he was black and born into slavery that George Washington Carver discovered the value and multiple uses of the peanut as a nutritious food. It was because he was a gifted child who was given an opportunity to develop those gifts. Henri de Toulouse-Lautrec was severely crippled, but that is not why the world remembers him. We honor Louis Braille, not because he himself was blind, but because of the printing and writing system for the blind that he developed. Recently, I happened to tune in late on a televised concert of the New York Philharmonic. It was the first time I had seen or heard the virtuoso violinist Itzhak Perlman. The Lincoln Center audience in New York gave him a thunderous ovation. He had performed seated, and it was only as he left the stage that I noted his canes. He had become a victim of poliomyelitis at the age of three.

The fact is that society's progress depends on the talents and gifts of a small group; the development of these talents and gifts is of primary importance to society's well-being and happiness. In the case of handicapped gifted, it is well to note that their giftedness should merit as much attention as their handicaps. They may never overcome the handicap, but they most assuredly can be given a rich and full life through the development of their gifts.

Parents of the gifted, who seem to be quite humble and reticent about their children's superior abilities, should never apologize or hesitate to demand the best possible education for their children. When they do make such requests, these parents are actually insuring progress and development for society, since the hopes of society are realized most often through gifted children.

If there is any doubt in the minds of modest parents, they have only to try to consider what today's world would be like if the following persons had not contributed their gifts to our society:

Curie	radioactivity
Edison	incandescent lamp, phonograph
Franklin	electricity
Bell	telephone
Morse	telegraph
Wright brothers	airplane
Braille	printing for the blind
Gutenberg	printing press
Fahrenheit	mercury thermometer
Watson and Crick	DNA, RNA
Waksman	streptomycin (tuberculosis)
Fleming	penicillin
Unknown hero/heroine	the wheel

A major factor in the increasing legislation for the gifted is the growing feeling that equality of education means that each child will be taught according to his or her needs. Obviously, this is the case for the handicapped. More and more parents of the gifted are insisting that their children have special needs and are entitled to equality of opportunity to realize their potential.

Part of the progress in legislation for the handicapped has been reinforced by lawsuits instituted by parents demanding more educational opportunities for their children. Under PL 94-142, detailed provisions were made for the handicapped. Martha McCarthy, speaking before the National Organization on Legal Problems in Education, stated that litigation might be instituted on behalf of other children *such as the gifted*, claiming that they should be sent to schools where *their* special needs will be met, at public expense. In any case, parents of the gifted in all parts of the country are beginning to ask for appropriate education for their gifted children and an occasional lawsuit has evolved from this quest.

STATE LAWS FOR THE GIFTED

Of the fifty states, fewer than twenty-one had any legal provisions for the gifted in 1972, most of which represented intent rather than implementation. Only twelve had anyone in their State Education Departments whose duties included either part-time or full-time responsibility for the gifted. As of 1981, forty-seven states had appointed such a person. California, as the home state of Lewis Terman, has had legislation for "mentally gifted minors" since 1961. Pennsylvania has state laws and regulations for the "mentally gifted and talented" that were established in 1964. Illinois has a regulation defining its gifted and has had a program for the gifted since 1963. Connecticut has a state regulation and Nebraska a state regulation *and* law defining their gifted populations. Data on the current status of such legislation in each state can be obtained from the Council for Exceptional Children. (See Chapter 11 for addresses.)

Actually, long before there was legislation, there were pioneer programs inaugurated by imaginative schools and educators that set the patterns for the legislation to follow. The Terman studies in California led many communities across the country to develop special programs for their gifted and talented. New York City inaugurated "Terman" classes in 1917, and followed this with an extensive program of education for its gifted youth through the high school years. Its specialized high schools, the Bronx High School of Science, Stuyvesant, Music and Art, The Performing Arts, and Brooklyn Technical have all acquired a highly justified national and international reputation. The Colfax Plan in Pittsburgh, Pennsylvania; the Major Works classes in Cleveland, Ohio; the Hunter College Elementary School in New York City; and others—all were in existence as models before federal or state legislation was enacted.

The significance of this bit of history lies in the fact that legislation cannot emerge in a vacuum. There must be some models, some applications of methods and procedures, to form guidelines for what eventually goes into the law. A second, extremely important aspect of this is the fact that parents cannot wait for action on a national or state scale before something is done for *their* children. Their children have an immediate need that must be met as soon as possible. It is much easier to initiate programs on a small scale at the local level than it is to persuade a national legislative body or a state legislature to pass a bill on their behalf.

There is wide variation in what takes place at the state level throughout the country. In each state, parents who wish to know what laws and regulations cover their children's rights should write to their State Education Department or to their representatives in the legislature. They should ask for a copy of laws and regulations related to the gifted and/or the name of the person assigned to the responsibility of supervising education of the gifted.

Parents can also write to the Council for Exceptional Children (CEC), 1920 Association Drive, Reston, Virginia 22091, for a copy of their bibliography *Gifted: Parenting/Legislation and Public Policy*, No. 636. The CEC has published a survey of current state legislation for the gifted, which is also available. The National/State Leadership Training Institute for the Gifted and Talented publishes, from time to time, a list of persons involved in federally funded programs for each state; these persons can be good sources of information. (See Chapter 11 for addresses.)

LOCAL LAWS AND REGULATIONS

Each city, town, village, community, and school building operates under local policies, rules, regulations, and laws. There is no universal answer to what one can expect to find in any one place. These are a few steps parents can take to become informed on what is available at the local level.

1. Speak to the principal of the school your child would normally attend. Find out about school policies and district regulations.
2. Go to the local school board for information on policies and budgets.
3. Make inquiries at the district headquarters offices.
4. Find out if there is a local parent group involved with education of the gifted. They may be familiar with regulations.
5. Make inquiries at local or nearby teacher training colleges. They may have special programs or know about them, especially if they have a Special Education Department that includes the gifted in its categories.
6. Write to your State Education Department.

Do Not

1. Accept the first negative response you receive. It is surprising how little knowledge the people giving out information have about their systems. The larger the system, the harder it is to track down special information.
2. Look for the impossible. If there are no provisions or programs, you cannot expect a school system to stop everything and create a class for your child. *But,* do seek ways of bringing about change.
3. Accept a local school board's statement that there is no money for the gifted. School monies should be allocated in such a way that *all* pupil populations receive a proportionate share of the total. The family with ten children manages to feed all ten on a fairly even basis. So, too, with education. Whatever there is must be spread over all the children according to their needs. Recognizing the existence of gifted children in the system and the fact that they, too, have special requirements is a critical step in long-range educational planning.

There are many parent groups throughout the nation dedicated to promoting appropriate education for the gifted. Sources for such lists appear in Chapter 11.

WHAT TO LOOK FOR IN LEGISLATION

There are some key elements in most legislation for the gifted that are of major concern and of which parents should be aware:

1. *Definition.* All legislation must define or describe its target population. Definitions of the gifted vary from state to state and can be very limiting or very broad. You should know what applies in your state.

2. *Identification Criteria.* There are many definitions of the gifted and talented and many ways suggested for identifying them. In California, for example, an IQ test was sufficient up to 1978. The federal government has usually specified that multiple criteria must be used. The important factors to bear in mind are that all criteria must have some proven, demonstrated reliability (consistency of results) and validity (relationship to the purpose of identification).

3. *Money.* You will need to know how much money, if any, the legislation authorizes and the limitations placed on it. Distinguish between authorization and allocation. The federal legislation in 1974 *authorized* 12.6 million dollars for the gifted. In practice, only 2.56 million was actually allocated in each of the following three years.

4. *Eligibility.* Find out who is eligible to receive the money and under what conditions. In some states monies are available only as grants for which local school districts must compete. In other states, such as California, monies are granted to schools which identify gifted pupils, as prescribed by law. Each state will follow variations of patterns based on grants, pupils identified, enrollment, and so on.

5. *Period of Funding.* Find out when the funding becomes available and for how long.

6. *Impact on Your Community.* Know how your community is affected by the legislation and what steps can be initiated at the local level to obtain a share of the funding.

7. *Inclusion of Trigger Clauses.* Look for "trigger" clauses that can insure that at least some monies will reach the maximum eligible population.

8. *Efficient Management.* Look for administrative procedures that reduce overhead costs and allow funds to reach the maximum eligible population.

9. *Practicality.* Many a desirable piece of legislation has bogged down because no one thought the problem through the actual implementation stages. The IEP (Individualized Education Plan) for the handicapped is an example of legislation that sounds desirable on paper but falls far short of its goals in implementation. Check to see how practical the plan is.

THE SCHOOL VS. HOME EDUCATION

Parents who choose to educate their children at home should make inquiries about local regulations and laws governing such procedures.

Parents should realize that for the very young, kindergarten attendance is rarely compulsory. In some states, children are not required to attend school until the ages of seven or eight. Others require rather early compulsory attendance, at age five or so. Some have compulsory kindergarten attendance laws, while others do not.

For those parents who anticipate that they will not send the child to any formal school even after the legal age limits have been reached, it is important to learn what local and state regulations must be observed. Some states require whoever will be teaching the child to have a teaching license or to have passed certain course requirements. Whatever these requirements may be, they take time to obtain; parents should plan far ahead to meet them if they intend to resort to home teaching. (See Chapter 4 for a discussion of the advantages and disadvantages of making this decision.)

SUGGESTED READINGS AND RESOURCES

Children's Defense Funds. Publications Department, 1520 New Hampshire Avenue, NW, Washington, D.C. 20036. Information resources for children's advocates. Include data on census, education. and health.

Gifted: Parenting/Legislation and Public Policy, No. 636. ERIC Clearinghouse, The Council for Exceptional Children, 1920 Association Drive, Reston, Va. 22091. Bibliography.

MARLAND, SIDNEY P., JR. *Education of the Gifted and Talented.* Report to the U.S. Congress by the U.S. Commissioner of Education. Washington, D.C.: U.S. Department of Health, Education and Welfare, 1971.

See also "The Gifted and Talented Children's Education Act of 1978" in the Appendix, pages 185–190, and the resources listed in Chapter 11.

Sources
of Information

This section provides listings of resources and references related to several aspects of education of the gifted. Please remember that there may be frequent changes of personnel in government and organization offices. It is wise to address your queries to the *current* director, president, or other supervising official associated with each. A telephone call to the office requesting the name of the official may be practical and desirable. Take advantage of "800" numbers which are, of course, toll free.

SOURCES CONCERNING LEGISLATION

Federal Law

Write or call your senator or congressman, requesting information on current legislation. Your call will serve two purposes. It will alert your legislative representative to your concerns for gifted children, and it will lead you to the most up-to-date information on the subject. Your local office in the appropriate political party is a good source of addresses, and if there are branch offices of the federal government in your community, you can obtain the information there.

Director of the Office of Gifted and Talented
U.S. Department of Education
Donohoe Building, 400 Sixth Street, SW, Room 3835
Washington, D.C. 20202
Hotline: 800-424-2861

The Association for the Gifted (TAG)
The Council for Exceptional Children
1920 Association Drive
Reston, Virginia 22091
800-336-3728

The National Association for Gifted Children (NAGC)
217 Gregory Drive
Hot Springs, Arkansas 71901

For current regulations on legislation, see

The Federal Register
(Published daily by Congress. Available in public libraries or by direct subscription.)

Write also to local chapters of TAG, NAGC, and parent groups listed in your telephone directory.

State Law

Laws concerning the gifted vary from state to state. An important source of information is your State Education Department. Try to find out the name of the state coordinator or supervisor of the gifted, the person in charge of curriculum and instruction, or the director of special education. The organization of state education departments varies and placement of a unit on education of the gifted follows no uniform pattern. Write also to your representative in your state legislature for information.

For up-to-date information, call these toll-free numbers:

The Council for Exceptional Children   800-336-3728
U.S. Office of the Gifted and Talented   800-424-2861

In the following listing for states, address your letter or inquiry to Programs for Gifted and Talented, State Education Department, followed by the address given below for each state, possession, or territory of the United States.

Addresses of State Offices

Alabama
868 State Office Building
Montgomery, Alabama 36130
205-832-3230

Alaska
Section for Exceptional Children
Pouch F
Alaska Office Building
Juneau, Alaska 99811
907-465-2970

American Samoa
Department of Special Education
Pago Pago, American Samoa

Arizona
Division of Special Education
State Department of Education
1535 West Jefferson
Phoenix, Arizona 85007
602-255-3183

Arkansas
Special Education Section
Arch Ford Education Building
Little Rock, Arkansas 72201
501-371-2161

California
721 Capitol Mall
Sacramento, California 95814
916-322-3776

Colorado
201 East Colfax
Denver, Colorado 80203
303-839-2111

Connecticut
P.O. Box 2219
Hartford, Connecticut 06115
203-566-3695

Delaware
Department of Public Instruction
The Townsend Building
Dover, Delaware 19001
302-678-4888

District of Columbia
Seaton Elementary School
10th and Rhode Island Avenue NW
Room 311A
Washington, D.C. 20001
202-673-7054

Florida
319 Knott Building
Tallahassee, Florida 32301
904-488-3103

Georgia
State Office Building
Atlanta, Georgia 30334
404-656-2425

Guam
Department of Special Education
P.O. Box DE
Agana, Guam 96910

Hawaii
1270 Queen Emma Street
Room 805
Honolulu, Hawaii 96813
808-548-6923

Idaho
Len B. Jordan Building
Boise, Idaho 83720
208-334-3940

Illinois
Illinois State Board of Education
100 N. First Street
Springfield, Illinois 62777
217-782-6601

Indiana
Division of Curriculum
State Department of Public Instruction
State House, Room 229
Indianapolis, Indiana 46204
317-927-0111

Iowa
Department of Public Instruction
Grimes State Office Building
East 14th and Grand Avenue
Des Moines, Iowa 50319
515-281-3191

Kansas
120 East 10th Street
Topeka, Kansas 66612
913-296-4944

Kentucky
Bureau of Instruction
1809 Capitol Plaza Tower
Frankfort, Kentucky 40601
502-564-4774

Louisiana
P.O. Box 44064, Capitol Station
Baton Rouge, Louisiana 70804
504-342-4411

Maine
Special Education Division
State House Station 23
Augusta, Maine 04333
207-289-3451

Marshall Islands
P.O. Box 1748
APO San Francisco, California 96555
808-422-8974

Maryland
Division of Instruction
P.O. Box 8717
BWI Airport
Baltimore, Maryland 21240
301-796-8300

Massachusetts
Division of Curriculum and Instruction
31 St. James Avenue
Boston, Massachusetts 02116
617-727-7934

Michigan
P.O. Box 30008
Lansing, Michigan 48909
517-373-3324

Minnesota
641 Capitol Square
St. Paul, Minnesota 55101
612-296-4072

Mississippi
Division of Special Education
P.O. Box 771
Jackson, Mississippi 39205
601-354-6950

Missouri
Special Education
Department of Elementary and
 Secondary Education
P.O. Box 480
Jefferson City, Missouri 65102
314-751-2453

Montana
Office of Public Instruction
State Capitol
Helena, Montana 59601
406-449-3116

Nebraska
301 Centennial Mall South
Lincoln, Nebraska 68509
402-471-2446

Nevada
Division of Special Education
400 West King Street
Carson City, Nevada 89710
702-885-5700

New Hampshire
Department of Special Education
105 Loudon Road, Building 4
Concord, New Hampshire 03301
603-271-3741

New Jersey
Division of Special Education
225 West State Street
Trenton, New Jersey 08625
609-292-7602

New Mexico
Division of Special Education
Room 125
Santa Fe, New Mexico 87503
505-827-2793

New York
320 A Main Building
Department of Education
Albany, New York 12234
518-474-4973

North Carolina
Department of Public Instruction
Education Building
Raleigh, North Carolina 27611
919-733-3004

North Dakota
State Capitol
Bismarck, North Dakota 58505
701-224-2277

Ohio
Division of Special Education
933 High Street
Worthington, Ohio 43085
614-466-8854

Oklahoma
2500 North Lincoln Boulevard
Oliver Hodge Memorial Building
Suite 382
Oklahoma City, Oklahoma 73105
405-521-3261

Oregon
700 Pringle Parkway SE
Salem, Oregon 97310
503-378-8460

Pennsylvania
Bureau of Special Education
333 Market Street
Harrisburg, Pennsylvania 17126
717-783-6887

Puerto Rico
Office of External Services
Department of Education
Hato Rey, Puerto Rico 00924
809-754-1100

Rhode Island
CIC Building
235 Promenade Street
Providence, Rhode Island 02908
401-277-2031

Saipan, Mariana Islands
Director of Education
Trust Territories of the
  Pacific Islands
Saipan, Mariana Islands 96950

South Carolina
Rutledge Building, Room 803
1429 Senate Street
Columbia, South Carolina 29201
803-758-2652

South Dakota
Division of Elementary and
 Secondary Education
Kneip Building, Church Street
Pierre, South Dakota 57501
605-773-3678

Tennessee
116 Cordell Hull Building
Nashville, Tennessee 37219
615-741-3665

Texas
Texas Education Agency
201 East 11th Street
Austin, Texas 78701
512-475-6582

Utah
250 East South Street
Salt Lake City, Utah 84111
801-533-6040

Vermont
Division of Elementary and
 Secondary Education
Montpelier, Vermont 05602
802-828-3111

Virginia
State Department of Education
P.O. Box 6A
Richmond, Virginia 23216
804-225-2070

Virgin Islands
Division of Special Education
Box 630, Charlotte Amalie
St. Thomas, Virgin Islands 00801
809-774-4399

Washington
Division of Special Service
Old Capitol Building
Olympia, Washington 98504
206-753-1140

West Virginia
Division of Special Education
Capitol Complex Building #6
Room B-315
Charleston, West Virginia 25305
304-348-8830

Wisconsin
Department of Public Instruction
126 Langdon Street
Madison, Wisconsin 53702
608-266-3560

Wyoming
Hathaway Building
Cheyenne, Wyoming 82002
307-777-7411

Local Laws and Regulations

When you are seeking information at the local level, it is usually advisable to begin with the school your child would normally attend. Approach the teacher, guidance counselor, principal, local supervisor, or superintendent, generally in that order. For regulations and local laws, consult your local library, legislative representatives, the mayor's office, school boards, and boards of education. Sometimes state supervisors know about local conditions and can give special assistance.

PARENT ADVOCACY GROUPS

The following organizations have lists of parent advocacy groups for the gifted in various parts of the United States. These lists are revised periodically to keep them up to date.

The Council for Exceptional Children   (See page 169)
The Association for the Gifted   (See page 174)

Other organizations and/or publications that provide lists from time to time are state and local education departments, state and local PTAs, and the periodicals devoted to gifted education. (See pages 182–183.)

PROGRAMS/SCHOOLS FOR THE GIFTED

Listings in this category vary from year to year as funding waxes and wanes. It is best to make inquiries starting at the local level and moving up the line: (1) local school; (2) local school board; (3) local board of education; (4) local colleges and universities; (5) state education departments.

From time to time, the following organizations and/or publications compile current lists of programs in operation:

Sources of Information

    U.S. Office of Gifted and Talented   (See page 261)
    Ask for the current list
    of programs or directors prepared by
    individual states or consortia of states
    LTI Bulletin   (See page 269)
    G/C/T   (See page 269)
    Gifted/Talented Education   (See page 269)

See also directories of private and public schools available through your public library, and the following reference books:

JENKINS, REVA C. W. *A Resource Guide to Preschool and Primary Programs for the Gifted and Talented.* 1979. Creative Learning Press, P.O. Box 320, Mansfield Center, Conn. 06250.

KARNES, FRANCES A., and HERSCHEL Q. PEDDICORD, JR. *Programs, Leaders, Consultants and other Resources in Gifted and Talented Education.* Springfield, Ill.: Chas. C Thomas, 1980.

The What and Where of Gifted Programs: A Report to the New Jersey Gifted Consortium. Theodore J. Gourley, Project Director. 1975. Educational Improvement Center, Pitman, N.J. 08071. Gives a good overview of programs for the gifted at levels kindergarten through grade twelve. Data on 130 programs are summarized and include identification, curriculum, in-service training, written information, program characteristics appropriate to the gifted, program exportability, objectives, evaluation, outcomes.

Other sources are the parent advocacy groups and such national organizations as CEC/TAG and NAGC (see page 174).

BULLETINS, PERIODICALS, NEWSLETTERS ABOUT THE GIFTED

Many organizations and parent advocacy groups publish newsletters, bulletins, or periodicals related to education of the gifted. Membership in some organizations usually includes a subscription to its journal, which may also be obtained separately. Other publications are independent of any organization. Listed here are several journals and other publications to which one can subscribe. Those associated with national organizations may be available in public libraries.

    G/C/T (Gifted/Creative/Talented)
    G/C/T Publishing Co.
    Box 66654
    Mobile, Alabama 36606
    Highly readable, colorful publication, with sections for parents. Articles of current interest. Some research. Book reviews.

Gifted Child Quarterly
National Association for Gifted Children
217 Gregory Drive
Hot Springs, Arkansas 71901
Professional journal, with reports of research activities in the field, ongoing programs, general discussion.

Gifted Children Newsletter
Gifted and Talented Publications, Inc.
530 University Avenue
Palo Alto, California 94301
General discussion of current topics. Reviews of books for children, toys and games. Pull-out section for children.

Gifted/Talented Education
P.O. Box 533
Branford, Connecticut 06405
Reports on current activities in the field. Reviews of programs in operation in many parts of the country.

JEG (Journal for the Education of the Gifted)
The Association for the Gifted (TAG/CEC)
1920 Association Drive
Reston, Virginia 22091
Professional journal. Reports on research and activities in the field. Book reviews.

Journal of Creative Behavior
Bishop Hall, SUNY
1300 Elmwood Avenue
Buffalo, New York 14222
Professional journal on research and discussions of relevant topics in creativity. Book reviews.

LTI Bulletin
Ventura County Superintendent of Schools
535 East Main Street
Ventura, California 93009
Listings of current events, locations of key personnel, programs. Reports on developments on the national scene.

Parent Communication
Roeper Publications
Roeper City and Country School
Bloomfield Hills, Michigan 48013
Topics of concern to parents. Discussions of teaching methods, new activities, critical issues of general concern.

PSYCHOLOGICAL SERVICES, TESTING, IDENTIFICATION

Psychological and testing services may be available through the local school system, frequently without cost. Other sources of qualified personnel are local college or university test guidance centers and the

American Psychological Association directories. Some hospitals and clinics that have social and psychiatric services may also be prepared to perform this service under limited conditions.

When using the services of private personnel, it is wise to ask whether the person is licensed under state law to administer psychological tests. Many states have this requirement, which is in accordance with recommendations of the American Psychological Association. The psychology departments of colleges or universities can usually answer this question for you.

Other possible sources of testing and evaluation are special programs funded under state or federal grants. Their availability will vary from state to state and also from time to time, depending on the status of government regulations. State and local coordinators of gifted programs may also have access to information about such personnel (see pages 175–181).

Professionals who are qualified to perform this service may be known as clinical or school psychologists, guidance counselors, or psychiatrists. The essential factor is whether the person doing the evaluation has been properly trained in the procedures and is qualified to interpret the data.

Individual intelligence tests and many group intelligence, aptitude, or performance tests must be administered by trained personnel. Many standardized achievement tests and other group tests are administered by teachers, with on-site preliminary training.

Appendix: The Gifted and Talented Children's Education Act of 1978

TITLE IX—ADDITIONAL PROGRAMS
Part A—Gifted and Talented Children

Short Title; Purpose

Sec. 901. (a) This part may be cited as the "Gifted and Talented Children's Education Act of 1978."

    (b) The Congress hereby finds and declares that—

    (1) the Nation's greatest resource for solving critical national problems in areas of national concern is its gifted and talented children.

    (2) Unless the special abilities of gifted and talented children are developed during their elementary and secondary school years, their special potentials for assisting the Nation may be lost, and

    (3) gifted and talented children from economically disadvantaged families and areas often are not afforded the opportunity to fulfill their special and valuable potentials, due to inadequate or inappropriate educational services.

    (c) It is the purpose of this part to provide financial assistance to State and local educational agencies, institutions of higher education, and other public and private agencies and organizations, to assist such agencies, institutions and organizations to plan, develop, operate, and improve programs designed to meet the special educational needs of gifted and talented children.

Definition

Sec. 902. For the purpose of this part, the term "gifted and talented children" means children and, whenever applicable, youth, who are identified at the preschool, elementary, or secondary level as possessing demonstrated or potential abilities that give evidence of high performance capability in areas such as intellectual, creative, specific academic, or leadership ability, or in the performing and visual arts, and who by reason thereof, require services or activities not ordinarily provided by the school.

Authorization of Appropriations; Apportionment of Appropriations

Sec. 903. (a) For the purpose of carrying out this part there are authorized to be appropriated $25,000,000 for fiscal year 1979, $30,000,000 for fiscal year 1980, $35,000,000 for fiscal year 1981, $40,000,000 for fiscal year 1982, and $50,000,000 for fiscal year 1983.

(b)(1) From the amounts appropriated under subsection (a) for each fiscal year, the Commissioner shall reserve 25 per centum or $5,000,000, whichever is less, for carrying out the provisions of section 905, relating to discretionary programs.

    (2) The remainder of the sums appropriated under subsection (a) for each fiscal year shall be available to carry out the provisions of section 904, relating to State programs.

State Programs

Sec. 904. (a) From the amounts available in any fiscal year under section 903 (b)(2), the Commissioner shall make grants to State educational agencies for the Federal share of the cost of planning, developing, operating, and improving programs designed to meet the educational needs of gifted and talented children at the preschool, elementary, and secondary levels. Such programs may include in-service training of personnel to teach such children.

    (b)(1) Except as provided in paragraph (2), to the extent funds are available in any fiscal year to carry out the provisions of this section, the Commissioner shall distribute funds so as to assure that each State educational

agency which submits an application which fully meets all requirements of this section and is approved by the Commissioner will receive not less than $50,000 in that fiscal year. If sums appropriated for any fiscal year for making payments under this subsection are not sufficient to pay in full the amount to which each state educational agency is entitled under the previous sentence, such amounts shall be ratably reduced.
(2) In any fiscal year in which appropriations under this part equal or exceed $15,000,000, the Commissioner shall allot the amount so appropriated in accordance with the provisions of section 906.
(c) Each State educational agency desiring to receive a grant under this section shall submit an application at such time, in such manner and accompanied by such information as is necessary for the purposes of this section. Each such application shall contain assurances that—
(1) funds paid to the State educational agency will be expended solely to plan, develop, operate, and improve programs and projects which—
(A) are designed to identify the educational needs of gifted and talented children,
(B) are of sufficient size, scope, and quality to hold reasonable promise of making substantial progress toward meeting such needs, and
(C) give appropriate consideration to the particular educational needs of disadvantaged gifted and talented children:
(2)(A) the State educational agency will reserve from funds made available under this section in each fiscal year not more than 10 per centum of such funds for the purpose of administration, technical assistance, coordination, and statewide planning related to program, and projects designed to meet the needs of gifted and talented children:
(B) the State educational agency will distribute, on a competitive basis, not less than 90 per centum of the funds made available under this section for payments to local educational agencies within the State which apply to the State educational agency, with due regard for the quality of activities proposed in the application of the local educational agencies;
(3) the State educational agency will use at least 50 per centum of the funds made available under this section for programs and projects which include a component for the identification and education of disadvantaged gifted and talented children from low-income families;
(4) the State educational agency and the local educational agencies within the State may use funds made available under this section to acquire instructional equipment only if such equipment will enhance the program or project for which such funds are furnished;
(5)(A) the requirements of section 406 of this Act (relating to participation of pupils and teachers in private elementary and secondary schools) are met unless such requirements cannot legally be met in the State (as determined by the State educational agency);
(B) the State educational agency will not approve the application of a local educational agency within the State for assistance under this section unless the State educational agency determines that in designing the proposal subject to the application the needs of children in nonprofit private elementary and secondary schools have been taken into account through the consultation with private school officials and by other appropriate means; and
(6) the State educational agency will provide to local educational agencies

within the State, which are unable to compete due to smaller size or lack of financial resources, technical assistance in preparing proposals and in planning, developing, and operating programs under this section.
(d) The Commissioner shall approve any application which meets the requirements of subsection (c) and not disapprove any such application without first affording an opportunity for a hearing.

Discretionary Programs
Sec. 905. (a) From the amounts available in any fiscal year under section 903(b)(1) the Commisioner may—
(1) make grants to State educational agencies, local educational agencies, institutions of higher education, and other public and private agencies and organizations, to assist them in establishing or maintaining programs or projects designed to meet the educational needs of gifted and talented children including the training of personnel in educating gifted and talented children or in supervising such personnel;
(2) make grants to State educational agencies to assist them, either directly or through arrangements by the State educational agency with other institutions, agencies, and organizations eligible to receive funds under this part, to provide training of personnel engaged in the education of gifted and talented children or supervision of such personnel;
(3) enter into contracts with, and make grants to, public agencies and private organizations including State and local educational agencies, to establish and operate model projects for the identification and education of gifted and talented children;
(4) make grants to, or enter into contracts with, public agencies, private organizations, or institutions which together or singly constitute a clearinghouse to disseminate information about programs, services, resources, research, methodology, and media materials for the education of gifted and talented children;
(5) make grants to State educational agencies to assist them in the statewide planning, development, operation, and improvement of programs and projects designed to meet the educational needs of gifted and talented children; and
(6) conduct, either directly or by grant or contract, a program of research, evaluation and related activities pertaining to the education of gifted and talented children and may transfer to the National Institute of Education pursuant to subsection (c) not more than 20 per centum of the sums available in any fiscal year to carry out the provisions of this section; to pay the Federal share of the cost of such grants or contracts. Not more than 20 per centum of the sums available in any fiscal year under this section may be used pursuant to clause (1) of this subsection for grants to institutions of higher education for the training of national leadership personnel.
(b)(1) No grant may be made and no contract may be entered into under this section unless an application is submitted to the Commissioner in such form, in such manner, and containing such information, as is necessary for the purposes of this section.
(2) The requirement of section 406 of this Act (relating to the participation of pupils and teachers in private elementary and secondary schools) shall apply to programs and projects under this section unless such requirements cannot legally be met in the State (as determined by the State educational agency of the State in which the applicant for funds under this section is located).
(c)(1) Notwithstanding the second sentence of section 405 (b)(1) of the Gen-

eral Education Provisions Act, the National Institute of Education may, in accordance with the terms and conditions of section 405 of such Act, carry out a program of research and related activities pertaining to the education of gifted and talented children from funds transferred pursuant to subsection (a)(6).
(2) For purposes of this section the term "research, evaluation and related activities" means research, research training, evaluation, surveys, and demonstrations in the field of education of gifted and talented children and youth, or the dissemination of information derived from such research, surveys or demonstrations, and all such activities, including experimental and model schools.

State Allotments
Sec. 906. (a)(1) In any fiscal year in which appropriations for this part are equal to or exceed $15,000,000 the Commissioner shall allot, from amounts available under section 903 (b)(2), not more than 1 per centum among—
(A) Guam, American Samoa, the Virgin Islands, the Trust Territory of the Pacific Islands, and the Northern Mariana Islands;
(B) programs for children and teachers in elementary and secondary schools operated for Indian children by the Department of the Interior; and
(C) programs authorized for children and teachers in overseas dependent schools of the Department of Defense,
in accordance with their respective needs.
(2) From the remainder of such sums in any such fiscal year, the Commissioner shall allot to each State which has an application meeting the requirements of section 904, an amount which bears the same ratio to such remainder as the number of children in the State aged 5 to 17 years, inclusive, bears to the number of children in all States, except that no State shall receive less than $50,000 in any such fiscal year.
(3) For the purpose of this subsection the term "State" means the several States, the Commonwealth of Puerto Rico, and the District of Columbia.
(b) The amount of any State's allotment under subsection (a) for any fiscal year which the Commissioner determines will not be required for such fiscal year shall be available for reallotment from time to time, on such dates during such year as the Commissioner may fix to other States in proportion to the original allotments to such States under subsection (a) for that year but with such proportionate amount for any of such other States being reduced to the extent it exceeds the sum the Commissioner estimates such State needs and will be able to use for such year; and the total of such reduction shall be similarly reallotted among the States whose proportionate amounts were not so reduced. Any amounts reallotted to a State under this subsection during a year from funds appropriated under section 903 shall be deemed part of its allotment under section (a) for such year.

Administration
Sec. 907. (a) The Commissioner shall designate an administrative unit within the Office of Education to administer the programs and projects authorized by this part and to coordinate all programs for gifted and talented children and youth administered by the Office of Education.
(b) Notwithstanding any other provision of law, any Indian tribe which operates schools for its children shall be deemed to be a local educational agency for the purposes of this part.
(c) No financial assistance may be made to a local educational agency for a period in excess of 5 years. The limitation contained in this subsection shall not

apply to any financial assistance extended prior to the date of enactment of the Education Amendments of 1978.

Federal Share

Sec. 908. The Federal share for any fiscal year shall be 90 per centum, except that the Federal share for the clearinghouse activities under section 905(a)(4), the research, evaluation and related activities under section 905(a)(6), and programs and projects involving the participation of students in nonprofit elementary and secondary schools shall be 100 per centum.

References

References

1. ANASTASI, ANNE. *Psychological Testing.* 4th ed. New York: Macmillan, 1976.
2. BLOOM, BENJAMIN S., ed. *Taxonomy of Educational Objectives: The Classification of Educational Goals. I. Cognitive Domain. II. Affective Domain.* Copyright 1956 by Longman, Inc. Reprinted by permission of Longman, Inc., New York.
3. BRIDGMAN, DONALD S. *The Duration of Formal Education of High Ability Youth.* Washington, D.C.: National Science Foundation, 1961.
4. BRONFENBRENNER, URIE. "Parent Education: It's Not Just for Parents." *Inside Education* 65, no. 2 (October 1978), 4–11.
5. BUROS, OSCAR. *Mental Measurements Yearbooks.* Highland Park, N.J.: Gryphon Press, 1933–1972.
6. CIHA, T. E., et al. "Parents as Identifiers of Giftedness, Ignored but Accurate." *Talents and Gifts* 17, no. 1 (1974).
7. College Entrance Examination Board. *ATP Guide for High Schools and Colleges.* College Board Publication Orders, Dept. C50, Box 2815, Princeton, N.J. 08541.
8. _____. *The Student Bulletin.* College Board Publication Orders, Dept. C50, Box 2815, Princeton, N.J. 08541.
9. CRONBACH, LEE J. *Essentials of Psychological Testing.* 2nd ed. New York: Harper & Row, Pub., 1960.
10. DENNIS, W., and P. NAJARIAN. "Infant Development under Environmental Handicap." *Psychological Monographs* 71, no. 436 (1957).
11. DEVLIN, JOHN C., and GRACE NAISMITH. *The World of Roger Tory Peterson.* New York: Times Books, 1977.
12. EHRLICH, VIRGINIA Z. "Acceleration and Enrichment." *G/C/T,* Issue Eight (May/June 1979), 42–43, 58.
13. _____. "Acceleration and Enrichment for the Gifted in New York City Public Schools." In *Educating the Gifted: Acceleration and Enrichment.* Edited by William C. George, Sanford J. Cohn, and Julian C. Stanley, pp. 202–204. Baltimore, Md.: Johns Hopkins University Press, 1979.
14. _____. *The Astor Program for Gifted Children: PreKindergarten through Grade Three.* 1978. Box 223, Teachers College, Columbia University, New York, N.Y. 10027.
15. _____. "Identifying Giftedness in the Early Years, from Three through Seven." In *Education of the Preschool/Primary Gifted and Talented.* 1980. Edited by Sherri Butterfield. National/State Leadership Training Institute, Ventura County Superintendent of Schools, 535 East Main Street, Ventura, Calif. 93009.
16. _____. *The Gifted Child Project: The Effect of Subject Specialists on Gifted Children and the School Program.* New York: Board of Education of the City of New York, 1967.
17. _____. "A Model Program for Educating Gifted Four- to Eight-Year-Old Children." *International Journal of Early Childhood* 2, no. 1 (1979), 115–123.
18. _____. *Program Planning for the Gifted.* 1978. AGATE Press, Dingman Point, Alexandria Bay, N.Y. 13607.

19. _____. "The Role of Reading in the Astor Program for Intellectually Gifted Preschool/Primary Children." 1979. Paper commissioned by the U.S. Commissioner of Education. AGATE Press, Dingman Point, Alexandria Bay, N.Y. 13607.
20. EINSTEIN, ALBERT. *Out of My Later Years.* Secaucus, N.J.: Citadel Press, 1950.
21. _____. *The World as I See It.* New York: Philos. Lib., 1949.
22. FONTEYN, MARGOT. *Autobiography.* New York: Warner Books, 1976.
23. *The Foundation Directory.* New York: The Foundation Center, Columbia University Press. Current edition.
24. FRENCH, JOSEPH L., ed. *Educating the Gifted: A Book of Readings.* Rev. ed. New York: Holt, Rinehart & Winston, 1964.
25. GALLAGHER, JAMES J. *Teaching the Gifted Child.* 3rd ed. Boston: Allyn & Bacon, College Division. 1979.
26. GETZELS, JACOB W., and PHILIP W. JACKSON. *Creativity and Intelligence.* New York: John Wiley, 1962.
27. GOERTZEL, VICTOR, and MILDRED GOERTZEL. *Cradles of Eminence.* Boston: Little, Brown, 1962.
28. GOWAN, JOHN C. *Development of the Creative Individual.* San Diego, Calif.: Robert Knapp, 1972.
29. GUILFORD, J. P. *The Nature of Human Intelligence.* New York: McGraw-Hill, 1967.
30. HALL, THEODORE. *Gifted Children: The Cleveland Story.* New York: World Publishing, 1956.
31. HARTSHORNE, H., and M. A. MAY. *Studies in Deceit.* New York: Macmillan, 1927.
32. HAYAKAWA, S. I. "Adventures of the Mind: How Words Change Our Lives." *Saturday Evening Post* 250, no. 9 (December 1978), 52.
33. HOLLINGWORTH, LETA S. *Children above 180 IQ (Stanford–Binet): Origin and Development.* New York: Arno, 1975. Reprint of 1942 edition.
34. _____. See above, Chapters 19 and 20.
35. HOLT, JOHN. Quoted in *Time,* December 4, 1978, p. 78.
36. HOYT, KENNETH B., and JEAN R. HEBELER. *Career Education for Gifted and Talented Students.* Salt Lake City, Utah: Olympus, 1974.
37. HULBERT, DAN. "Tips from a Maverick Adviser." *New York Times,* Section 12, October 14, 1979, p. 71. © 1979 by The New York Times Company. Reprinted with permission.
38. JACOBS, J. C. "Effectiveness of Teacher and Parent Identification of Gifted Children as a Function of School Level." *Psychology in the Schools* 8, no. 2 (1971), 140–142.
39. JENSEN, ARTHUR R. *Bias in Mental Testing.* New York: Free Press, 1980.
40. KEATS, EZRA JACK. *Jennie's Hat.* New York: Harper & Row, Pub., 1966.
41. KHATENA, J. *The Creatively Gifted Child: Suggestions for Parents and Teachers.* New York: Vantage Press, 1978.
42. KRUEGER, MARK L., ed. *On Being Gifted.* National Student Symposium on the Education of the Gifted and Talented. New York: Walker, 1978.

43. LONDON, JACK. *Martin Eden.* New York: Airmont, 1969.
44. LONGFELLOW, HENRY WADSWORTH. *The Poetical Works of Henry Wadsworth Longfellow.* Boston: Houghton-Mifflin, 1975.
45. MAKER, C. JUNE. *Providing Programs for the Gifted Handicapped.* 1977. The Council for Exceptional Children, 1920 Association Drive, Reston, Va. 22091.
46. MARLAND, SIDNEY P., JR. *Education of the Gifted and Talented.* Report to the U.S. Congress by the U.S. Commissioner of Education. Washington, D.C.: U.S. Department of Health, Education and Welfare, 1971.
47. MARTINSON, RUTH A. *A Guide toward Better Teaching for the Gifted.* 1976. National/State Leadership Training Institute, Ventura County Superintendent of Schools, 535 East Main Street, Ventura, California 93009.
48. MAYER, MILTON S. "Mother of Comptons." *Scientific Monthly,* November, 1938.
49. MEEKER, MARY NACOL. *The Structure of Intellect: Its Interpretation and Uses.* Columbus, Ohio: Chas. E. Merrill, 1969.
50. MILL, JOHN STUART. *Essential Works of John Stuart Mill.* Edited by Max Lerner. New York: Bantam, 1961.
51. New York City Board of Education. *The Gifted Child in the New York City Schools: A Memorandum and Bibliography.* New York: Board of Education of the City of New York, 1959.
52. _____. *Guidance Newsletter,* Bureau of Educational and Vocational Guidance, no. 7 (1978–1979).
53. *New York Times.* "Careers in the 80's," National Recruitment Survey. Section 12, Sunday, October 14, 1979, p. 68. © 1979 by The New York Times Company.
54. _____. "What Is an Educated Person? 3 Experts Share Answers," Section 4, May 18, 1980, p. 22E. © 1980 by The New York Times Company. Used with permission.
55. ODEN, MELITA H. "The Fulfillment of Promise: 40-Year Follow-Up of the Terman Gifted Group." *Genetic Psychology Monographs,* 77 (1968), 3–93.
56. PEGNATO, C. W., and J. W. BIRCH. "Locating Gifted Children in Junior High Schools: A Comparison of Methods." *Exceptional Children* 25 (1959), 300–304.
57. ROEDELL, WENDY C., and HALBERT B. ROBINSON. *Programming for Intellectually Advanced Preschool Children.* Seattle, Wash.: University of Washington, September 1977. Child Development Research Group, Guthrie Annex II, NI-20, Seattle, Wash., 98198.
58. San Diego City Schools. *Programs for the Gifted in San Diego City Elementary Schools.* San Diego, Calif.: The System, Publication No. ID-72-1, 1972.
59. SCHWEITZER, ALBERT. *Out of My Life and Thought.* New York: Holt, Rinehart & Winston, 1972.
60. SIDLIN, MURRY. "Talentcide, or How I Almost Became a Pharmacist." Keynote address, AGATE (Advocacy for Gifted and Talented Education) Annual Conference. Albany, N.Y.: September 26–27, 1980.

61. *South Pacific*. Music by Richard Rodgers. Lyrics by Oscar Hammerstein II. "Carefully Taught." Copyright 1949 by Richard Rodgers and Oscar Hammerstein. Copyright renewed, Williamson Music, Inc., owner of publication and allied rights throughout the Western Hemisphere and Japan. International Copyright Secured. All rights reserved. Used by permission.

62. SPITZ, R. A. "Hospitalism: An Inquiry into the Genesis of Psychiatric Conditions in Early Childhood." In *The Psychoanalytic Study of the Child*. Vol. I. Edited by A. French and others, pp. 53–74. New York: International University Press, 1945.

63. _____. "The Role of Ecological Factors in Emotional Development in Infancy." *Child Development* 20 (1949), 145–156.

64. STANLEY, JULIAN C., DANIEL P. KEATING, and LYNN H. FOX, eds. *Mathematical Talent: Discovery, Description, and Development*. Proceedings of the Third Annual Hyman Blumberg Symposium on Research in Early Childhood Education. Baltimore, Md.: Johns Hopkins University Press, 1974.

65. STEINHILBER, A. W., and C. J. SOKOLOWSKI. *State Law on Compulsory Attendance*. Washington, D.C.: U.S. Department of Health, Education and Welfare. OE-23044, Circ. No. 793, 1966.

66. TERMAN, LEWIS M., and MAUD A. MERRILL. *Stanford-Binet Intelligence Scale: Manual for the Third Revision—Form L-M*. Boston: Houghton-Mifflin, 1973.

67. TERMAN, LEWIS M., ed. *Genetic Studies of Genius*. 2nd ed. Vol. I: *Mental and Physical Traits of a Thousand Gifted Children*. Stanford, Calif.: Stanford University Press, 1954.

68. _____. *Genetic Studies of Genius*. 2nd ed. Vol. II: *The Early Mental Traits of Three Hundred Geniuses*. By Catharine Morris Cox. Stanford, Calif.: Stanford University Press, 1953.

69. _____. *Genetic Studies of Genius*. Vol. III. *The Promise of Youth: Follow-Up Studies of a Thousand Gifted Children*. With Barbara S. Burks and Dortha W. Jensen. Stanford, Calif.: Stanford University Press, 1958.

70. _____. *Genetic Studies of Genius*. Vol. IV. *The Gifted Child Grows Up: Twenty-Five Years' Follow-Up of a Superior Group*. With Melita H. Oden. Stanford, Calif.: Stanford University Press, 1947.

71. _____. *Genetic Studies of Genius*. Vol. V. *The Gifted Group at Mid-Life: Thirty-Five Years' Follow-Up of the Superior Child*. With Melita H. Oden. Stanford, Calif.: Stanford University Press, 1959.

72. TERRASSIER, JEAN-CHARLES. "Gifted Children and Psychopathology: The Syndrome of Dyssynchrony." In *Gifted Children: Reaching Their Potential*. Edited by James J. Gallagher, pp. 434–440. Proceedings of the Third International Conference on Gifted Children. Jerusalem, Israel: Kollek & Sons, 1979.

73. THORNDIKE, ROBERT L., and ELIZABETH HAGEN. *Measurement and Evaluation in Psychology and Education*. 4th ed. New York: John Wiley, 1977.

74. TORRANCE, E. PAUL. *Creativity*. Belmont, Calif.: Dimensions Publishing, 1969.
75. ———. *Rewarding Creative Behavior*. Englewood Cliffs, N.J.: Prentice-Hall, 1965.
76. U.S. Congress. *Education Act of 1978*. Washington, D.C.: Government Printing Office, 1978.
77. U.S. Government Printing Office. *Occupation Index*. Washington, D.C.: Government Printing Office. Current edition.
78. WIENER, NORBERT. *Ex-Prodigy: My Childhood and Youth*. New York: Simon & Schuster, 1953.
79. WILLIAMS, EMLYN. *The Corn Is Green*. In *Sixteen Famous British Plays*. Compiled by Bennett A. Cerf and Van H. Cartmell, pp. 933–1000. New York: Random House, Modern Library, 1942. Reprinted by permission.

Index

INDEX OF EMINENT PERSONALITIES

(An "r" following the page number indicates citation in readings.)

A
Alexander the Great, 5
Angell, Sir Norman, 67

B
Beethoven, Ludvig van, 3, 43, 61
Bell, Alexander Graham, 168
Braille, Louis, 167, 168
Brandeis, Louis, 67
Bromfield, Louis, 112, 136
Brontë, Charlotte, 21
Browning, Elizabeth Barrett, 38
Byrd, Richard, 67

C
Carroll, Lewis, 138
Caruso, Enrico, 85
Carver, George Washington, 35r, 43, 135, 167
Casals, Pablo, 39
Cassatt, Mary, 35r
Cato, Marcus Porcius, 40
Cézanne, Paul, 11
Chaucer, Geoffrey, 40
Churchill, Winston, 35r, 136
Cicero, Marcus Tullius, 38
Columbus, Christopher, 12, 38
Compton, Arthur, 137
Compton, Karl, 137
Crick, Francis, 86, 141, 168
Curie, Marie Sklodowska, 35r, 67, 135, 168

D
Darwin, Charles, 20, 35r
da Vinci, Leonardo, 5, 39, 42
Davis, Sammy, 5
Descartes, René, 5
Disraeli, Benjamin, 35r

E
Eban, Abba, 35r
Edison, Thomas Alva, 35r, 43, 46, 62, 168
Einstein, Albert, 3, 5, 11, 35r, 39, 53, 85, 87, 133
Eliot, George (Mary Ann Evans), 35r
Erasmus, Desiderius, 20

F
Fahrenheit, Gabriel D., 168
Fleming, Sir Alexander, 11, 168
Fonteyn, Dame Margot, 35r, 111, 136
Franklin, Benjamin, 39, 42, 168
French, Daniel, 5

G
Galilei, Galileo, 12, 38
Gandhi, Mohandas, 126
Goethe, Johann Wolfgang von, 21, 35r, 39, 40, 42, 134
Gutenberg, Johann, 168

197

H

Hayes, Helen, 40
Hearst, Randolph, 67
Homer, Winslow, 5
Hughes, Charles Evans, 67

J

Jefferson, Thomas, 39, 42
Jesus, 38

K

Kahn, Michael, 43
Keats, John, 38
Keller, Helen, 35r, 135

L

LaFarge, John, 67
Lear, Edward, 138
Leopardi, Giacomo, 35r, 38
Lincoln, Abraham, 38
London, Jack, 133
Longfellow, Henry Wadsworth, 40

M

MacArthur, Douglas, 35r
Marconi, Guglielmo, 43, 141
Mendelssohn, Felix, 20, 35r
Menuhin, Yehudi, 35r, 40
Michelangelo (Buonarroti), 3, 38, 39
Mill, John Stuart, 5, 35r, 40, 62, 134
Montessori, Maria, 35r, 138
Morse, Samuel F. B., 168
Mozart, Wolfgang Amadeus, 21, 35r, 40, 61

N

Nijinsky, Vaslav, 85

P

Pascal, Blaise, 35r
Perlman, Itzhak, 167
Peterson, Roger Tory, 35r, 45, 134, 141
Picasso, Pablo, 35r, 39, 43, 141
Puccini, Giacomo, 43, 112

R

Ricci, Ruggiero, 40

S

Salk, Jonas, 167
Sand, George (Aurore Dupin), 21
Schweitzer, Albert, 35r, 39, 40, 42, 133
Shakespeare, William, 3
Sidis, Henry, 52
Sidlin, Murry, 33
Simonides of Ceos, 40
Singer, Isaac Bashevis, 35r
Socrates, 38
Sophocles, 40
Stern, Isaac, 5
Stevenson, Robert Louis, 38, 55

T

Tallchief, Maria, 5
Tesla, Nicola, 38
Theophrastus, 40
Thorpe, Jim, 5
Toulouse-Lautrec, Henri de, 38, 167

V

Verdi, Giuseppe, 40

W

Waksman, Selman, 168
Watson, James Dewey, 86, 141, 168
Weizmann, Chaim, 35r
Wiener, Norbert, 35r, 38, 50, 52, 62
Williams, Emlyn, 126
Woolf, Virginia, 35r, 141
Wright Brothers (Orville and Wilbur), 168

GENERAL INDEX

A

Acceleration, 13–14, 48, 71
ACH (*Achievement Tests* of CEEB), 157
Achievement tests, 153–54
Achiever, 9–10
Addresses (for information), 174–84
Anastasi, Anne, 151, 152
APP (*Advanced Placement Program* of CEEB), 158
Aptitude tests, 155–56
Astor Program, 42, 47, 54, 61fn, 65, 70–71, 80, 104, 124–26
ATP (*Admissions Testing Program* of CEEB), 156–58

B

Basic skills, 79–82
Behaviors (*see* Characteristics)
Binet, Alfred, 7
Binet-Simon Tests, 3
Bloom's *Taxonomy*, 82–83
Boredom, coping with, 54–56
Bridgman, D. S., 33, 39
Bridgman, P. W., 4
Bronfenbrenner, Urie, 63
Bronx High School of Science, 169
Brooklyn Technical High School, 169
Buros, Oscar, 151, 152

C

Career choice (see also Career education):
  early specialization, 86
  during early years, 133-34, 140-41
  educational requirements, 140. 145 (Table 4), 145-47
  and the handicapped, 136
  hobbies and special interests, 140-41
  minority groups, 136
  and multiple talents, skills, 138, 143
  and student effort, 136
  and student priorities, 136-37
Career education (see also Career choice):
  college vs. industrial training, 66
  definitions, 131
  exposure to variety of occupations, 87
  and future needs, 143-47
  and mechanical skills, 143
  and parents' roles, 111-12, 139-43
  phases, 139
  and school roles, 139-43
  significant factors in, 135-39
  and talent development, 133, 137
  when to start, 131-33
Career guidance (see Career education)
CEEB (see College Entrance Examination Board)
Characteristics (see also Identification):
  aloofness, 53
  boredom, knowing too much, 54-56
  checklist, 23-29, Table 2
  concentration, 48-49
  developing positive, 91-92
  dyssynchrony, 46-48
  in early childhood, 30-32
  impatience with detail, 43-46
  love of truth, 49
  nursery, prekindergarten, 30-32
  problem related, 41-58
  sensitivity, empathy, sympathy, 51-52
  understanding too much too soon, 56-58
  unfair demands, 52-53
  versatility of interests, 42-43
Cleveland Public Schools, 71
Coaching (see also Tests, coaching), 158-59
Coeur d'Alene School, 70
Cognitive domain, 82-83
Colfax Plan, 169
College attendance (see also Career education):
  alternatives, 66-67, 143
  vs. industrial training, 145
College Entrance Examination Board (CEEB), 156-58:
  ACH, 157
  APP, 158
  ATP, 156
  PSAT/NMSQT, 157
  SAT, 156
Compulsory education laws, 61
Compulsory school attendance, 61
Convergent thinking, 11, 12
Council for Exceptional Children, 106, 169, 175, 181
Cox, Catharine Morris, 20

Creativity, 11-12
  definition, 11
  tests, 155
Crick, Francis H. C., 86, 141
Cronbach, Lee, 151, 152
Crystal, John C., 146
Curriculum planning, 78-92
  basic skills, 79-82
  developing positive characteristics, 91
  essential information, 84-85
  knowledge, 85-87
  social, civic responsibilities, 87-89
  thinking skills, 82-84
  values, 89-91
  vocational guidance, 87

D

Definitions, 2-15
Divergent thinking, 11, 12
Dyssynchrony, 46-48

E

Ehrlich, Virginia Z., 28, 116
Einstein, Albert, 3, 53
Enrichment, 13-14
ESEA (Elementary and Secondary School Act), 163-64

F

Funding (see also Legislation), 164-65
  federal, 186-90
  private, 119
  public, 119

G

Genius, 3, 5
Getzels, J. W., 12
Gifted (see also Giftedness):
  definition, 4-5
  in regular classroom, 32
  and talented, 4-5
  trials, tribulations, 38-58
Gifted and Talented Children's Act, 1978, 4, 164-65, 185-90
Giftedness (see also Gifted):
  acceptable evidence for schools, 77
  in negative behavior, 116
  unrecognized, 33, 116
Goertzel, Victor and Mildred G., 67
Grade equivalents, 154
Guilford, J. P., 6

H

Hagen, Elizabeth, 151, 152
Hartshorne, H., 41
Hebeler, Jean R., 131
Heterogeneous grouping, 13
Hollingworth, Leta S., 47, 58
Holt, John, 60

200 Index

Home schooling, 107–10
  advantages, disadvantages, 63–66
  vs. formal education, 62–63, 65
  general considerations, 62
  in kindergarten years, 61
  and the law, 60–61, 172
  vs. nursery schools, 63–64
Homework, 92–95
Homogeneous grouping, 13
Honors programs, 71
Hoyt, Kenneth B., 131
Hulbert, Dan, 146
Hunter College Elementary School, 169

I

Identification (see also Characteristics), 18–35
  in classrooms, 32, 116–17
  effects of unrecognized, 33–34
  by parents, 29–32, 104
  by teachers, 32, 116–17
    teacher failure in, 29
Innovations, introducing in classroom practice, 118–19
Intelligence, 5–6
  definitions, 5–6
  physiological theories, 6
Intelligence quotient, 7–9
Iowa Tests of Basic Skills, 154

J

Jackson, P. W., 12
Jacobs, J. C., 29
Javits, Senator Jacob, 165
Jennie's Hat, 19
Jensen, Arthur R., 6
Jobs (see also Career education) for the future, 143–47
Johnson, President Lyndon, 163

K

Kahn, Michael, 43
Kemeny, John G., 144
Kindergarten (see also Prekindergarten):
  advantages, disadvantages, 64–65
  attendance, 61
  identification of giftedness in:
    by parents, 29–32
    by teachers, 29–32
  model programs, 70–71
  programming for, 69–70
Knowledge:
  essential, 84–85
  need for broad range of, 85–87
  taxonomy, 82

L

Landers, Ann, 46
Law (see also Legislation):
  federal (ESEA), 163–65
    Gifted and Talented Children's Act, 186–90
    sources of information, 174
  and home schooling, 60–62, 172
  local, 170
    sources of information, 181
  state, 168–70
    sources of information, 175–81
Learning, specialization in, 86–87
Legislation (see also Laws):
  allocations, 164
  arguments favoring, 167–68
  essentials to look for, 171–72
  history, 163–65
  Marland Report, 33, 164
  origins, 165–66
  and parents' roles, 166, 167–68
  promoting, 165–66
Leiter Performance Scale, 9
London, Jack, 133
Longfellow, Henry Wadsworth, 40

M

McCarthy, Martha, 168
Major Works Classes, 169
Marland Report (see also Legislation), 33, 164
Marland, Sidney, 165
Martinson, Ruth A., 119
May, M. A., 41
Meeker, Mary, 6
Metropolitan Achievement Tests (MAT), 154
Miller, George, 144
Moral, ethical, spiritual values, 89–91
Model programs, prekindergarten/primary, 70–71
Music and Art High School, 169
Myths about giftedness, 38–41

N

National Association for Gifted and Talented (NAGC), 174
Normal probability curve, 9
NOVA Program, 71
Nursery schools, 63–64

O

Oden, Melita, 130
Overachiever, 11

P

Parent advocacy groups, 81
Parents:
  as career guides, 111–12
  as defenders, 105
  as disciplinarians, 105–6
  as educators (see also Home schooling), 60–66, 107–10
  as identifiers of giftedness, 29–32, 104
  and legislation, 166, 167–68
  as listeners, 107
  as partners with schools, 111
  as promoters of talent, 110
  roles, 103–13, 139–43

as social models, 104–5
as social planners, 106
as time managers, 106–7
Percentiles, 154
Prekindergarten (see also Kindergarten):
  advantages, disadvantages, 63–64
  classroom activities, 69–70
  identification by parents, 29–32
  identification by teachers, 30–32
  model programs, 70–71
Preschool child, suitable activities, 109–10
Program planning, 78–92
  college, 72
  grades one to twelve, 71–72
  prekindergarten, kindergarten, 69–70
Programs, models (see Model programs)
Programs, schools for gifted, 70–71, 181–82
PSAT/NMSQT (*Preliminary Scholastic Aptitude Test/National Merit Scholarship Qualifying Test*), 157
Psychological services, 183–84
Publications, 182–83

R

Raven's Progressive Matrices, 9
Recognizing giftedness and talent (see also Identification), 18–35
  at home, 29–32, 104
  in school, 29, 32, 116–17

S

SAT (*Scholastic Aptitude Test*, CEEB), 156
Schooling (see also Home schooling):
  formal, 65–66
  time out, 67
Schools, selection criteria, 67–72
  college, 72
  general, 67–69
  grades one through twelve, 71–72
  prekindergarten, kindergarten, 69–70
School transfers, problems in, 96–99
Sequential Tests of Educational Progress, 154
Simon, Théodore, 7
SOI (Structure of the Intellect), 6
Spearman, Charles, 5
Specialization of learning, 86–87
SRA Scholastic Series, 154
Stanford Achievement Tests, 154
Stanford-Binet Scales, 3, 8, 153
Stanley, Julian, 14, 71fn
State offices, addresses, 175–81
Stuyvesant High School, 13, 169

T

TAG (The Association for the Gifted), 106, 174
Talent development, 110–11
  and commitment, 136–37
Talented, definition, 4–5
Taxonomy of Educational Objectives, 82

Teachers:
  evaluating qualifications of, 119–23
  as identifiers of giftedness, 29
  as innovators, 118–19
  parent expectations of, 123–27
  roles in educating gifted, 115–27
Teaching, in regular classrooms, 117–19
Terman, Lewis M., 20, 22, 39, 41, 104, 130, 168
Terman children, 3
Terman classes, 169
Terrassier, Jean-Charles, 46
Tests (See also College Entrance Examination Board):
  achievement, 153–54
  aptitude, 155
  coaching, 158–59
  creativity, 155
  intelligence, 152–53
    group intelligence, 153
    individual intelligence, 152
  purposes, 150
  recency of data, 153
  standardized, 151, 153
  teacher-made, 151
Thinking skills:
  Bloom's *Taxonomy*, 82–83
  convergent, divergent, 11, 12
  mastery of, 82–84
Thorndike, Robert L., 151, 152
Thurstone, L. L., 5
Time out from schooling, 67
Torrance, E. Paul, 12
Traits (See Characteristics; Identification), checklist, 24–27
Transfers, related problems, 96–99
TSWE (*Test of Standard Written English*, CEEB), 157

U

Underachiever, 10–11
Unfounded beliefs about gifted:
  burn out, 40–41
  fending for themselves, 39–40
  frailty, 38–39
U.S. Office of Gifted and Talented (OGT), 174

P

Values (See Curriculum planning), 89–92

W

WAIS (See Wechsler Scales)
Watson, James D., 86, 141
Wechsler Scales (WAIS, WISC, WISC-R, WPPSI), 8, 152
Wide Range Achievement Tests, 154
Wiener, J., 119
Wiener, Norbert, 38, 50, 52, 62
WISC, WISC-R (See Wechsler Scales)
WPPSI (See Wechsler Scales)

For a Free
Catalog
of Materials
for the Education
of Gifted & Talented
Children
Write

Trillium Press
Box 921
Madison Square Station
New York NY 10159